621 117 129

Movies

About

the

Movies

Movies
About
the
Movies

Hollywood
Reflected

Christopher Ames

THE UNIVERSITY PRESS OF KENTUCKY

Publication of this volume was made possible in part by
a grant from the National Endowment for the Humanities.

Scholarly publisher for the Commonwealth,
serving Bellarmine College, Berea College, Centre
College of Kentucky, Eastern Kentucky University,
The Filson Club Historical Society, Georgetown College,
Kentucky Historical Society, Kentucky State University,
Morehead State University, Murray State University,
Northern Kentucky University, Transylvania University,
University of Kentucky, University of Louisville,
and Western Kentucky University.

Editorial and Sales Offices: The University Press of Kentucky
663 South Limestone Street, Lexington, Kentucky 40508-4008

01 00 99 98 97   5 4 3 2 1

Library of Congress Cataloging-in-Publication Data

Ames, Christopher, 1956-
    Movies about the movies : Hollywood reflected / Christopher Ames.
        p.   cm.
    Includes bibliographical references and index.
    ISBN 0-8131-2018-7 (cloth : alk. paper)
    1. Motion picture industry in motion pictures.   I. Title.
PN1995.9.M65A43   1997
791.43'657—dc21   96-52946

Manufactured in the United States of America

The idea of Hollywood is the most original idea
Hollywood ever had—the only one that it ever
made up by itself. . . . In its impact on the world,
it's the most powerful idea it ever had.

—Richard Schickel (*Hollywood on Hollywood,*
American Movie Classics documentary, 1993)

Contents

Acknowledgments

People love movies—even when they criticize them. This paradox is one manifestation of the cultural ambivalence about motion pictures examined in this study. People also love to talk about movies, and I have benefitted from the suggestions and insights of many during my work on *Movies About the Movies*. Here I would like to thank some of those who gave me much needed advice and assistance.

My gratitude goes first to those colleagues who made important suggestions regarding this work in progress: Tim Gustafson, Eric Mallin, and Peggy Thompson. Special thanks go also to the inquisitive students of English 230, who always seemed to ask the right questions. I am grateful for support of various kinds from Roberta Ames, Michael Ames, Karen Miller, Richard Bliss, Emily Gwynn, Linda Hubert, Jennie Payne, Lee Payne, and Tim Regan.

Much of this study was completed on a sabbatical generously provided by Agnes Scott College. I was aided by a Fleur Cowles Fellowship for study at the Harry Ransom Humanities Research Center at the University of Texas at Austin. While there I was helped considerably by Charles Bell. Though my work at the Huntington Library, supported by a Haynes Foundation Fellowship, was primarily for another project, some of that research and time in southern California proved useful for this book as well.

All photos are courtesy of Photofest, New York City.

Finally, I would like to dedicate this book, with love, to my wife, Lauren Ames, who, among many other gifts and graces, knows more about movies than anyone I know.

Introduction:

Hollywood Stories

It's a Hollywood story." Throughout the history of American film, this phrase has been used to classify and define those movies that take the world of movies—Hollywood—as their subject. Yet one of the first truisms about Hollywood is that it is not a place but a state of mind; as John Ford famously put it, "Holly-

In the most famous film about Hollywood, *Sunset Boulevard,* Norma Desmond (Gloria Swanson) descends the staircase of her mansion, believing she is making her triumphant return to motion pictures. The cameras are for the newsreel photographers chronicling her arrest for the murder of screenwriter Joe Gillis.

wood is a place you can't geographically define."[1] Critics have resorted to a variety of metaphors in the attempt to define Hollywood. Some call it a factory town and refer to "the industry" and its products. Geoffrey O'Brien, thinking of the ubiquity of filmed images, refers to Hollywood as "wallpaper." That is, one does not have to travel to California to experience Hollywood, since it surrounds us wherever movies are screened. Anne Friedberg moves further from geography and treats film-viewing as an activity in the historical context of spectatorship, a context that includes store windows, arcades, amusement parks, museums, and shopping malls. Hollywood is difficult to locate or define because the term "Hollywood" embraces a bundle of associations conveyed by movies and the mass of writing about them. One step toward understanding what Hollywood means in American culture is to study the myths that are fostered and debunked when Hollywood depicts Hollywood.

All Hollywood movies are about Hollywood; some just happen to be set there as well. That is, all Hollywood films contribute to the larger story of film and celebrity that gives "Hollywood" its complex meaning. Film audiences read the literal plot of a movie simultaneously with that developing metanarrative of Hollywood to which each film contributes a piece. For example, we often refer to characters in a film by the names of the actors, not the characters they portray: we speak of "Bette Davis" saying "Fasten your seat belts!" in *All about Eve* or "Humphrey Bogart" responding "I was misinformed" in *Casablanca*. This familiar phenomenon is one manifestation of how films tell stories about Hollywood in addition to their purported narratives. Each film we view adds to the repertoire of impressions we bring to bear in imagining specific actors and, ultimately, in envisioning Hollywood itself. What "Bette Davis" means to an individual filmgoer is a compound created from her movie roles, her publicity in fan magazines and tabloids and interviews, information gleaned from her memoirs or her daughter's book, and so forth. The double focus experienced by the film audience—immersed in plot and yet conscious of actors with full careers and celebrity images engaged in playing parts that will further their careers and celebrity—is not, of course, an exclusive property of the film medium. Reading a Henry James novel, the reader will be conscious of character and plot and dialogue, but also of the technique of a manipulating author. And the reader will add this new reading experience to whatever "Henry James" figure already exists in his or her mind. Similarly, the spectator at a play can be conscious of the portrayed action, the playwright's technique, and the performance of a particular actor. All mimetic arts allow for an immersion in the represented narrative that does not exclude other levels of awareness of the artist, the craft, and the medium. But movies are different. Film foregrounds its own mythology more insistently than do other media. This insistent foregrounding arises partly because movies are a twentieth-century mass medium: their status as technological novelty is still in recent memory, and the discourses of magic, illusion, and wonder still influence how the moviegoing experience is depicted and marketed. Almost from the beginning of the film industry, its artistic productions have been associated with the glamour and luxury of those who make them. And though Hollywood is more than a geographic location, its association with southern California, a region settled in a series of heavily hyped "booms," is no small part of its mythology. The construct of Hollywood remains a "world" both figurative and literal, and individual films map its contours.

Hollywood maps are deceptive, however, since location or setting is one of the first illusions of filmmaking. Whether we watch Tarzan in Africa, cowboys in the West, or police tracking a suspect over New York City rooftops, the scene is likely to have been filmed in southern California. Whether shot on the back lots, soundstages, or in the California hills, the literal Hollywood becomes our cinematic Africa, mythic West, or urban scene. Most movies are about Hollywood because Hollywood is what they show—in terms of geography as well as celebrity. The geographic double focus—a cinematic setting that is both Zenda and California, for example—is one of the most obvious ways in which movies tell stories about Hollywood while they tell other stories. Because movies contribute to the developing general concept of Hollywood as they relate their specific narratives, they also fuel a desire to see more movies. Sequels and series and genres and stars all exploit this phenomenon: Hollywood incessantly advertises itself.

So all Hollywood films are about Hollywood, but some are explicitly set there, and these Hollywood films of Hollywood make a fascinating genre for study because they offer insights into what that mysterious, multiple signifier—"Hollywood"—means. The study that follows is the first part of a two-book investigation into the cultural meaning of Hollywood. The next book will look at the genre of the Hollywood novel and will explore how the many fictions composed by writers working in the movie industry both create and critique myths of Hollywood. But those fictions exist in a context of other fictions of Hollywood: narratives told in fan magazines, scholarly books, mass-market exposés, documentaries, entertainment columns and reviews, even theme parks and restaurants—and in the movies themselves. Here I propose to look at a particular kind of self-referentiality: the movie about Hollywood.

The moment that Hollywood films take Hollywood as their narrative subject, they encounter a series of paradoxes. Films about Hollywood purport to take the viewer behind the scenes and behind the cameras, but by definition what appears on the screen must be taking place in front of the camera. When cameras are depicted filming a scene (as they often are in these movies), we know that it cannot literally be the scene we are watching. This obvious paradox is but one instance of the larger contradiction of Hollywood films about Hollywood: they simultaneously demystify and mystify their subject. "The Truth about Hollywood" was the working title of the important movie that became *What Price Hollywood?* and that original title describes what most films about Hollywood claim to offer—truth as opposed to myth. Often these movies criticize Hollywood myths and dreams, but as would-be successful popular movies they are generally made by people pursuing and profiting from those very myths. Speaking of the familiar story that cautions against the perils of success at any cost, Michael Wood explains, "All the film's real energies come to it from the myth it sets out to criticize, and it ends up not as a correction of the myth but as another fine instance of it" (95). This nice formulation applies especially well to films about Hollywood because they are almost inevitably engaged in debunking the very myths that animate them. This paradox manifests itself in terms of technique, ideology, and genre. The built-in contradiction of the self-referential Hollywood film poses challenges about what to reveal and conceal, challenges that generate technical or thematic responses with ideological consequences. Individual scenes enact the tension of revealing and concealing that ultimately shapes the attitude toward Hollywood that the film as a whole communicates. And that attitude may create further conflicts with a film's genre (musical comedy and film noir, for example, demand different resolutions, but when Hollywood myths are inserted into those genres they may clash with the generically appropriate plot structure).

The contradiction working in movies about Hollywood reveals the tensions between realism and illusion characteristic of film as a medium. "Moving pictures," "motion pictures," "talking pictures"—all of these terms are oxymorons, terms that attempt to express the collision of static media of visual representation with kinetic media of narrative: the photograph and the drama, the painting and the novel. The motion of motion pictures—the very quality that makes them seem so real—is, of course, an illusion. Film, famously, has a dreamlike quality—shifting images played out on a visual field and capable of moving far beyond what the eye of an individual observer could see. And yet the photographic realism of film gives it a mimetic immediacy that exceeds the mimetic illusions of book and stage. Leo Braudy identifies filmic realism as virtually inevitable, "a necessary characteristic that [film] grapples with. . . . realistic illusion is basic to film" (33). From the start, movies have valued documentary realism—seeing, witnessing, being there. Yet they are filled with illusion and "special effects" (fake rainstorms, painted backdrops, stunt doubles, soundtracks, dubbed dialogue and song, and so on). Films thus invoke only an illusion of being there, a simulacrum of witnessing. "Dream" and "magic" are terms that have been associated with the medium from its inception, and Hollywood has been complicit in furthering those associations. Yet the dream and magic involve precisely the magic of realism, the sense of being there or witnessing human drama while actually watching passively.

Some early critics worried that films that showed behind-the-scenes making of movies (and there are many from the silent days, including documentary short subjects) would spoil the illusionary magic of films, but this has not proved the case. In 1937, the year that saw the most important early film about Hollywood, *A Star Is Born,* the *New York Times* compared such Hollywood exposé films to a striptease. The article claimed that Hollywood used to deny that "it was all done with mirrors," but that, thanks to the flood of movies about Hollywood, the public discovered "that every one in a studio bellows 'Quiet' before a scene is shot. It learned that even male stars primp and powder. It practically tripped over cameras and microphones, arcs and cables, papier-mache bricks and breakaways" (Nugent). The article argued, however, that Hollywood revelations still present a romanticized Hollywood full of "glamour and romance" and "directors [who] wear berets." The Hollywood striptease, the *Times* concluded perceptively, is "not nearly so candid as it seems." The author of the piece in the *Times* persisted, however, in believing that Hollywood would not reveal its more elaborate tricks—"the secrets of the process shot, the studio tank, miniatures, the split screen, the voice double and the playback system of recording." But motion picture history has belied this prediction—all of those effects have been revealed in films about Hollywood and yet the illusionary magic remains effective, as the *Times* noted that it did in 1937. In recent years, television specials and video releases on "the making of" various movies have made special effects, particularly computer animation, an object of fascination that augments interest in the movies rather than detracting from it.

The public's hunger to *see* extends to seeing behind the scenes, and the illusion, to a remarkable degree, remains preserved. This triumph of illusionary art lies in showing how the trick works and still making the trick work. Because the self-reflexive character of films about Hollywood exposes the mechanics of illusion, it turns the question of the movie's attitude toward the real into a theme for critical exploration. When movies about the movies reveal cinematic fakery or show, they generally put forward an alternative reality that contrasts with the illusion of the movies. But because the entire film inevitably is trapped in the cinematic realm for the viewing audience, the identification of a genuine "truth about Hollywood" becomes ironic or paradoxical.

One of the oft-cited qualities of classical Hollywood cinema is its invisibility. Richard Sylbert sums up this effect simply: "Hollywood makes you pay attention to the pictorial world, not the means by which it brings it to you" (qtd. in Basinger 21). The predominance of narrative over technique defines a style in which such qualities as seamlessness in editing have been assumed desirable. In this context, films about filmmaking threaten to disrupt the illusion that encourages the audience to forget about camera placement or lighting or cutting. Since films about filmmaking promise to show what transpires behind the scenes, their appeal is precisely in stripping away the illusion of seamlessness. And yet, as mainstream Hollywood films, they remain within the dominant invisible style. Thus the content of these films is often at odds with their style. To put it in ideological terms, the content demystifies while the style mystifies; the content at least purports to reveal what is ordinarily hidden while the style continues the convention of hiding the mechanics of cinematic construction.

This contradiction has specific historical roots, roots that are located in the geographical move of the film industry to southern California from the East Coast. As Bordwell, Staiger, and Thompson have demonstrated, the basic elements of the realist style (what came to be known by critics as "classical Hollywood cinema") were established in the mid-teens, when the move to Hollywood was just beginning. The overarching aesthetic paradigm—the notion that movies would convey narratives in a way that created the illusion of realistic witnessing—was so thoroughly established that one can see almost all the subsequent technical refinements of filmmaking as advances in service of that aesthetic. But the concentration of the film industry in southern California coincided with the growth of the institution of stardom and the ancillary modes of publicity that grew out of and promoted celebrity—fan magazines, gossip columns, self-promoting newsreels, tours of the stars' homes, and so forth. Lary May argues that the traditional reasons given by film historians for the move to Los Angeles—for the sunny climate and to flee Edison's trust—are inadequate (168). Rather, he argues persuasively, the tourism boom of southern California inspired a utopian and consumerist view of leisure that appealed to film stars and vicariously to their audiences: "At a time when the birth of the modern family and consumption ideals might have remained just a cinematic fantasy, Hollywood showed how it could be achieved in real life" (167). Thus, in various ways, the film industry found it worthwhile to promote audience interest in the lives of movie stars, to present stars as "liv[ing] the happy endings, in full view of the nation" (167). This discovery coincided with the overall marketing of southern California as a paradise on earth, a tradition of boosterism that dates back to the 1870s but was revivified in the 1920s.[2] So, while it is true that southern California stands in for geographical locations across the globe, it also may stand in for itself, as evidenced by the extensive location shooting in many films about Hollywood (such as *What Price Hollywood?*, *A Star Is Born* [1937 and 1954], *The Star*, *In a Lonely Place*, and *Sunset Boulevard*).

The Hollywood film about Hollywood thus has sources in studio self-promotion and southern California boosterism. And coming after the realist aesthetic was firmly established in filmmaking, the self-referential Hollywood film was not likely, ultimately, to challenge the core assumptions of filmmaking and film-viewing. As the *Times* article suggests, the fear that movies about movies might shatter mimetic illusions was perceived in Hollywood, but it was a fear that never proved true. The contradictions of the Hollywood-on-Hollywood film highlight contradictions of the film industry as a whole, which simultaneously positions the spectator to consume films as illusionistic slices of life and to unmask that illusionism through privileged glimpses behind the scenes. The paradoxical genre of Hollywood on Hollywood owes its vitality to a coincidence of commercial factors very unlike the development of literary modernism, which, though occurring at much the same time, defined itself in opposition to bourgeois values instead of in furtherance of them.

Nevertheless, cinematic self-reference, as in modernist and postmodernist literature, retains the power to undermine the realist illusion; it calls attention to the work as an artifact rather than unmediated experience. When we are reminded that we are reading a novel or viewing a film, the realist frame is temporarily broken. But self-reference in film typically does something that self-referentiality in literature does not: it foregrounds the circumstances of artistic production and reception, the dynamics of industry and audience. Self-reference in James Joyce or John Barth (or Laurence Sterne, for that matter) may remind us of the writer as shaping artist, but it does not call attention to the intricacies of the publishing industry, the technology of printing, or the tracking of sales and reviews.[3] The movies about Hollywood, to varying and limited extents, do reveal those circumstances of production and reception. Richard Maltby and Ian Craven argue that "one of Hollywood's most telling characteristics is that, while appearing to draw attention to the mechanisms of its industrial processes, it masks one level of its operations by selectively highlighting another" (93-94). In examining individual examples of the genre, we will be alert to which aspects of film production and reception are brought to the attention of the viewer and which elements remain concealed. But even as the technical base of a profit-driven industry is examined in these films, they still ultimately enhance the charm of moviegoing; mainstream films by definition are limited in how adversarial they can be.

We will see many manifestations of this basic paradox, but it would be a mistake to interpret the contradiction as an artistic weakness or as an ideological failing, as some critics do. Judith Hess Wright, for example, criticizes genre films because "they produce satisfaction rather than action, pity and fear rather than revolt. They serve the interests of the ruling class by assisting in the maintenance of the status quo" (41). Such criticism has its value, particularly when it reveals conservative ideologies masked in apparently subversive works. But it has significant limitations: not only does it assume a limited audience that presumably accepts social revolt as the one true aim of art, but it also measures a popular art form against an ideological standard wholly alien to it. Thus, such an ideological analysis not surprisingly reaches the same conclusions about film after film and genre after genre. I think it is more useful to ask what the fundamental contradictions in films about Hollywood reveal about cultural ambivalences toward motion pictures, not what they fail to offer in blatant critique. Speaking from within the film industry to audiences that view movies as pleasurable entertainment, these works naturally celebrate the medium they interrogate. In the best films of the Hollywood-on-Hollywood genre, many of which I focus on in the pages to come, these ambivalences become a source of strength, an insurance against oversimplification. The paradoxes of the Hollywood film about Hollywood are more than simply genre constraints; rather, the paradoxes reveal the nature of Hollywood's—and America's—conflicted cultural stance toward its most powerful narrative medium.

Relevant here is Christian Metz's critique of the "*cinematic writer* (critic, historian, theoretician, etc.) [who maintains] a good object relation with as many films as possible, and at any rate with the cinema as such" (9). Metz is concerned with delineating an analytical, even scientific, position for film critics, a position that is neither in thrall to movies or in intransigent opposition to them ("the persecutory aspects of blind polemic" [10]). He offers the insight that oppositional criticism is very often the other side of the coin of cinema advocacy, since attacking one type of film provides the grounds for asserting the superiority of some alternative, idealized conception of filmmaking. But as well as recognizing that films exert a strange power over those who write about them, "the film's inaudible murmuring to us of 'Love me'" (14), Metz's formulations help us understand the further conflicted status of film critique when it occurs as a discourse within the Hollywood film. Those contradictions that make writing about film "another form of cinematic advertising" apply all the more vividly to the genre of Hollywood exposé films. Indeed, such films are literally inside the institution they criticize, a condition that Metz asserts is the figurative reality of much film criticism. Yet Metz's conclusion—that "to be a theoretician of the cinema, one should ideally no longer love the cinema and yet still love it" (15)—is a paradoxical condition analogous to the self-contradictory ideological space occupied by the Hollywood film critical of Hollywood.[4]

Films about filmmaking date from the silent era and include comic treatments of filmmaking by Mack Sennett, Charlie Chaplin, Buster Keaton, and Harold Lloyd.[5] The genre includes numerous stories of Hollywood hopefuls seeking fame and fortune, of stars encountering tragedy and decline, of producers and directors ruthlessly seeking success, of screenwriters struggling to make a living, of fans absorbed by the spectacle of cinema. Virtually all aspects of the moviemaking industry have received film treatment at some time. In the process, many films do reveal a good bit about filmmaking techniques; and many films provide biting critiques of the excesses and absurdities of the Hollywood system. Despite the richness of this genre, however, it has not received much critical attention. James Agee's 1950 review of *Sunset Boulevard* is generally cited as the first critical discussion of the Hollywood-on-Hollywood film as a distinct genre. Agee does little more than acknowledge the recurrent theme and contrast it favorably with the outsider fiction of Hollywood novelists. He does, however, note a slipperiness to the self-criticism seemingly inevitable to movies about Hollywood, the paradoxes of "the view from inside" (414). Aside from his perceptive article and an article by Theodore Huff three years later,[6] there were no detailed treatments of the genre until a spate of books appeared in the mid-seventies. Rudy Behlmer and Tony Thomas's *Hollywood's Hollywood* (1975), Patrick Donald Anderson's *In Its Own Image: The Cinematic Vision of Hollywood* (1976), Alex Barris's *Hollywood according to Hollywood* (1978), and James Robert Parish and Michael R. Pitts's *Hollywood on Hollywood* (1978) all appeared in a four-year period. These works are broad surveys of the several hundred films of the genre. Behlmer and Thomas's book and Barris's volume are heavily illustrated works that divide the films of the genre into various thematic classifications. Parish and Pitts's volume is an alphabetical reference work that provides, for each listed film, production and cast information as well as a brief synopsis and quotations from contemporary reviews. Without the research of Behlmer and Thomas and of Parish and Pitts—research that includes screening many out-of-circulation films and uncovering synopses of lost films—this study would not have been possible.

Anderson's work provides the most sophisticated thematic analysis. He discusses how the films in this genre treat the idea of success and argues a historical thesis that sees 1950 as the dividing point between the "Merton of the Movies" cycle, which celebrates success, and an anti-Merton cycle that criticizes the evils of the industry. An unpublished dissertation by Laurence Soroka, "Hollywood Modernism: Self-Consciousness and the Hollywood-on-Hollywood Film Genre" (1983), follows Anderson's historical thesis but argues that the earlier treatments of the genre are too exclusively thematic. Focusing on self-referentiality as a technique of literary and dramatic modernism, Soroka examines Hollywood self-referentiality in *Sunset Boulevard, Singin' in the Rain,* and *The Last Movie* and concludes that they evidence a "hybrid modernism" that uses modernist techniques but not for the wholly demystifying function generally associated with New Wave or avant-garde cinematic modernism. Robert Stam in his *Reflexivity in Film and Literature: From Don Quixote to Jean-Luc Godard* (1992) discusses self-referentiality as a filmic gesture, but almost entirely in the context of non-Hollywood films, thus furthering the connection assumed between filmic reflexivity and avant-garde modernism. My approach also focuses on the most self-referential moments of films, but rather than measuring cinematic self-reflexivity against a modernist yardstick, I explore how the self-referentiality (and the narrative contradictions it reveals) illuminates the conflicted cultural significance of motion pictures in American society. For this purpose, mainstream or classical Hollywood cinema is particularly revealing.

It is worth considering why these several genre surveys emerged within such a short time. One reason is certainly that the seventies marked the beginning of wide-ranging academic study of motion pictures, and the idea of filmic self-reference (with its literary parallels) has an academic appeal. But the historical surveys may also have been reacting to a burgeoning of films about Hollywood, most of them nostalgic, in the seventies: *The Way We Were* (1973), *Hearts of the West* (1975), *The Wild Party* (1975), *The Great Waldo Pepper* (1975), *Nickelodeon* (1976), *Silent Movie* (1976), *W.C. Fields and Me* (1976), *Gable and Lombard* (1976).[7] The period also saw film versions of two of the best-known Hollywood novels: *The Day of the Locust* (1975) and *The Last Tycoon* (1976). I have the luxury of discussing a variety of interesting films about Hollywood that have come out in the decade and a half since these earlier studies were published (four of the movies I discuss in detail are from this period). Perhaps we are again entering a period in which the movie about Hollywood is especially popular. The nineties have already seen *Postcards from the Edge, The Player, Mistress, Chaplin, True Romance, I'll Do Anything, Jimmy Hollywood, Get Shorty, Swimming with Sharks, Living in Oblivion,* and *My Life's in Turnaround.* In any case, the continued popularity of films about Hollywood and the growth of critical studies of those films as a coherent genre belies the old maxim that films about Hollywood are box-office losers.[8] The continued interest in films about Hollywood also manifests itself on television: a cable television special, "Hollywood on Hollywood," was written and produced for American Movie Classics by Richard Schickel in 1993.

I examine fifteen artistically successful films of the genre in depth here. With the thematic analyses provided by the earlier surveys in mind, I want to look at how these films exploit the narrative potential of the self-referential paradoxes of Hollywood films about Hollywood. That is, how do the specific tensions of revealing and concealing, mystifying and demystifying, get played out both technically and thematically? The mediated self-examination that characterizes these films offers a good starting point for examining the complexities of what Hollywood means in our culture. The best films about Hollywood struggle with ambivalences that our culture has about movies and their role in our lives: the viability of the American dream of material success, the cultural struggle between highbrow and lowbrow definitions of art and entertainment, and the conflict between corporate capitalism and the belief in individual heroes or creative geniuses. Sometimes these tensions or conflicts are readily apparent, part of the explicit themes of the movie; more often they are implicit, intelligible in moments of self-referential crisis, where the limitations of the medium become apparent. The self-referential moments of these movies are like fissures in the Hollywood style that allow us to discern the paradoxes and conflicts common to the genre though manifested in different, particularized ways.

The most-commented-on ambivalence concerns the American myth of success. Anderson argues that "the 'compensatory illusions' which the films about Hollywood and the motion picture industry offered its audiences all relate . . . to the central myth of the culture: the American dream of success. Since its very inception, this dream has been an ambiguous one and the films in the Hollywood genre . . . reflect this ambiguity" (331). The ambiguity is manifold: those films that exhibit a simple dreams-come-true pattern offer wish-fulfillment fantasies to viewers, but they often show success conferred haphazardly or accidentally; the films that show success turning into tragedy comfort the unsuccessful by suggesting that their failure may result from good character or may be fortunate after all. In a society that gives prominence to the myth that anyone can succeed, the reality that many do not remains troubling. Movies have a dual relationship with this American mythology, as the oxymoron "dream factory" suggests. As wish fulfillments, movies often narrate success stories and depict characters that ordinary folk can dream of emulating. As a "factory," or actual workplace, the film industry has offered millions the hope of making money in films (though it has actually conferred fame and fortune on only a few). That is, films depict the good life, while the film industry offers a chance of achieving it. That dual focus comes together in films about Hollywood. *What Price Hollywood?, A Star Is Born,* and *The Star* (discussed in chapter 1) provide a fascinating trilogy of Hollywood treatments of rising and falling stars, of the promises and deceptions of movie fame. In these films Hollywood analyzes its most precious and ultimately mysterious creation—stardom. Paradoxically, these films invite the audience to sympathize with figures they would ordinarily envy. This sympathy complicates the action of desire by presenting glamorous stars who long for the simple life of the masses who envy them. And by showing the star on and off screen, these films create a fiction that represents the supposedly authentic person behind the screen persona. This contradiction manifests the essential paradox of Hollywood-on-Hollywood movies: movies cannot truly take us behind the cameras, behind the screen, or behind the myth.

Stardom, success, and the nature of Hollywood celebrity make up one nexus of issues common to films about Hollywood. But the genre also raises other questions about the role of movies in American society. The conflicted nature of the artistic function of film arises from two contradictory motives of filmmaking: to show what's hidden (that is, to reveal or even educate) and to provide diversion or pleasant escape. Whether films should reflect social problems or provide a holiday from them is the focus of *Sullivan's Travels.* But the issue also lurks in the self-referential show musicals *A Star Is Born* and *Singin' in the Rain* and in the dark and disturbing "anti-musical" *Pennies from Heaven.* In differing ways, these films (discussed in chapters 2 and 3) reveal the gap between the optimism of musical comedy (and movies in general) and the dark realities of contemporary society. They explore the various stances that film can take toward its imperative to entertain and its desire to reveal and expose. Interrogating the validity of musicals, comedy, escape entertainment, and happy endings, these films all struggle with their own generic identity: are they ultimately optimistic comedies offering escape or somber films offering content at odds with the demands of cinematic comedy? Their complexity emerges from their attempts to be both kinds of film.

This tension is manifested in the fiction of the audience, a fiction that points two ways: toward the individual spectator and toward the industry that defines the mass audience and guesses what will satisfy it. In *The Purple Rose of Cairo* and *Last Action Hero* (discussed in chapter 4) the border between screen and spectator is broken down: movie figures roam real streets and the spectator enters the movie world. The conceit allows for a fanciful satire of genre conventions, of the unreality of screen realism, but it also probes the attitude of the spectator toward the film. Do the movies provide diversion in an otherwise complex and meaningful life, or do the movies become the ironic source of vitality and meaning in an otherwise vapid existence? Dealing with very similar themes, these two films aim at quite different audiences. Their bittersweet endings (in which the viewers must part from the screen heroes who have befriended them) evidence the irresolvability of the questions they address.

In the process of exploring the adversarial relationship between business and art, movies that focus on the financial side of moviemaking also examine the audience as a fictional construct. *Stand-In* and *The Bad and the Beautiful* (discussed in chapter 5) examine (in contrasting styles) the way in which the structure of the film industry, and particularly the personality and motives of the producer, shape the creative process. The marketplace is implicated in all artistic creation, but the mass public medium of film has always been particularly embroiled in the vagaries of the box office. The rule of the dollar is typically seen as the bane of Hollywood, and yet Hollywood's strength is its mass appeal. This contradiction is underscored in films that critique the business side of Hollywood while seeking to make a tidy profit as well as a statement.

The tension between business and art is further explored in films that examine the special place of the writer in filmmaking. The writer is obviously less central in filmmaking than in book or magazine publishing, yet film writers have traditionally been better rewarded financially. This circumstance, most pronounced in the early years of talking pictures, when screenwriters were widely recruited from print media, places screenwriters in an adversarial position toward their livelihood. When that adversarial stance results in a screenplay for a picture about Hollywood, further contradictions emerge. Several films explore the dicey place of the writer in Hollywood: *Boy Meets Girl* and *In a Lonely Place* (discussed in chapter 6), and *Sunset Boulevard* and *The Player* (discussed in chapter 7). All of these films draw intriguing parallels and contrasts between the movies we see being written within the films and the framing films themselves. Films about screenwriters also contain numerous scenarios or story pitches, mini-narratives that comment on how the movie medium influences narrative design. Thus films about screenwriters unmask the practical constraints that shape the construction of film narratives.

The Player also explicitly examines the aesthetic conflicts occasioned by the persistent demand for happy endings in film. This question is implicated in all of the themes and all of the films outlined above. The role of movies in that central American quest—the pursuit of happiness—affects how they depict ambition and success, how they envision their artistic function, how artistic creation is related to financial success, how the experience of the spectator is imagined, and how films get conceived, written, and produced. The happy ending reinforces the comic sensibility, promotes social integration, and suggests that things are as they should be—at least in the fiction of the individual film. But happy endings can also be corrupting—as they are explicitly in *The Player*—and they can seem distorting and inappropriate, even an artistic cheat. Throughout this study, we will see how the creation or avoidance of the happy ending foregrounds issues of the cultural function of movies.

Not surprisingly, films about Hollywood interrogate the role of movies in our culture. In all these films, the self-examination is signified in moments of self-referentiality, the moments in which movies, through a variety of recurrent devices, call attention to themselves as movies and intentionally break or suspend the mimetic illusion. Accordingly, I focus on these moments of slippage, moments that reveal the "man behind the curtain" and emphasize the paradoxical nature of the movies about the movies. Perhaps the most blatant sign of self-consciousness occurs at the beginning and end of the original *A Star Is Born*, when we are shown the shooting script of "A Star Is Born." The image is literally a picture of what is ordinarily hidden behind the scenes, but, here, rather than bracketing the screen image, it eclipses it. Scenes of framing are more common, usually in the movie-within-the-movie. The bracketed movie may be film of daily rushes (such as the modern noir we get a glimpse of in *The Player*), screen tests (as in Bette Davis's test in *The Star* or Constance Bennett's in *What Price Hollywood?*), the test preview of a motion picture (as in the test of "The Duelling Cavalier" in *Singin' in the Rain* or of "Sex and Satan" in *Stand-In*), a premiere (as in the opening of *Singin' in the Rain* or the opening and closing of the 1954 *A Star Is Born*), or a private screening in a star's home (as in Norma Desmond's screening of *Queen Kelly* in *Sunset Boulevard*). Or it may simply be a film being watched by an audience on an ordinary day, as in the fictional films within *The Purple Rose of Cairo* and *Last Action Hero*, or the use of *Follow the Fleet* in *Pennies from Heaven*, or the melodrama triple bill screened in the middle of *Sullivan's Travels*. In almost all of these examples, the screen is shown, at least once, with a frame that shows a theater and a partial view of an audience. And usually, at least once, the film-within-the-film occupies the full screen so that it briefly becomes the film we are watching. Directors can manipulate and cut between those perspectives—framed and whole screen—for a variety of self-conscious effects. The framed screen becomes a metaphor for cinematic self-consciousness.

Another kind of framing occurs when the movie shows us a film being made on a studio lot or soundstage. Here, part of what we see on the screen is what the camera making the film-within-the-film sees, but we see that image surrounded by cameras, lights, technicians, and so forth—the factory part of the dream. Once again, a director can zoom in and eclipse the technical apparatus and show us something close to what the fictional filming camera sees or pull back and show the actors in the crowded context of the soundstage. The framed-screen shots call attention to the audience and the experience of watching a motion picture; the studio shots call attention to the making of a motion picture. Together they exemplify how the genre calls attention to its circumstances of production and reception. Both techniques also highlight the gap between illusion and reality; indeed, the latter shot of an acted scene in the midst of cameras and technicians is common in still photography and emphasized in the Smithsonian exhibit "Hollywood: Legend and Reality." Eleven photographs in the catalog from the exhibit use this technique. In the most dramatic, a high-angle shot shows the light technician's view of the filming of *The Razor's Edge*. Tyrone Power and Gene Tierney embrace intimately in the foreground of a lavish set while some fifty workers look on amidst lights, scaffolding, cameras, and microphones (Webb 53). By enlarging the photographic frame, the contrast is highlighted between what the movie camera (and movie audience) sees and what the reporter offering the truth about Hollywood shows. The photograph emphasizes the exhibit's dualistic theme—"legend and reality"—a paradigmatic theme for cinematic treatments of Hollywood as well.

The framed screen and the studio shot raise the self-referential question: how does what is being said about the bracketed film apply to the film we are watching? How does "The Duelling Cavalier" comment on *Singin' in the Rain*? Or how does "Sex and Satan" comment on *Stand-In*? Does this movie practice what it preaches, or is it guilty of the excesses it criticizes in others? The answers to these questions are rarely simple; the relation of framed film and framing film is generally conflicted. When certain elements of the Hollywood-on-Hollywood film represent the world of moviemaking and other elements represent the real world outside the cinematic illusion, we encounter the basic paradox of the genre: the supposedly extra-Hollywood reality cannot escape its Hollywood genesis. Such moments of self-referentiality initiate the questioning about the role of movies that is important to all these films. Like similar moments in postmodern fiction, these self-referential signatures can break the mimetic illusion or ironically heighten it by seeming to present the truth behind the fiction.

In the contemporary spirit of situating the critic, a few words about my critical method may be in order. This work is essentially a genre study in that it examines a variety of works linked by common themes and stylistic similarities. Yet it also cuts across genres by considering films about Hollywood that might be classified as musicals, film noir, melodramas, comedies, and even action-adventure films. I have tried to avoid the acknowledged weaknesses of thematic study: the tendencies to emphasize content over technique, to ignore historical context, and to elide theoretical concerns. To put that in positive terms, my thematic analysis examines the stylistic aspects of filmic self-reference and considers the way in which particular films engage their immediate historical context (as in the representation of fan magazines in *What Price Hollywood?*, the oblique and paradoxical reflection of labor unions in *Stand-In*, or the concern with the relation between movie violence and urban crime in *Last Action Hero*). These considerations serve the larger goal of exploring the role of motion pictures in American culture as it is articulated within mainstream movies themselves.

The relationship of this study to contemporary film theory is more complex. This work is not an exercise in theory and is not likely to interest those who see theory as the primary critical front in cultural studies. At the same time, this study is not "innocent" of theory: I try to articulate particular theoretical assumptions in the context of specific discussions (the nature of stardom in chapter 1, genre theory about the musical in chapter 2, theories of the audience in chapter 3, and so forth). Nevertheless, this book reflects a conscious decision to address a wide audience, one that includes but is not restricted to people working in film studies. As such, the book is not primarily a conversation with or survey of critics; I have noted only those critics who have been most influential in shaping my ideas. I have opted to discuss individual movies in detail.

The focus on a small number of films about Hollywood is perhaps the most important choice shaping this study. It is motivated, first of all, by a desire to supplement the work already done—there are already excellent wide-ranging surveys of the genre (see the first section of the bibliography). I also want to engage in a dialogue about films that are widely known. Though I provide brief plot summaries of all the movies I discuss, I assume that most readers will be familiar with a majority of the films treated in depth. This familiarity allows me to examine how filmic self-reference manifests itself in individual scenes and shots as well as in the overall structure of a film. While it is important to note scenes, images, and stereotypes common to a great many films, it is also important to see how concepts (in this case, ways of envisioning Hollywood) are worked out over the course of a narrative. That is, I examine how the story is told, visually and verbally, with attention to the trajectory of the entire narrative, particularly to how conflicts are established and resolved. Only this full narrative context allows the contradictions of the genre to emerge with clarity. I have argued that in the best films about Hollywood, these contradictions enrich the movie by engaging cultural ambivalences rather than running from them or simplifying them out of existence. As the film *Boy Meets Girl* emphasizes, the Hollywood environment encourages the formulaic (for example, "boy meets girl, boy loses girl, boy gets girl"); films that avoid simplistic plots or caricatures distinguish themselves from the mass of Hollywood product.

Most of the films discussed here have been admired and singled out for praise by film critics, reviewers, and the Motion Picture Academy. That films critical of Hollywood are roundly praised in Hollywood is one of the paradoxes discussed throughout this study. *A Star Is Born* (1937), *Sunset Boulevard,* and *The Bad and the Beautiful* received screenplay Oscars; *What Price Hollywood?, Pennies from Heaven,* and *The Purple Rose of Cairo* also were nominated for best story or screenplay. *A Star Is Born* (1954) and *The Player* were nominated for multiple major Oscars,

and *The Star* earned Bette Davis a nomination for best actress. *Singin'
in the Rain* (nominated only in Supporting Actress and Scoring categories) has risen significantly in critical esteem since its release and is now
common to several critics' lists of the ten best films of all time (the 1982
Sight and Sound poll of the best movies of all time ranked it second).
Sullivan's Travels, although politically controversial and neglected entirely
by the Academy, is always grouped with Preston Sturges's run of great
films in the forties. *In a Lonely Place* figures significantly in most studies
of film noir and is particularly revered in France, where Nicholas Ray
received more serious critical attention early on. *Stand-In* and *Boy Meets
Girl* are lesser known but certainly critically respected and initially successful films; I believe they are somewhat undervalued because they are
light comedies (and certainly *Stand-In* was overshadowed by *A Star Is
Born* in the 1937 Oscars). I have included, however, two idiosyncratic
choices, films that have been admired but also reviled, even considered
"megaflops": *Pennies from Heaven* and *Last Action Hero*. Given their
box-office failure and the critical controversy surrounding them, I discuss the critical reception of these pictures in the appropriate chapters. I believe that in both cases these movies' very self-reflexiveness and mixing
of genres led to their poor reception. I do not wish to retreat from thorny
questions of aesthetic value, and, though I believe that one can profit
from studying cultural artifacts of all levels of quality, my particular investigation is best served by detailed study of well-respected films.

Ultimately, Hollywood-on-Hollywood films are just one of many ways
in which Hollywood acquires cultural meaning, just one genre of Hollywood insider stories. But unlike Hollywood novels, fan magazines, or celebrity memoirs, movies about Hollywood depend on the cinematic medium to explore the culture that has grown around it. They frame the
screen and turn it into a distorting and two-way mirror: the screen on
which images of fictional or far-off places is projected flashes back to the
sites where those images are created, and in doing so, the screen projects
to the audience a coded vision of how the audience is imagined by the
artists, technicians, and businesspeople who create the movies. The movies about Hollywood resist the extremes of Hollywood evaluation—from
the paeans to cinema as an uplifting and therapeutic medium to the jer-
emiads of cultural decline. These movies or moments in movies offer
instead meditations on the cultural significance of films intriguingly produced by parties with an active interest in preserving screen mythology

and a perspective for seeing through that mythology. As the first century of cinema comes to a close, we are surer of the importance of movies in American culture and less sure of their meaning or ideological force. Looking at the movies about the movies, we can analyze a century of self-examination, repeatedly testing the limits of the screen, telling and retelling the Hollywood story.

1 Cautionary Tales

What Price Hollywood? (RKO 1932). Producer: David O. Selznick. Director: George Cukor. Screenwriters: Jane Murfin, Ben Markson, Rowland Brown, Gene Fowler, based on a story by Adela Rogers St. Johns.

A Star Is Born (United Artists 1937). Producer: David O. Selznick. Director: William Wellman. Screenwriters: Dorothy Parker, Alan Campbell, Robert Carson, based on a story by Robert Carson and William Wellman.

The Star (20th Century-Fox 1952). Producer: Bert Friedlob. Director: Stuart Heisler. Screenwriters: Dale Eunson and Katherine Albert.

What Price Hollywood? illustrates the power of fan magazines in advertising the Hollywood Dream. Young hopeful, Mary Evans (Constance Bennett), places herself in a magazine photograph with Clark Gable, demonstrating how the fan imaginatively identifies with the pictured star.

When David O. Selznick defended *A Star Is Born* to the Hays Office during production, he wrote that the film would function as "a warning to girls of how strong the chances are against them."[1] Indeed, the movie includes at least one such explicit cautionary scene at Central Casting. As Esther Blodgett observes a host of switchboard operators telling hopefuls that no extra work is available, the receptionist warns her that her chances are "one in a hundred thousand." But, of course, *A Star Is Born* is not a disillusioning movie in this sense. Esther responds tentatively, "But—maybe—I'm that one," and *A Star Is Born* proves her right. This little scene—and Selznick's moralistic synopsis of the story's meaning—epitomizes the mixed message that is inherently a part of Hollywood exposé films. Cautionary tales about stardom end up glamorizing the phenomenon they are cautioning viewers about.

The simplest cautionary tale in Hollywood fiction follows the dreamer who comes to Hollywood in search of stardom and finds only poverty and exploitation. Examples include the silent films *The Extra Girl* (1923, directed by Mack Sennett), *Stranded* (1927, written by Anita Loos), and *Hollywood* (1923, directed by James Cruze and based on a story by Frank Condon). The cautionary story also frequently organizes Hollywood novels of disillusionment, such as Horace McCoy's *They Shoot Horses, Don't They?* (1935) and *I Should Have Stayed Home* (1938). But this cautionary tale needs to be understood as a reaction to the more familiar rags-to-riches tale of achieving fabulous success in Hollywood. Particularly popular in the twenties and thirties, these films follow the formula made famous in Harry Leon Wilson's popular novel *Merton of the Movies* (1922) and the play and films based directly on it.[2] Patrick Anderson in his *In Its Own Image* catalogs a host of films—silents and talkies—that evoke "this first and most fundamental myth about Hollywood . . . a belief that opportunity was unlimited (and hence available to everyone)" (74). These success stories are generally given a comic twist and become stories of "accidental success" where a screen hopeful's dramatic acting is unintentionally but successfully comical, or where a resemblance to a star helps an unknown's career. Against the background of these formula films, movies in which the screen hopeful does not succeed stand out. The film *Hollywood* (of which no copies survive) is a particularly interesting case of a movie's explicitly serving a cautionary function, since James Cruze made it at the suggestion of Will Hays. The original story by Frank Condon, published in *Photoplay*, was a deliberate satire of the success myth, in which the heroine, Angela Whitaker (played in the movie by the aptly named Hope Drown), fails to find work in pictures while the members of her horrified family who come out to rescue her blunder into screen roles by accident.

But, for obvious reasons, films about the wholly unsuccessful quest for stardom have a limited appeal. As a result, the most common cautionary tale in Hollywood works a distinct variation on the straightforward tale of disillusionment. It follows the dreamer who achieves stardom and *then* encounters tragedy and unhappiness. We see this complexly mixed message in three excellent films about stardom: George Cukor's *What Price Hollywood?*; the William Wellman film based on it, *A Star Is Born*; and Stuart Heisler's *The Star*. All three of these films conceive of stardom within the paradigm of rise and fall, the ancient pattern of Fortune's wheel given a contemporary Hollywood spin. *What Price Hollywood?* and *A Star Is Born* have an hourglass structure: the rise of the female star parallels the decline of the male star, while the movie chronicles their fruitful but doomed intersection. The trajectory of *The Star*, on the other hand, is remorselessly downward (except for a glimmer of hope at the end): it begins with an auction of the possessions of one-time star Margaret Elliot. Her rise to stardom and success precede the film, which shows us only her decline. Thus all three films ostensibly serve the cautionary function. They warn the viewer that the privileges of fame and riches do not guarantee happiness and that the height of the celebrity's rise predicts the pain of the eventual fall.

The theme of happiness sacrificed to ambition was popular in fan magazines, although the fan magazines extolled the Hollywood dream more powerfully than they cautioned against it. "Fame is the consolation prize which is given when everything else has been sacrificed," writes one fan-magazine reporter in an article entitled "The Price They Pay for Fame" (Busby 94).[3] Richard Maltby and Ian Craven note how such articles purporting to show "the price they pay for fame" "obscure the profit motive that drives [movies] by substituting a discourse on loss" (94). But the catalog of heroic risks taken by devoted actors only heightens their romantic appeal, and though fan magazines frequently published warnings to young girls and cautionary tales about the perils and disappointments of Hollywood, they played an unquestionably major role in creating actors' fame and representing the luxury of their lives to the public. Gaylyn Studlar argues that, "by providing glimpses of the stars' most personal thoughts and relying on the reader's wealth of pre-established knowledge," the fan magazine made readers complicit with the stars even while demystifying the star system (13).[4] Films about movie stars tend to create the same sort of complicity by offering an insider's view of stardom. In particular, the Cukor and Wellman movies inevitably glamorize the Hollywood they warn against and invite the viewer to identify with the lucky star.

Stardom is Hollywood's most powerful and most mysterious phenomenon. Everyone knows the story of how early film producers failed to predict audiences' interest in the actors and actresses who portrayed characters in photoplays.[5] But when that interest emerged in about 1909, studios were quick to capitalize on it, as the formation of the Famous Players film company by Adolph Zukor signifies. In the glory days of Hollywood, the nature of stardom shaped how films were written, produced, and marketed, and this remains true in the post-studio-system era. Interest in stars as individuals propelled the fan magazines and newspaper gossip columns that in turn fed audience interest in the movies themselves. *What Price Hollywood?, A Star Is Born,* and *The Star* reveal Hollywood exploring its greatest fictional creation. They ask: What makes someone a star? What is the experience of being a star like? What is the relationship between celebrity and audience? What causes stars to fade into obscurity? In treating those questions, these films display honesty and insight, but not at the expense of glamour. If anything, celebrity glamour is enhanced by depictions of the stars as strong individuals wrestling with the extraordinary demands of a larger-than-life existence. These films ask us to sympathize with figures we would ordinarily envy, and in doing so they create a complicated reciprocal desire that ultimately enhances star appeal.

In *What Price Hollywood?* and *A Star Is Born* the double message is reflected in the doubling of the protagonists: though both of these films show the decline and suicide of a once successful Hollywood figure, they juxtapose that tragedy with the spectacular rise of an actress to superstardom. *A Star Is Born* ends explicitly with Vicki Lester returning to film, after mourning the death of her husband. *What Price Hollywood?* finds Mary Evans renewing her marriage and attempting a comeback after the scandal that results from the death of the director who made her a star. Both films render the rags-to-riches myth but make that myth seem more truthful by placing it in the context of another star's tragic decline.

The Star critiques the myth evoked in these earlier films; remarkably, it ends with the star's flight from Hollywood. Here, the two characters of these other films have become one: the actress who has risen to tremendous fame now falls herself into unpopularity, drunkenness, and mental breakdown. No rising star provides a hopeful myth to place alongside the cautionary tale (except for a minor figure, a youthful actress whom the main character envies and despises). Perhaps it is just as useful to see the other films dividing the single story of a rise and fall into two characters (and thus lessening the cautionary elements). In any case, *The Star* provides an instructive contrast to the related earlier films, *What Price Hollywood?* and *A Star Is Born,* perhaps because it is a product of the fifties, a period of unease, reorganization, and financial decline in the film industry.[6]

What Price Hollywood? (originally titled "The Truth about Hollywood") follows the fate of a Brown Derby waitress, Mary Evans (Constance Bennett). Mary meets the drunken director Max Carey (Lowell Sherman) at the restaurant. They attend a premiere together and become friends. He gets her a test at the studio, and, after two tries, her work impresses the benevolent producer Julius Saxe (Gregory Ratoff), who gives her a contract and makes her a star. Mary Evans and Max Carey become great friends, though never lovers, and she witnesses his drunken decline. She marries a dapper playboy, Lonny Borden (Neil Hamilton), who exhibits a growing dislike of Max, Mary's other Hollywood friends, and being married to a celebrity—being "Mr. Evans." Before long, he leaves Mary. Max eventually hits bottom and has to be bailed out of a drunk tank by Mary. Recovering in her house, he is overcome by despair and shoots himself. His death in her house creates a scandal, and Mary flees Hollywood for seclusion in France. Lonny has a change of heart and goes to France to revitalize his marriage; he brings with him a comeback movie offer from Julius Saxe. Mary accepts Lonny's return and the film ends with their embrace.

A *Star Is Born* follows a similar pattern. It traces the trip to Hollywood from North Dakota of young Esther Blodgett (Janet Gaynor) and follows her abortive attempts to get employment as an actress. Her fortunes turn when she meets a drunken actor, Norman Maine (Fredric March), at a party where she is a waitress. He falls for her and gets her a screen test that leads to a contract. Eventually Esther stars opposite Norman and her popularity eclipses his. The success of Esther's fresh-faced vitality seems linked to the decline of the mature screen star Norman Maine. Under the stage name Vicki Lester, she becomes a sensation, and she marries Norman. Though he experiments with sobriety, he continues to falter in his career. Eventually he retires and tries to be happy as Esther's husband. After a stint in a sanitarium, a fight with his old agent sets Norman on a drunken spree that ends in jail. After Esther bails him out, he fears that he is standing in the way of her career, and he kills himself by walking into the Pacific Ocean. Following his death, Esther decides to retire, but her grandmother, Lettie (who lent her the money to come to Hollywood years earlier), urges her to continue her career. Esther agrees to stay in Hollywood and attends the premiere of her latest picture, identifying herself at the microphone as "Mrs. Norman Maine."

What Price Hollywood? begins with a fan magazine. The pages are flipping, and the viewer is looking over the shoulder of the as-yet-unseen Mary Evans. Three times we see a photo in the movie magazine fade to a glimpse of Mary copying it: trying on first stockings, then a dress, then "kissable lipstick." Then we see Mary in a medium shot looking from the movie magazine in one hand to a hand mirror in the other. Content with her successful imitation, she folds over a picture of an actress kissing Clark Gable, places her own face against his, and speaks in a Garbo imitation. Cukor then disrupts her fantasy in three ways: she switches from the Swedish accent to her normal tough-girl voice ("Time to scram"); she shuts off the record player (so that what had seemed extra-diegetic soundtrack is revealed as merely her Victrola); and she puts up her Murphy bed and hurries to her job as a waitress at the Brown Derby. It is a wonderfully revealing scene. The opening alternation from the perspective of Mary Evans to shots *of* her demonstrates how these movies invite us to identify with the star at the same time that they objectify and ostensibly demystify the star. They invite us to participate in the very action they depict: identifying with a movie star. When the camera places us over Mary's shoulder reading her magazine, it engages us in the same sort of action as Mary's holding Gable's picture next to her face.

That Mary Evans is copying styles from fan magazines is hardly a surprise: *Vogue* magazine told readers in 1937 that "the way you make up your lips, apply your rouge . . . ten to one it came from Hollywood" (Webb 187). The emphasis on photographic and mirror images recurs frequently in Hollywood films about movie stars. The photo magazine and mirror call attention to the importance of the visual image in screen celebrity, a significant difference from stage acting. The mirror and magazine also suggest the dynamics of imitative desire. To make the image in the mirror match the image on the screen—that is the key to the magical transformation that celebrity brings about. And, of course, *acting* is imitation itself. When Mary gets a job serving hors d'oeuvres at a big Hollywood party, she tries to impress the directors and producers by imitating Greta Garbo, Mae West, and Katharine Hepburn. But imitation is not just an onscreen technique: the movie magazine, showing the stars off camera, encourages fans to imitate celebrities' styles in order to be more like the stars' supposed offscreen selves. Makeup, costume, and fake accents point out the extent to which stardom involves a literal remaking, a physical transformation of ordinary person into screen image.

Of course Mary Evans is not a star yet, but Constance Bennett *is*—a familiar double focus in Hollywood films. The self-referential quality of Hollywood films about Hollywood invites speculation about how the actors relate to the characters they portray. Often there are interesting parallels: Lowell Sherman was a director as well as an actor, for example, and Bette Davis of *The Star* was an aging actress dissatisfied with the roles she was being offered (as we will see, the most famous and most discussed parallel of this sort occurred in the casting of Gloria Swanson in *Sunset Boulevard* as the silent-picture actress Norma Desmond). At other times, a contrast between actor and role is apparent: Fredric March, for example, was at the height of his career (and a far bigger star than Janet Gaynor) when *A Star Is Born* was made, and in the 1954 remake, Judy Garland, who portrays Esther, was in a career decline more similar to Norman Maine's. That we see the figure on screen both as a character and as an actor/celebrity generates ambiguities that the movies about the movies exploit.

Star movies reveal the multiple fictions of which stardom is compounded: the ordinary person—whether Mary Evans or Esther Blodgett—imitates celebrity photos, which are posed "candid" shots representing the fictional personality invented by the studio for the actor or actress whose job on screen is the impersonation of other fictional characters. Richard Dyer in *Stars* notes how the characters portrayed by actors were often perceived as "revealing the personality of the star, [but] that personality was itself a construction known and expressed only through films, stories, publicity, etc." (22-23). In these rags-to-riches star stories, the humble aspiring actress is portrayed by a glamorous and already famous star—so her success seems strangely assured.[7] Such multiple fictions become commonplace in films about Hollywood.

A Star Is Born begins far from Los Angeles geographically, but not far from the reach of the movies. Esther Blodgett returns to her Dakota farmhouse from the local movie theater, a fan magazine clutched in her hand. Her mother mocks her love for Hollywood and recounts the sort of imitative behavior that Mary Evans exhibits in What Price Hollywood? The mother complains about "the house all cluttered up with movie magazines" and asserts with horror that "the other day I caught [Esther] talking to the horse in a Swedish accent" and "making faces in the mirror and talking to herself." Ring Lardner and Budd Schulberg, working as backup (and ultimately uncredited) writers on the script, wanted to cut these pre-Hollywood scenes and essentially begin the story in Los Angeles, the same way What Price Hollywood? begins. But these scenes in the Dakota wilds not only establish Esther's naïveté and the long reach of Hollywood, but also introduce the resonant metaphor of moviemakers as pioneers.

Grandmother Lettie, played by May Robson, makes the comparison explicit. She urges Esther to ignore the warnings of her mother because "everyone in this world who's ever dreamed about better things has been laughed at." But she asserts that "there's a difference between dreaming and doing" and adduces for support her own experience crossing the plains in a prairie schooner: "There'll always be a wilderness to conquer—maybe Hollywood's your wilderness now."

Indeed, the migration to Hollywood was a revitalized westward movement, a gold rush in quotation marks that followed the real gold rush in 1849 and the oil and land grabs of the early twentieth century. This pioneer context is crucial to the self-mythologizing of the movies. The desire to be transformed to the image on the screen thus becomes not self-deceptive narcissism but a version of the American dream of self-improvement, a venturing to the newest frontier, the technology of motion pictures. When Esther Blodgett arrives in Los Angeles, a screen title identifies the city as "the beckoning El Dorado . . . the Metropolis of Make-Believe." "Make-Believe" and "El Dorado" imply the false hopes of a cautionary tale. But despite early setbacks, Esther becomes that "one in a hundred thousand"; thus the movie affirms her idealistic delusions as pioneer determination. Mary Evans in What Price Hollywood? exhibits that same faith: "I'm no wise guy, but I believe in myself. All I need is a break."

"The break" is a key component of the Hollywood myth—Lana Turner's being discovered in the Schwab's Drugstore. "The break" reveals truthfully how arbitrary Hollywood success or failure can be, as well as how much it may depend on personal connections. In revealing this arbitrariness, as we will see, the narrative of the break minimizes the issue of talent and skill. In both of these films the break comes about as a result of an encounter with a drunk and cynical Hollywood celebrity beginning his downward slide from popularity and fame to obscurity and despair. Both drunks are initially presented as comical and eventually become tragically self-destructive. They are remarkably complex character studies, especially given the Hays Office's insistence that scenes of intoxication be kept to a minimum and be clearly unattractive. The drunkenness of director Max Carey and actor Norman Maine provides a license for truth-telling about Hollywood as well as a comic lance for puncturing solemnity and gloom. Max Carey's blustering but benevolent entrance into the Brown Derby dispensing gardenias lampoons the image of the director dispensing favors and "breaks" (right before Max enters, Cukor shows Mary Evans rebuffing an unscrupulous lesser producer who is trying to pick her up, casting-couch style). When Mary waits on Max and confesses, "I'm looking for a break—and I'm going to get it," he invites her to the premiere of his latest film; he takes her to the premiere in a ramshackle jalopy that he offers to the parking attendant as a tip. His style of entrance to the premiere, like that of his entrance to the Brown Derby, is a refusal to respect matters about which Hollywood is deadly serious. Max's behavior reinforces the one piece of advice he offers Mary: "You know the motto of Hollywood: it's all in fun."

Norman Maine's drunkenness is more bitterly antisocial. Before Esther meets him, she witnesses his drunken tantrum in which he smashes a reporter's camera at the Hollywood Bowl. When she works at a wrap party as a waitress and vows, "I'll *make* them notice me," the drunken, alienated Norman is the only one who does—precisely because he is aloof from the usual social machinations of the Hollywood party. Esther's break is signaled by literal breaks—Norman's breaking dishes as he helps her clean up and his girlfriend's breaking a plate over his head in frustration at his drunken rudeness. This "cute meet" also foreshadows how Esther and Norman will fail in their attempt at married domesticity. Nevertheless, Norman is attracted to Esther precisely because she is outside the circle of Hollywood insiders with whom he has become disenchanted. He respects genuineness and is attracted by her beauty: "Whatever I do, I still respect lovely things—and you're lovely."

Norman's drunken disgust extends to himself. Gulping tumblers of scotch at the party, he identifies his epitaph as the motto on the back of a home slot-machine token: "Good for Amusement Only." Max and Norman exemplify a familiar Hollywood cycle: decline in popularity leads to bitterness and drunken cynicism, which turns the industry and audience against celebrities for good. In other words, it is never made clear whether Max and Norman drink because they have lost the fickle audience they once commanded or whether they have lost the audience because they drink. Alcoholism is Hollywood's primary way of signifying character dissolution, whether the drinking is seen as cause or effect or both. The dramatic potential of drunkenness aside, Max and Norman have a host of real-life models. The portrait of Max Carey has been linked to John McCormick and to silent-film director Tom Forman; Norman Maine has been seen as a composite of John Barrymore, John Gilbert, and John Bowers (Behlmer 81).[8]

Perhaps because they are invigorated by the youth and naïveté of the unspoiled Blodgett and Evans, Maine and Carey each grant the young starlet the desired break. And both Carey and Maine warn the starlets of what awaits them. They serve as cautionary figures by word as well as by example:

> Maine: You're foolish enough to want to go into pictures.
> Blodgett: Why foolish? Look at you.
> Maine: Yeah, look at me.

> Evans: I'm . . . I'm in pictures! Mr. Carey, I'm in pictures!
> Carey: Well, don't blame me.

But to some extent these men are to blame—not for offering a kid a break, but for contributing to the powerful allure of motion pictures that drove the starlets to Hollywood in the first place. Similarly, these very films, in spite of their cautionary elements, would inspire countless young would-be actors. The promotion of *A Star Is Born* even included contests in which the winners were flown to Hollywood for screen tests.[9] And Selznick publicized the story of how a wardrobe assistant, Joan Carlyon, was "discovered" by director William Wellman and "given a role in the Academy Award ball sequence . . . marking the end of her wardrobe career, and the beginning of a career as an actress."[10] These publicity gimmicks reveal that the cautionary tale is a blind for what the studio thought of as essentially a story of magical success.

Once Esther and Mary are given their breaks they have to prove themselves in screen tests. The screen test, one version of the film-within-a-film in self-referential Hollywood movies, is a favorite behind-the-scenes episode. Both *What Price Hollywood?* and *A Star Is Born* devote considerable time to showing the making, or "birth," of their stars, beginning from the moment of the screen test. But Hollywood exhibits an unresolved ambivalence about how stars are born, about the mystery of star quality. As a result, the nature of the star's appeal and talent almost always remains ambiguous.

Mary Evans has a test in which she must descend a staircase and speak a single line: "Hello Buzzy, you haven't proposed to me yet tonight." She blows it horribly, and she knows it. But at home (in the familiar boarding house of Hollywood hopefuls), Mary practices her line until she gets it right. This scene is important in showing that acting involves talent and work—even in a single line reading.[11] She begs for another test, and it is that successful test that we see in a framed screen. We watch from Mary's viewpoint in the projection room: the screen occupies the background, the heads and propped-up feet of director and producer in the foreground. "Terrific!" exudes producer Julius Saxe. "Who is that gorgeous creature? Sign her up immediately." Julius inspects Mary: "Let me look at you. Fine. . . . I have discovered a new star." Although the test shows acting as a difficult craft, it still inevitably depicts stardom as something conferred upon a young woman because of her looks and screen presence. Alexander Walker in *Stardom* describes the primacy of physical appearance as the "uniqueness of the star whose physical looks, deepening into the personality he or she projected, would invite instant recognition at every appearance and connect with an audience's dreams and aspirations in ways that lay below the level of their awareness" (29). Acting unquestionably involves talent and hard work, but screen acting obtains a magical aura from the spellbinding effects of the enlarged visual image.[12] Mary Evans does a good job with her single line—but it remains a single line.

A Star Is Born is even more frank about the importance of look or "type" over talent. Though the movie shows, in some detail, the technical preparations for Esther's test, it elides the test itself. The film fades from the moment before the test to the signing of the contract, as if she wins the

part by magic, or as if the content of her performance were not important. The producer, Oliver Niles (Adolphe Menjou), explains that he is
signing Esther because he thinks "the public will like you." That estimation is not based on any signs of talent, but on Oliver's hunch that tastes
are going to change in favor of the "natural" and "mild." The omission of
Esther's test performance suggests that star quality is too difficult to depict or too potent to demystify on screen. A similar lacuna characterizes
Joseph Mankiewicz's Hollywood film, *The Barefoot Contessa* (1954), a
story about the making of a movie star somewhat modeled on Rita
Hayworth.[13] "Scouting for a new face" in Madrid, a group from the studio
watch Maria Vargas (Ava Gardner), a flamenco dancer. They are entranced, but the camera shows us only their reacting faces, never the actual dance. Maria accepts the offer to go to Hollywood, but only after
director Harry Dawes (Humphrey Bogart) promises to teach her the craft
of acting and make her a real actress, not just a screen beauty. Maria is
unusually savvy in anticipating the difficulties that await a starlet selected
arbitrarily by producers. When Maria has her screen test, Harry's voice-
over narration apologizes that though it is "one of the most tiresome clichés
of show business, . . . that first screen test of Maria Vargas lit up all the
lights of Hollywood." Once again, we see only the entranced audience,
not the test itself; her electric performances (aside from a brief dance
with some gypsies) are left entirely to the imagination.

Mankiewicz and Wellman may be suggesting that it is the reaction
to the test and not the test itself that is important. But we need to be
attentive to what the films that purport to show the truth behind the illusion of Hollywood choose to keep concealed. A survey of films about
Hollywood suggests that the unsuccessful screen test is much more commonly dramatized, often for comic purposes, as in *The Extra Girl* (1923);
Souls for Sale (1923); *Free and Easy* (1930), starring Buster Keaton; *Movie
Crazy* (1932), starring Harold Lloyd; and *It's a Great Feeling* (1949), starring Doris Day. Later we will see the serious dramatic potential of the
failed screen test in *The Star.* In any case, pretending to act badly often
offers an opportunity for a dramatic tour de force. Showing a successful
screen test risks exposing what these films require to be kept mysterious:
the nature of talent, the stuff of stardom.

The decision to leave blank the performance of the rising star, to
keep those performances off screen, has interesting consequences. Often it means that the narrative of the making of a star is told comically as

the invention of a personality by the studio's machine of makeup artists, wardrobe specialists, posture coaches, and, above all, publicity agents. The starlet remains virtually passive. Mary Evans is allowed to keep her name, but Julius Saxe decides on the spot to mount a national publicity campaign to market her as a "typical American girl—America's pal," an allusion to the marketing of film's first great star, Mary Pickford. Mary Evans's rise to stardom is communicated in a remarkable montage of less than a minute's length: first a close-up of her face in rippling light with swelling music and her eyes rising, as star-shaped lights dot the background; then her full figure in long shot, growing in size, superimposed over the fading close-up while fireworks seem to spout from her form, as if she were a roman candle; then cuts to three marquees with her name in lights, first as costar and then as star with name above the title; then a dissolve to a kaleidoscope of clapping hands, with stage lights refracted into star shapes and fireworks. Since showing actual performances of the star appears to be taboo, Cukor (with the aid of montage expert Slavko Vorkapich) resorts to symbolism and the economic montage—here the tropes of rising and of celestial bodies (stage lights, fireworks, stars in the heavens). In less than a minute, Mary Evans becomes a star, and she is next seen flirting with playboy Lonny Borden at the Santa Barbara Polo Fields.

A Star Is Born is somewhat more detailed in depicting the rise to fame, but "questions of talent and training are obscured," as Maltby and Craven note (96). After Esther Blodgett is signed, she is shown being transformed and manipulated in a series of comic vignettes: the PR man dubs her a "Cinderella from the Rockies," posture and diction coaches cluck their tongues at her, makeup artists give her a Joan Crawford mouth and eyebrows that make her look "always surprised." Above all, she is renamed Vicki Lester in a wonderfully comic scene that shows not only how stage names conceal old-fashioned or overly ethnic names but how they symbolize the studio fabrication of a personality. But after all this effort, she secures only a one-line speaking part, until Norman intervenes and begs Oliver Niles to make her his costar in the costume drama "The Enchanted Hour." This move is presented realistically as a risk that will require intensive work on the part of the new Vicki Lester.

Vicki Lester's success is shown through the screening of a preview that Norman and Vicki attend together. Wellman, working in early technicolor, uses black and white to set off the film-within-the-film, as well as the traditional technique of framing. He cuts four times from "The Enchanted Hour" to Norman and Vicki in the audience. As the screen lovers kiss, the actors in the audience hold hands. We even hear a line or two of romantic dialogue from the framed film, but still we only learn of Vicki's success from the audience comments that Oliver overhears. That is, what Wellman shows us of Vicki's performance offers no real clue to her talent or potential for success. But the audience loves the new Vicki Lester and thinks she outshines the fading Norman Maine. Norman senses this too and tells Vicki that "a star is born." Here the focus on audience reaction suggests a further mystery to star quality, a sort of tyranny of the masses, who are capable of discarding one favorite for another on a whim.

As Norman and Vicki look out over "the crazy quilt" of nighttime Los Angeles (the same background against which the opening credits roll), he tells her, "It's a carpet spread for you. It's all yours now." The view of nighttime Los Angeles as a vast blanket of twinkling lights (or stars)

Viewing the movie-within-the-movie, Norman Maine (Fredric March) and Vicki Lester (Janet Gaynor) in the 1937 A Star Is Born witness the birth of the star in Vicki's preview.

recurs in other films about Hollywood. The dramatic location epitomizes the importance of geographic place intertwined with the quest for success. In *A Star Is Born,* this dramatic moment is the pivot of the picture's hourglass structure: it certifies Vicki's rise and Norman's fall, and it is paired with his confession of love for her. Norman admits that he thinks he has found his happiness too late.

Thus *A Star Is Born* turns to the subject of Hollywood's destructive effect on marriage, a theme that emerges also in *What Price Hollywood?* even though Mary Evans marries a Hollywood outsider, not her mentor-director. However, it is the drunken cynic Max Carey in that movie who expresses the truth about Hollywood marriages in an exchange with Lonny Borden:

> Max: It'll never last.
> Lonny: What won't last?
> Max: My liver—and a movie star's marriage.

Both films use a wedding and marriage to argue that stars sacrifice an essential privacy in return for their fame. The wedding of Mary Evans and Lonny Borden in *What Price Hollywood?* becomes a Hollywood spectacle, with a wedge of magazine and newsreel photographers blocking our view of the bride. In the midst of dizzying close-ups, Mary throws her bouquet to her fans, who respond by trying to rip off her wedding veil (an image echoed in the funeral scene in *A Star Is Born*). The honeymoon is then postponed for film retakes. Eventually we see Lonny languishing in boredom while Mary works and frolics with her Hollywood friends. Not long after being called "Mr. Evans," he leaves her.

In *A Star Is Born,* the fate of Norman and Vicki's marriage is implied in the proposal scene, which is set at a boxing match. Norman proposes as the fighters exchange blows; Vicki demands that he reform his drinking if they are to marry; as he agrees we see the two fighters knock each other down. The juxtaposition presages how their marriage will be a struggle in which both will fall. Though dubbed "America's Dream Lovers" by the zealous press agent, Norman and Vicki elope and are married with their original given names, Albert Henkel and Esther Blodgett. Their honeymoon in a trailer represents an abortive flight from Hollywood (an inverted take on Grandmother Lettie's prairie schooner migration). Some scripted scenes where they try to avoid their fame and recognition by dining in blackface were mercifully omitted from the film. Their brief escape from Hollywood ends when they trade in their trailer for the palatial and swan-bedecked estate that Norman has bought for them as "our castle." Vicki's career continues to rise as Norman's continues to flounder. We see this in a vivid and economical shot as a billboard reading "Norman Maine in 'The Enchanted Hour'" is changed to "Vicki Lester in 'The Enchanted Hour.'" For a brief moment in between it reads "Vicki Maine."

Lack of privacy is only one reason that Hollywood seems inimical to happy marriages. These movies suggest that the Hollywood creation of an artificial persona forces the star to sacrifice genuine human relationships. Rita Hayworth said of her many marriages: "They all married Gilda [Hayworth's most famous character] but they woke up with me." In these films, the reverse seems true: Norman Maine marries Esther and wakes up with Vicki Lester, the movie star, who, like Mary Evans, struggles to find time to forge the domestic life with her increasingly idle husband.

"You're not slipping," Oliver tells Norman; "you've slipped." Even though he's stopped drinking (temporarily), Norman Maine has become "the screen's most finished actor," and he becomes the rich but bored househusband that Lonny Borden was unable to sustain in *What Price Hollywood?* A variety of brilliantly conceived scenes chronicle Norman's decline: his brutal and drunken interruption of Vicki's Academy Award acceptance speech, a poignant scene in which Oliver visits him in a sanitarium, and a pathetic fistfight with his vindictive press agent, Libby (Lionel Stander), at Santa Anita. Ultimately, his suicide expresses his inability to accept his return to a so-called normal life, as well as his perception that he has become a burden to the star he helped create. The demise of his screen persona leads to his own death.

The fatal tension between screen celebrity and the pleasures of a normal life becomes the sentimental myth central to both films, the myth that asks us to sympathize with these figures who have achieved their dreams. *A Star Is Born* expresses that tension in its play on naming and renaming. When Norman and Vicki marry, they use their real names, and this gesture, as we have seen, inaugurates their search for a life apart from their Hollywood personalities. It is also our first sign that Norman Maine's name is a stage name, though we might have expected it, with its echoes of normality and Main Street. Fabricated as America's Dream Lovers, Norman and Vicki seek to escape their celebrity selves. The billboard scene and a scene where Norman is addressed as "Mr. Lester" call further attention to the ways in which Hollywood naming runs counter to American social expectations. But after Norman's death, Esther's grandmother urges her to assert herself as *Vicki Lester,* as the personality she has worked to achieve. She takes her grandmother's advice but modifies it in the film's final line, identifying herself as "Mrs. Norman Maine." Esther Blodgett thus moves through four names and identities: Esther Blodgett, the girl from North Dakota; Vicki Lester, the Hollywood star; Mrs. Albert Henkel, the loving wife in the trailer; and Mrs. Norman Maine, the star who acknowledges that she has risen from the ashes of her husband's career. In this play with naming, *A Star Is Born* shows the double bind of female celebrity. That the stage name prohibits an actress from taking a married name symbolizes the tension between celebrity and marriage. But the tension proves equally destructive to the men, including Max Carey, who seems to have long since given up on romance.

The suicide of Max Carey is the most remarkable scene in *What Price Hollywood?* The film makes it clear that Max's dissolution is a loss of self, and it implies that this loss of identity may be the ultimate consequence of the acquisition of a celebrity persona: "You mustn't be unhappy over a man who doesn't exist any more," he tells Mary. "I'm not the Max Carey you once knew. I'm all burned out, Mary. Don't you see I'm dead inside?" Recuperating at Mary's house from an extended drunk, Max admits, "From where I am, they don't come back. . . . [But] now that you're the top of the heap, I'm happy." Mary goes to bed and Max wanders about the darkened house, pours himself a drink, looks for a match and finds a gun instead. Finally he lights his cigarette in front of a mirror and examines his ravaged face in the flickering light. His eyes fall to a framed picture of himself—younger and healthier, of course. He now stands between a photograph and his mirror image in a reversal of Mary's actions in the opening scene. Like Mary, he wishes the two images were the same, but while the disjunction signified ambition for Mary, it represents failure for Max. The visual echo suggests that the two contrasts are opposite ends of a single trajectory, that the price of becoming an image is losing one's self. Though Max is a director, he too suffers from the cult of youth Hollywood has become famous for. In this scene, he appears old and world weary in an environment that celebrates youthful vitality. As Max stares in the mirror, blurry scenes from his past emerge, a strange whirring sound intensifies, and a rippling whirlpool of light surrounds the center of the screen where his drawn face is seen in close-up. He takes the gun and shoots himself in the heart. With the pistol shot the whirring noise ceases, and a quick series of images of Max's former self flash on the screen.

Stardom, these films suggest, becomes a devil's bargain. Esther's grandmother in *A Star Is Born* makes this point explicit in her moralistic lecture at the end of the film, in which she chastises Esther for leaving Hollywood: "It seems to me that you got more than you bargained for: more fame, more success, even more personal happiness. Maybe more unhappiness. You *did* make a bargain and now you're whining over it." But if stardom is a Faustian bargain, who represents the devil? What agency wrecks the happiness of these figures who, against great odds, have achieved their dreams? In these films at least, the devil is not the studio (which is characterized with unbelievable benevolence), the devil is the audience. In asking us to identify with and sympathize with the star, these movies vilify the audience.

At some points the vilification of the audience or the public is mediated through the press, which becomes the surrogate villain. In *What Price Hollywood?* the downfall of Mary Evans comes about from the scandal of Max Carey's death at her home. Cukor uses that old favorite Hollywood montage, the sequence of newspaper headlines; he shows the progression from press suspicion to public vilification, taking us from "Director Max Carey Dies of Wounds in Star's Home" to "Mary Evans Denies Romance Entered Life with Director" to "Women's Clubs Ban Pictures of Mary Evans from Theaters." When that final headline appears, we see dirt shoveled on it, presumably to indicate that the press is digging up dirt, or, for that matter, desecrating Carey's grave. Cukor then specifically recalls the montage of Evans's ascent to stardom, but in reverse: against a background of whirling newspapers, her figure shrinks beneath the star-shaped lights, while her eyes in the superimposed close-up of her face turn downward. Again, the visual echo connects the fall to the rise. When reporters surround her estate and climb the balconies, Julius Saxe must explain to her, "The public don't understand relations like between you and Carey. . . . You're a motion picture star; you belong to the public. They make you and they break you." Broken, she flees Hollywood, much as her husband had a year earlier with his dramatic speech to her: "You live in a world where people are cheap and vulgar without knowing it. And if you weren't cheap and vulgar yourself, you couldn't stand it." Given that they both come to reject Hollywood, their reunion makes for a logical happy ending. But the implied return to Hollywood for a comeback doesn't make sense, and the forced happy ending once again exposes the cautionary tale at war with its own implications: Hollywood promotes itself through movies regardless of their content.

The implied attack on the audience in *A Star Is Born* begins with the press as well. After Norman Maine's suicide, the headline cruelly reports "Ex-star Perishes in Tragic Accident" (anticipating the derogatory quotation marks around "singer" in the headline shot in *Citizen Kane*). Press agent Libby continues the cruelty, regaling a bartender with the witticism "First drink of water he's had in twenty years, and then he had to get it by accident." The cruelty of the public emerges clearly in the funeral scene, in which the mourning widow is besieged by fans demanding autographs, one counseling her, "Don't you cry, dearie, he wasn't so much," and another brutally ripping off her veil. The unveiling of Vicki's now famous face unmasks the public claim to ownership: having made her a star they demand to see her. The screen fills with her screaming face, and then the film cuts to a photograph of Norman Maine peeling potatoes on their rustic honeymoon. Faced with this clear contrast, Vicki Lester replaces her veil and vows to leave Hollywood, screening herself off from the screen.

But her grandmother arrives for yet another unmasking—this one supposedly a liberating one. She removes Vicki's veil and unveils a chair covered for the closing of her Malibu home. She lectures Vicki on the need to surmount heartbreak, and she asserts, "I was proud to be the grandmother of Vicki Lester—it gave me something to live for." Her plea succeeds, and we fade to Vicki's name in lights at her biggest premiere at Grauman's Chinese Theatre: "The girl who has won the hearts of Hollywood! The girl who has won the hearts of the world!" enthuses the radio announcer broadcasting the premiere to a world of fans, fans we have just seen portrayed as heartless and crass. The movie shifts the spectator back from the star's perspective to the more familiar place of the audience. As they all applaud, Grandmother Lettie speaks to the world and explicitly reverses the cautionary message: "Maybe some of you people listening in dream about coming to Hollywood, and maybe some of you get pretty discouraged. Well, when you do, you just think about me. It took me over seventy— . . . sixty years to get here, but here I am and here I mean to stay." As Vicki approaches the microphone on Oliver's arm, she sees Norman Maine's footprints in the famed sidewalk. She grows faint, and I think we are meant not only to marvel at how far she has come since she first gaped at those footprints on her arrival in Hollywood but also to wonder how far she will follow in those footsteps that lead from stardom to suicide.

When Vicki speaks her famous line—"This is Mrs. Norman Maine"— the ovation is tremendous, and now at the end of the film we are invited to join that ovation, to join that vast audience the film has shown to be such a thankless master. And if we do not sense that the ovation is tremendous, we read it—"The ovation is tremendous"—for the movie cuts to the final page of its screenplay. This self-referentiality reminds us of the movie's complex fictionality. At the beginning of the film, showing us the screenplay was a way of taking us behind the scenes to see what the final shooting script looked like. Yet what we see in the opening shot is the familiar disclaimer asserting the film to be a fiction ("any similarity to persons living or dead," etc.). And just as the self-referential beginning makes problematic the film's claim to show the truth about Hollywood, so too is the final shot self-canceling: once we cut to the screenplay the camera no longer can show us what the screenplay describes (indeed, we miss seeing enacted the very last stage direction, where Vicki looks into the distance). And of course the framed screenplay does not read, "Cut to shot of screenplay." The frame is putatively outside the fiction and cleverly reminds us that there are limits to what truths the films about Hollywood can tell. The metafictional gesture paradoxically undermines verisimilitude by calling attention to the film's ultimately irreducible fictionality.

The Star combines many of the elements of these earlier cautionary tales in a structure that criticizes them, or at least sheds new light on them. The star of the title is Margaret Elliot (Bette Davis), and most of her fall from popularity precedes the opening of the film. Indeed, the movie begins with an ending of sorts: the auction of her personal possessions to pay creditors. Through Margaret's conversations with her agent, her daughter, and her ex-husband's wife, we learn that she hasn't made a film in three years. Though she was once one of the greatest stars, she now cannot pay the rent on a small apartment. She grabs her Oscar statuette and tears off on a drunken ride through Beverly Hills. She crashes near her old mansion and ends up in jail. Jim Johannson (Sterling Hayden) posts her bail and offers her a place to live. Jim is a figure from her past, a carpenter to whom she once gave a starring film role. He abandoned

Hollywood after his one film, fought in the Pacific, and now operates a shipyard. He represents the clean-cut, morally healthy alternative to Hollywood (he describes himself as "a wet nurse for sick boats"). As Margaret comes to suspect, he has been secretly in love with her. She tries a normal job as a sales clerk at a department store, but flees when fans recognize her and ridicule her arrest for drunk driving. Desperate, she begs for another film role and is offered a small part in a film starring a younger, up-and-coming actress. But she fails the screen test by trying to act as a flirtatious coquette in a role that calls for an old and bitter housewife. When, the next day, a director at a Hollywood party offers her a role playing a washed-up actress, she vows to quit Hollywood and runs to Jim Johannson, presumably to marry and not return to the movies. Aside from the brief happy ending, this film focuses entirely on the decline of an aging star, what makes for the middle section of *What Price Hollywood?* and *A Star Is Born*. Davis's extraordinary (and Oscar-nominated) performance as a proud and bitter actress desperate to cling to her status drives the film.

The absence in *The Star* of a Hollywood success story to counter the falling-star tragedy (and the more negative view of Hollywood that absence implies) reflects historical changes in the film industry. The financial decline of the industry (in part because of the popularity of television) and the concomitant reduction in the number of features produced may be connected to the spate of negative portrayals of Hollywood in films of the fifties: *Sunset Boulevard, The Bad and the Beautiful, The Barefoot Contessa, In a Lonely Place, The Big Knife*. More specifically, the incisive critique of *The Star* was made possible by the critical success of *Sunset Boulevard* and *All about Eve*, two earlier portraits of bitter and aging actresses, and the rise of film noir conventions that licensed a "dark" vision of life and even permitted unhappy endings. This era also saw an entire generation of actresses forced to confront, as Margaret Elliot does, the unfair consequences of aging. For the previous generation of motion picture stars, the rough transition to sound interrupted (or, in some cases, ended) maturing careers and obscured the relation between aging and star status. Molly Haskell identifies the fifties as the decade in which the centrality of women to film stardom finally gave way: "It is only recently that men have come to monopolize the popularity polls, the credits and the romantic spotlight. . . . Back in the twenties and thirties, and to a lesser extent the forties, women were at the center, [as was] amply reflected in the billings" (11-12). These trends may help explain the gender shift in the figure of decline from *What Price Hollywood?* and *A Star Is Born* to *The Star*, and they may help explain why *The Star* deals with such strikingly similar material in different ways.

   The Star opens with a huge searchlight in the left foreground and the small figure of Margaret Elliot in sunglasses in the right background. The searchlight suggests an opening, but the sounds of an auction signal an ending. As the searchlight turns, Margaret walks into the foreground and looks up at a glamour photograph of her younger self and the advertisement for the auction of her "personal effects." As in *What Price Hollywood?* the contrast between present and past is shown through the star confronting an old photograph. But in *The Star*, the decline of the celebrity is linked more directly to age. The older Margaret Elliot contemplating her younger self reminds us of the power of movies to immortalize youth. The ability to capture a moving human form on film was initially heralded as offering an immortality of sorts, but it also chronicles the aging of a star across a career and offers repeated reminders of the difference between the aging actor and the ageless image.[14] Geoffrey O'Brien describes the movies as "a medium in which the dead continued to walk about . . . an education in time . . . a multiscreen documentary on the aging process" (57). Director Stuart Heisler cuts from the glamour photo to a close-up of the older Margaret, who slowly removes her sunglasses and winces. In the background the auctioneer provides a remarkable eulogy to her:

>   Auctioneer: This beautiful onyx vase—what am I offered?
>   Bidder: One dollar.
>   Auctioneer: One dollar! You don't seem to realize, Mister,
>   that this stuff didn't just belong to anybody; it belonged to
>   Margaret Elliot, one of the most exciting actresses to ever
>   hit the silver screen. She was your favorite movie star;
>   you stood in line to see her latest picture; she made you
>   laugh; she made you cry; you were secretly in love with
>   her. Show Margaret Elliot you haven't forgotten her. And
>   now, ladies and gentlemen, what am I offered?
>   Bidder: Two dollars.
>   Auctioneer: Going, going, gone. . . .

This brief scene poignantly establishes the height of Margaret Elliot's fame and the depth of her fall from popularity. The past tense of Margaret's stardom will be interrogated throughout the movie, most directly by her daughter, Gretchen (Natalie Wood). When Margaret tells her daughter, "Your mother is a star," Gretchen responds, "I know you *were*, but are you now?" Her mother replies with an article of faith, "If you're a star, you don't stop being a star." The film shows both the truth and falsity of this credo. Margaret Elliot has lost her star quality in the eyes of the audience, but she continues to live with the mentality and self-image (if not the elegant trappings) of a star. The disjunction between her self-perception and the reality drives her to despair. She comes to see the auctioneer's call of "going, going, gone" as a verdict on herself and her career.

As if overhearing the auctioneer were not disheartening enough, Margaret encounters her agent leaving the auction with her chandelier. In the scenes that follow with him and others, we learn quickly of her decline. She talks of "telephoning directors that I put into this business and their not phoning back." Her agent tells her that she has lost "that fresh, dewy quality" and that "something else" has taken its place. When she visits her daughter and her ex-husband's wife, we learn that her marriage failed in exactly the way the marriages in *A Star Is Born* and *What Price Hollywood?* failed: "His name was Morgan, and he didn't like being Mr. Elliot." He needed a "real wife" and not a busy celebrity. Ironically, since their breakup John Morgan has become a successful western actor, shooting on location in Arizona (reminding us that men are allowed to age in Hollywood).

The character of Margaret Elliot gives new dimension to the plight of the falling star by connecting it with aging, a topic about which the earlier films are silent. Indeed, aging has always been tougher on women than on men in the movies, in part because of the very factors that once made actresses the center of the screen world: the mixture of innocence and youthful sex appeal, that "fresh, dewy quality." Haskell points out that actors like Fred Astaire and Cary Grant played romantic leads for generations "while their early partners were forced to play mothers or character parts or go wilting into retirement" (16). She notes how *Sunset Boulevard* and *All about Eve* both treat this problem and exemplify it in presenting "women whose success has been based on looks more than acting ability and for whom age, therefore, is more catastrophic" (245).

The treatment of aging in *The Star* brings together a variety of themes handled critically in the earlier movies: the mystery of "star qual-ity" and its distinction from acting talent, the fickleness and potential cruelty of the audience, the star as a prisoner of the imaginative projec-tions of others. *A Star Is Born* and *What Price Hollywood?* never hint that Margaret Elliot's fate awaits their heroines, but of course it is the rule, and youthful actresses who develop a successful screen persona in middle age and beyond are the exception. Bette Davis is one such famous excep-tion, but her career was filled with anxiety about the limited roles she was given. *The Star* comes just three years after her break with Warner Broth-ers, and it is one of a variety of projects from a difficult decade of declin-ing popularity for the one-time superstar. Margaret Elliot was intended by the writers as a nasty takeoff on Joan Crawford, and Davis took up the part with some malevolence ("That bitch is getting her revenge on me," Crawford confided to Hedda Hopper [qtd. in Quirk 345]). But the role of Margaret Elliot also had many elements of Davis herself in it. The review in *Time* noted that Bette Davis "is still her own best imitator," a remark aimed at other actresses who copied her style, but a revealing one with regard to this autobiographical role. That Davis would later achieve success in horror films comments further on the tyranny of ag-ing in the celluloid world of the perpetually young.

Drunkenness is used to show mental crisis and dissolution of char-acter in films about Hollywood, and *The Star* is no exception. Though Margaret Elliot is not depicted as a consistent problem drinker, she does get roaring drunk in her despair following the auction. In a well-conceived scene, she takes her Oscar statuette on an inebriated tour of the homes of the stars in Beverly Hills. The sequence begins with a point-of-view shot: looking over Margaret's shoulder out the windshield at night, some on-coming headlights, Oscar standing on the dash, and a pint of whiskey visible in Margaret's right hand. As she weaves through the streets, Mar-garet bitterly intones the names of the youthful stars in their mansions: "How young can you get?" Finally she pulls up to the house in which she once lived: "And that, Oscar, was the home of the wealthy, exciting, glam-orous Margaret Elliot. I remember the day you came home. That was a day. Going, going, gone."

Like Max Carey and Norman Maine, Margaret Elliot ends up in the drunk tank and the headlines. But the figure who comes to rescue her is a surprise, a minor figure from her past. Jim Johannson is designed to embody all that Hollywood isn't: he's sunny and healthy, straightforward, hardworking (in outdoor physical labor), and unpretentious. Margaret had once gotten him a movie role, even though he hadn't been seeking one (she later confesses she got Jim the role only to pique an actor who refused to costar opposite her). For a very brief while, Jim was known as Barry Lester. But he abandoned the movies, a choice that distinguishes him from virtually all the major figures in these three films. The stars in the earlier films flirt with leaving Hollywood behind—Norman and Vicki in their camping trailer; Mary Evans in seclusion in France—but they fail, as they must in a film that is designed ultimately to affirm the Hollywood dream. Jim Johannson, having rejected his stage name and career, is designed as a ticket out, and that may be why he is rather unconvincing. Drawn as a big, good-hearted paragon of virtue, he seems out of place in the otherwise sophisticated milieu created by the scriptwriters. Nevertheless, he serves as a sort of reverse of the grandmother in *A Star Is Born*, offering Margaret anti-Hollywood lectures on morality: "That's not the way real people live," he chastises Margaret at one point; "I once thought you were a woman. But I was wrong—you're nothing but a career," he moralizes at another. But in spite of his tendency to self-righteousness, he is an essential figure in the film's critique of Hollywood, a far more convincing foil than Lonny Borden in *What Price Hollywood?*

When Jim's criticism becomes too much, Margaret flees his shipyard home, and the scene that ensues is a crucial one in Hollywood's analysis of stardom. Earlier scenes have established Margaret's love for an expensive perfume called "Desire Me," which she can no longer afford. Her daughter, too, associates her mother's scent with her beauty, glamour, and fame. The name of the perfume makes an obvious but important point about the nature of stardom: the star desires to be the object of desire. The ineffability of stardom manifests itself as a quest to shape the desires of masses of other people. Margaret enters a drugstore to buy sleeping pills. She sees a large display for Desire Me on the counter and it lures her, much as the craving for star status has driven her behavior since her career began. In desperation she shoplifts a display bottle of the perfume and runs back to the shipyard, now appalled at how low she has sunk: "I stole this," she wails. "I haven't stolen anything in my life. . . . I don't *need* perfume; nobody needs perfume. What's wrong with me?" Jim, in a rather contemporary self-help fashion, identifies her perception that something is wrong as the first step to recovery. Calmed, she opens the perfume and dabs some on her wrist, only to discover that it is "noth-

ing but colored water." Attracted by the gaudy display of a magical product promising to induce desire, the fallen star discovers that the potion is
an illusion: "When you grabbed it you thought it was real—that's the story
of your life, isn't it?" comments Jim (in case we miss the point). In this
single episode, *The Star* offers a critique of the mythology of stardom
that could apply to the earlier star films as well. From the fan's viewpoint,
star worship exemplifies what René Girard calls imitative or mimetic
desire: the longing for luxury or consumer goods masks an essential desire to become like, to imitate, the one who possesses those objects of
desire.[15] From the star's viewpoint, this mediated desire is further distanced: one desires to become the object others will imitate.

But when Margaret tries to lead a normal life by taking a sales job
in ladies' lingerie at a department store, the attempt fails. A couple of
shoppers recognize and criticize her for her drunk-driving arrest, and she
rails at them: "Take a good look, ladies. So there's no doubt. I am Margaret Elliot. And it *is* a disgrace: Margaret Elliot waiting on a couple of old

The desire to be desired: Fading star Margaret Elliot (Bette Davis) prepares to shoplift
a display bottle of her favorite perfume in *The Star*.

bags like you. I am Margaret Elliot and I intend to stay Margaret Elliot."
Bette Davis vents Margaret Elliot's rage: rage at being notorious rather
than famous, rage at having been cut off from her livelihood while unfit
for other kinds of work or life.

So Margaret Elliot attempts a comeback, something we never see
in *A Star Is Born* or *What Price Hollywood?* She has fallen so far that
she must test for a minor role. But what bothers her is not the test but that
she must portray an aging and unattractive woman. The treatment of the
test spends a lot of time showing how she is made up and costumed to
look older. Then, before the filming, Margaret sneaks into the dressing
room of young actress Barbara Lawrence (playing herself), the one who
has essentially taken her place in the studio. Facing the mirror in the
dressing room of the actress she'd like to be, Margaret remakes herself,
in another comment on the nature of mimetic desire: one desires not an
object or quality but to imitate a person who possesses that object or
quality. With skill, Margaret redoes her hair, removes the extra wrinkles
added by makeup, unbuttons the neck of her dress, and reties her scarf.
She does this so effectively that the director worries that she looks "a
little young for the part." Margaret responds, "Women of forty-two these
days don't have to look ready for the old ladies' home." Here she echoes
Gloria Swanson, who had refused to be made up to look older for her role
in *Sunset Boulevard* two years earlier (rather, she demanded they make
William Holden look younger). But Swanson, whose work in *Sunset Boulevard* is clearly an important inspiration for Davis in *The Star*, was portraying an elegant movie star. Margaret Elliot is testing for a poor and
run-down woman, as the director explains. The tension between two views
of the actress emerges: as one who realistically plays a variety of characters, or as one who embodies on screen a particular kind of elegance and
glamour, regardless of the part. It is this latter concept of the actress that
has put Margaret Elliot out of work; it is the former concept that, in actual
life, allowed Bette Davis to be successful through a long career.

Margaret chooses the way of glamour and blows the test. *The
Star* shows us the failed test in great detail: in rehearsal, in shooting,
and in screening. Having a great actress play a bad actress is dramatically powerful and, it seems, allowable, whereas, as we have noted, showing positive screen tests seems to be taboo. Margaret plays the bitter
woman in a flirtatious manner, talking to the camera and beaming. She
ignores the director's advice and demands a change in the key light to

accentuate her beauty. She leaves convinced she has gotten the part.

But Margaret Elliot is too savvy a pro to stay fooled, and the scene in which she watches her screen test the next day is the most powerful one in the movie. Once again we see the framed movie, the sign of the self-referential film, as Margaret watches the test alone in a darkened screening room. The camera focuses on her reaction and we see the contrast between Bette Davis the actress and Margaret Elliot the actress: the scenes in the framed screen show an actress awkwardly hitting a one-note expression at odds with the dramatic requirements of the scene, where the close-ups of Margaret Elliot in the screening room show Davis registering a range of emotions from shock, to fury, to disappointment and regret. Finally, she screams at her screen image, "Shut up! Shut up! You don't know anything." While the scene recalls the opening shots of Margaret confronting her glamour photo, it emphasizes revelation rather than illusion. She leaves the studio broken in spirit.

Recovering at her agent's house, Margaret stumbles into his exclusive Hollywood party. Though people treat her kindly, the experience turns ugly. First she overhears another actress announcing that she got the very part Margaret had tested for. Then young actress Barbara Lawrence enters and electrifies the gathering, becoming instantly the center of attention, as Margaret Elliot must once have been capable of doing. But the final dishonor comes when a screenwriter-director pitches a role to her:

> It's a Hollywood story, but it might have happened any-
> where. . . . In my script, she happens to be a movie star,
> so we can take advantage of the bizarre atmosphere.
> Now she's been on a sleigh ride, but she can't face the fact
> that it's over, like half the people in this town. . . . This is
> your simon-pure movie star, like the ones that play it
> twenty-four hours a day: thinking of themselves and what
> they look like, what kind of impression they're making;
> demanding, driving, ambitious—for what? Power, to stay
> on top. And like all climbers that have reached such a
> precarious pinnacle, they can't look down lest they fall—so
> they stand, clutching what they have with fear their lonely
> companion. That's the character of the heroine, if you can
> call her that, of "Falling Star."

Margaret is horrified. This man has just pitched her life, or, from the audience point of view, he has just pitched the movie we have seen, another exploitation of the self-referentiality of Hollywood films about Hollywood (we will see this same technique at the end of Robert Altman's *The Player*). But our movie is *The Star*, not "Falling Star," and I suppose the brief ending that follows this scene is meant to distinguish Margaret from the pitiful figure the writer described. She flees the party, picks up her daughter, and rushes to the shipyard and Jim's arms. The end.

The influence of *Sunset Boulevard* is apparent throughout *The Star*, perhaps most pointedly in the pitch at the Hollywood party. In 1950, two years before *The Star* was released, both Gloria Swanson and Bette Davis were nominated for Academy Awards for their portrayals of aging actresses (Davis had played a stage actress in *All about Eve*). Swanson later commented of her portrayal of Norma Desmond that perhaps she had "played the part too well. . . . I had somehow convinced the world of that corniest of all theatrical clichés—that on very rare occasions the actor actually becomes the part." Swanson complained that most of the scripts she was offered after *Sunset Boulevard* "dealt with aging, eccentric actresses" (Swanson 270). That prospect drove Swanson, like Margaret Elliot, out of acting (though Davis would play an aging actress again, in *Whatever Happened to Baby Jane?*). These films of the fifties demonstrate a new frankness about the gendered double standard of movie celebrity.

Critics were dissatisfied with the ending of *The Star*. The happy ending seems tacked onto a tragic plot, and no real romance between Margaret and Jim is allowed to develop. Margaret's abandonment of Hollywood seems to go against everything her character represents, though it is of course consistent with the anti-Hollywood message embodied in Jim. It is interesting to compare this escape from Hollywood not only with the abortive flights from the film industry in *What Price Hollywood?* and *A Star Is Born* but also with a comic takeoff on this theme in Jean Harlow's *Bombshell* (1933, also titled *Blonde Bombshell*). In that movie, Harlow plays Lola Burns, a star actress shown repeatedly as the victim of her unscrupulous press agent, Space Hanlon (Lee Tracy), who cooks up fake scandals to get her name in the paper. The movie is a cheerful, fast-paced comedy, one of those movies where everyone seems to be shouting. When Space's antics finally drive Lola batty, she flees Hollywood for Palm Springs, where she falls in love with the handsome and healthy

Gifford Middleton (Franchot Tone). Gifford is essentially a cross between Jim Johannson of *The Star* and Lonny Borden of *What Price Hollywood?* He is a healthy outdoorsman but he's from a blue-blooded family that scorns the movies as vulgar. Gifford and Lola become engaged and plan to flee the Hollywood world, but he fears breaking the news to his parents. The parents are so condescending toward Lola that she abandons Gifford and returns to Hollywood with relief (recalling Mary Evans's initial preference for her Hollywood buddies over Lonny Borden's snobbish set). But this plot has a twist: Gifford and his family are all character actors planted by Space to cure Lola of her desire for a wholesome life away from pictures. His deception works. So in *Bombshell*, the alternative to Hollywood is equally illusory—the star cannot escape her world of celebrities and actors. Harlow's character can't stop being a celebrity; Davis's character can't regain her celebrity status. Both sides of Margaret Elliot's credo become apparent—"If you're a star, you don't stop being a star."

The paradoxes that are seemingly inherent in the Hollywood cautionary tale are not, finally, weaknesses. All three of these movies avoid simplistic stances toward the phenomenon of stardom. They show movie stars as complex figures, as dedicated workers who are oddly distanced from the effects of their labors, as individuals who experience extraordinary rewards and disappointments. Douglas Fairbanks said of *A Star Is Born*, "I have never been so completely moved by any picture in my memory. The delight of the first part and the heart tearing quality of the second part, made one of the rarest combinations that I have ever seen."[16] Fairbanks's praise realizes ambivalence as a potential strength in a movie. Perhaps such a realization helped generate more complex films about Hollywood and made producers less wary of a genre they considered (before *A Star Is Born*) to be unprofitable.

Is it possible for films that covertly celebrate stardom to offer useful insights about it as well? Can cultural criticism operate under the aegis of cultural chauvinism? I think so. For, ultimately, the ambivalence about Hollywood expressed in these films complicates the image of the star as figure of desire. We have noted how celebrities epitomize mimetic desire when the desire for consumer goods (with which they are often explicitly associated) is expressed through the fan's desire to become the person who possesses such goods. In a way, movie celebrities personify, or give human form to, the materialistic elements of the American Dream. But the fallen or struggling stars in these films exhibit a reciprocal desire for the simple domestic life associated with the nameless masses of the audience. This flattering counter desire, in which the figures you desire to imitate envy your simplicity, compounds rather than subverts celebrity appeal. The critiqued myth of stardom ironically humanizes the star and chastises an ungrateful audience. The step from idealized figure to tragic figure becomes a reconfiguration or heightening of idealization, a characterization that allows for the demystification and remystification of stardom. By complicating the myth of celebrity, these films revitalize it; in celebrating the myth, they complicate it.

2 Singin' on the Screen

Singin' in the Rain (MGM 1952). Producer: Arthur Freed. Directors: Gene Kelly and Stanley Donen. Screenwriters: Betty Comden and Adolph Green. Music: Nacio Herb Brown. Lyrics: Arthur Freed.

A Star Is Born (Warner Brothers 1954). Producer: Sidney Luft. Director: George Cukor. Screenwriter: Moss Hart, based on an original story by Robert Carson and William Wellman and a screenplay by Dorothy Parker, Alan Campbell, and Robert Carson. Music: Harold Arlen. Lyrics: Ira Gershwin.

Hollywood movies advertise themselves. In the closing moments of *Singin' in the Rain,* Don Lockwood (Gene Kelly) and Kathy Selden (Debbie Reynolds) embrace before a billboard advertising their upcoming feature.

Early in the 1954 remake of *A Star Is Born*, Norman Maine (James Mason) finds Esther Blodgett (Judy Garland) at the Downbeat Club, where she is jamming after hours with her orchestra after finishing a show at the Cocoanut Grove. Earlier in the evening, Esther and Norman had met on stage and she had cleverly saved him from drunken embarrassment by incorporating him into her act. Now that he has sobered up he wants to thank her and, the movie implies, pursue a romance with her. Norman walks into the smoky nightclub with chairs and ashtrays stacked and a few bartenders closing up. He remains hidden in the back of the club watching Esther and her orchestra rehearsing a new tune. Esther starts tentatively from sheet music, singing "The Man That Got Away," but she soon puts the music aside and launches into an all-out performance, replete with dramatic hand gestures. The camera keeps her centered in a medium shot as she snakes through her seven-piece band, dressed in blue and bathed in half-light. It is a bravura performance, certainly one of the two or three best renditions by Garland, one of the greatest singers of the screen. The Arlen-Gershwin composition allows for dramatic shifts in dynamics and mood and provides a superb showcase for Garland's voice. However the performance affects us in the film audience, it alters Norman's mission: he is now intent on persuading Esther to apply her tremendous talent to movies. He tells her, "You've got that little something extra that Ellen Terry talked about . . . star quality."

This musical number transforms the story of Esther Blodgett from the narrative of the 1937 original by giving Esther one quality she didn't exhibit at the start of the earlier film: talent. Indeed, it almost reverses the combination of talent and ambition. The Esther of the 1937 film had the desire to be an actress but no experience or demonstrated talent; the Esther of the 1954 film has tremendous talent but no ambition beyond continued success in music. Garland's Esther is thus more experienced and worldly than Gaynor's, and the process of making her a star does not wholly elide the question of talent as the 1937 *A Star Is Born* does. We are allowed to see exactly what enchants Norman Maine and what will delight the film audiences within the movie. As my analysis of the films in chapter 1 suggests, the addition of a clearly demonstrated talent to Esther's character partially demystifies the metanarrative of stardom.

We know, of course, that Esther has been transformed into a singer in order to make *A Star Is Born* into a musical. But that knowledge raises more questions than it answers. What happens when a non-musical movie is turned into a musical? Certainly it is possible simply to insert musical numbers illustrative of the action into the existing narrative (as appears to be the strategy in recent Broadway musicals made from non-musical films such as *Big*, *Kiss of the Spider Woman*, and *Sunset Boulevard*, the last example doubly ironic since the silent film star who couldn't make the transition to talkies must now express herself primarily through song). But the musical in which non-musical characters suddenly burst into song in operetta fashion has always seemed uncomfortable on the screen. So the alternative is to transform at least one character into a singer, which provides a realist justification for having her (or him) perform songs. Thus *A Star Is Born* becomes a backstage or "show" musical,[1] a musical about a musical performer making a musical. We see a similar metamorphosis in the film-within-the-film in *Singin' in the Rain*. When Monumental Pictures executives consider turning "The Duelling Cavalier" into a musical, they don't just add songs to the existing narrative; rather, they recast the film as a show musical. Cosmo Brown (Donald O'Connor) explains: "How's this? We throw a modern section into the picture. The hero's a young hoofer in a Broadway show, right? He sings and he dances. But one night backstage he's reading *A Tale of Two Cities* in between numbers, see? And a sandbag falls and hits him on the head. And he dreams he's back during the French Revolution." This strategy apparently solves their problems, not only by allowing for modern musical numbers but also by ensuring a principal character who can sing and dance.

The strategy is also important because it responds to one manifestation of the continuing tension between generic conventions and what is loosely and problematically called "realism," a tension important to reflexive Hollywood films that celebrate the movie medium. Tzvetan Todorov has argued with regard to literature that realism or verisimilitude is strictly genre dependent: "Discourses are not governed by a correspondence with their referent but by their own laws. . . . there are as many verisimilitudes as there are genres" (81, 83). So, for example, to have the most likely suspect be guilty violates the verisimilitude of the murder-mystery genre, just as having characters burst into song enhances the generic verisimilitude of a musical. Todorov's formulation has its limits, however, because it does not admit the possibility that audiences may find an entire genre more or less realistic, in the sense of the formal realism that Ian Watt has defined as a convention that presents itself as "a full and authentic report of human experience" (32).[2] Thus it is precisely the innocence of the most likely suspect (and similar conventions) that makes the mystery genre appear unrealistic (and different from—but not less valuable than—the realist novel or film). It is precisely the habit of characters who are not singers bursting into song that makes musicals seem particularly unrealistic.

The problem comes when the joyfully unrealistic genre of the musical is wedded to the remorselessly realistic medium of motion pictures. Even the generic license of the musical does not free the filmmaker from audience expectations about believability. Thus the backstage or show musical represents a particular kind of (limited) answer to this problem. In *A Star Is Born* virtually all the musical numbers are performances by actors portraying singers delivered in occasions that call for a song, and often the accompanying musicians are provided as characters in the scene. The movie's first song, "You Gotta Have Me Go with You," is performed by Esther and her orchestra at a Hollywood benefit. "The Man That Got Away" is an after-hours rehearsal. The jingle for Coconut Oil Shampoo is a television commercial. The lengthy production number "Born in a Trunk" is part of Esther's first film, screened as a film-within-the-film at a preview. "What Am I Here For?" is shown as a studio recording with live orchestra for a film. "Somewhere There's a Someone" is performed by Esther in her home using props at hand and accompanied by a practice record she puts on a turntable. "Lose That Long Face" is a rehearsal of a song-and-dance number for a film. The only slight exception occurs with "It's a New World." On their honeymoon, Norman and Esther hear the song on the radio, but Norman shuts it off and asks Esther to sing it to him personally. She begins unaccompanied, but after the first verse, an accompanying orchestra creeps in extra-diegetically, a technique Rick Altman defines as an "audio dissolve" (63).

I have risked belaboring these observations to point out that the 1954 *A Star Is Born* is an extreme example of a musical in which the numbers are grounded in the backstage frame; they do not interrupt the narrative with a discrete production number that surrounding characters pretend not to have heard. The backstage musical is reflexive by nature— and doubly so in a film about making film musicals. Thus the strategies for preserving the illusion of a realist narrative flow are technical manifestations of the thematic concern with whether musicals (and eventually movies in general) are shallow or inconsequential because of the ways in which they deviate from a certain mainstream representational realism.

But the backstage conceit does not solve the representational prob-lem. Indeed, most film musicals include both numbers framed as perfor-mances within the realist convention and songs that advance the narra-tive but are not framed as performances by entertainers (Feuer 24). Though it would seem that numbers that interrupt the narrative would be, by definition, less realistic, since they call attention to the movie as a musical, this is not necessarily the perception of audiences and critics. Many critics of the movie musical measure the unity and realism of a musical not by the diegetic grounding of the occasion for song but by the degree of integration of the song content with the narrative. That Esther Blodgett is singing in the nightclub is certainly consistent with her charac-ter, but the lyrics of "The Man That Got Away" have little to do with her dramatic situation. Show musicals are particularly liable to presenting framed performances that do not advance the narrative, while operettas (and musicals tending toward the operetta style) insist on the song and dance advancing, rather than interrupting, the story. In this context, we can see both strategies—the integrated musical, in which the numbers transform the narrative into a world brimming with music, and the show musical, in which the conceit of the show justifies the recurrent emer-gence of song—as solutions to the tension between film's inherent realism and the musical's generic tendency toward fantasy.

To make a film that is about Hollywood into a musical, though, the choice between the two strategies is clear: a show musical heightens the self-referentiality already woven into the plot. "Musicals about Hollywood almost always become musicals about making musicals" (Feuer 45). A Star Is Born and Singin' in the Rain are essential to this study because they demonstrate what happens when the self-referential genre of the movie about Hollywood meets the self-referential genre of the musical. Altman explains how back-stage musicals exhibit the paradox of movies about Hollywood: "Because we are permitted 'backstage' within the film, we fail to recognize that there is no such thing as backstage in the film world, only 'onstage.' We never go behind the set but only behind the stage part of the set" (223). While Altman argues that the illusion of seeing behind the set obscures the paradox, I be-lieve it can also serve to call attention to it, as it does in these musicals about Hollywood. Peter Wollen, in a study of Singin' in the Rain for the British Film Institute's Film Classics series, notes how that movie has "benefited critically from an increased interest in self-reflexive cinema [and] the foregrounding of conventionally concealed technology" (53).

With regard to the relation between primary diegesis and song and dance, *Singin' in the Rain* is a more hybrid example than *A Star Is Born*. It is, of course, a show musical, and the people who sing and dance are established as singers and dancers. And several numbers are framed performances ("All I Do Is Dream of You," performed by Kathy Selden at the premiere party; "Would You?," performed in the movie-within-the-movie, "The Dancing Cavalier"; and "Singin' in the Rain," when it is performed after that premiere). Some numbers are clearly *not* framed performances, however (the parodic Busby Berkeley–like montage about the coming of sound that segues into "Beautiful Girl"; Don Lockwood's confession of love, "You Were Meant for Me"; and the trio treatment of "Good Mornin'"). Still others are harder to place with regard to how much they suspend the narrative (the working-on-the-set numbers "Make 'Em Laugh" and "Moses Supposes"; the Gene Kelly version of the title song on the rainy street; and the highly problematic "envisioned" number, "Broadway Melody"). Nevertheless, *Singin' in the Rain* restricts the song and dance to characters identified as singers and dancers, and this restriction has important consequences in the exclusion of Lina Lamont. As in most musicals, part of the energy of the narrative is directed at endorsing music itself, what Jane Feuer calls "the genre's overall rhetoric of affirming itself" (55-56), against those Malvolio-like forces opposed to it. This propensity links the show musical to the movie about Hollywood, in that both are engaged in demystifying but ultimately celebrating the world of entertainment. This tension between competing views of Hollywood (critical and celebratory) animates the self-referentiality of both the 1954 *A Star Is Born* and *Singin' in the Rain;* both films intertwine the question of the value of cinema with the question of the value of musical entertainment. Both films—in very different ways—also explore what gets left out of the musical comedy.

The classic history of Hollywood presents two great crises for the film industry: the coming of sound and the coming of television (the latter coinciding with the break-up of studio control of exhibitors); *Singin' in the Rain* is set during the first crisis and filmed during the second. The film begins with the premiere of a Lockwood-Lamont silent film. Though the film is a success, an ominous threat is signaled at the celebratory party when a talking picture is screened to a disbelieving audience. Eventually the studio will decide to transform its next picture, a swashbuckling romance entitled "The Duelling Cavalier," into a talking picture. On the way to the party, Don Lockwood (Gene Kelly) meets and falls for Kathy Selden (Debbie Reynolds). He is charmed by her frankness in telling him she finds his pictures and other silents unimpressive, "just . . . a lot of dumb show." Though she claims to be interested only in serious drama, Kathy turns out to be a song-and-dance girl, like Don's old self (he came to silent acting from vaudeville) and his musician partner, Cosmo Brown.

While Don pursues Kathy there is trouble on the set. Not only does the new sound technology pose problems, but Lina Lamont (Jean Hagen) has a screechy, unrefined voice thoroughly at odds with her glamorous screen persona. After a disastrous preview of the talking version of "The Duelling Cavalier," Don and Cosmo and their producer, R.F. Simpson (Millard Mitchell), decide to turn it into a musical and use Kathy Selden to dub Lina's speaking and singing voice. The making of the renamed "The Dancing Cavalier" becomes the quest of the film, paralleled with Don's quest for Kathy's love. The film is successfully produced, but when Lina discovers her rival is doing the dubbing, she demands that Kathy be fired rather than given a chance to act on her own, as the studio proposes (Lina's contract evidently gives her this power). Only a public humiliation of Lina at the premiere (when the curtain lifts to reveal Kathy Selden singing behind her for a special encore) succeeds in derailing her malevolence. The movie ends with the successful premiere, the romantic union of Don and Kathy as they sing the duet "You Are My Lucky Star," and a shot of a billboard advertising the movie we have just seen—"Singin' in the Rain"—but starring Don Lockwood and Kathy Selden.

Singin' in the Rain thus includes a relationship between an aging star and a young hopeful (as in *A Star Is Born* and *What Price Hollywood?*), though here the young starlet succeeds in helping the older man regain his popularity. As is standard in backstage musicals, the union of the romantic couple parallels the creation of a successful show. But the self-celebration of the musical acquires interesting significance, given the treatment of the silent-to-talkies transition. That is, the value granted to song implicitly presents talking pictures as a drastic improvement over silent films, and the movie is surprisingly un-nostalgic (though refreshingly comical) in its treatment of Hollywood's past. Feuer describes the film's ideological stance this way: "*Singin' in the Rain* demystifies silent movies, serious theater and early talkies while glorifying musical comedy" (91). While this analysis is accurate, it is important to recognize that the movie also demystifies musical comedy, though it does so in the paradoxical process of celebrating it. Indeed, the plot of the film is as much about dubbing as it is about singing, and the story becomes complexly implicated in the interplay between illusion and reality. Though it is always easy to tell the good guys from the bad in this picture, it is not easy to see how that character valuation relates to issues about truth and illusion.

We see this interplay in the film's much-discussed opening scene. Approaching the microphone at the premiere, Don Lockwood is invited to describe "the story of your success [which] is an inspiration to young people all over the world." Don narrates the story of his career as a dignified ascent through dramatic training to serious acting, but while he narrates to a radio audience, the film shows scenes of his career that ironically comment on the publicity myth he is voicing. "Perform[ing] for Mom and Dad's society friends" is pictured as tap-dancing for tips at a pool hall; "accompanying Mom and Dad to the theater" is depicted as sneaking into monster films; "vigorous musical training at the conservatory of fine arts" is playing in a crowded barroom; and the tradition of the "most exclusive dramatic acting" is vaudeville. Don's Hollywood career is shown—in the visual interpolations only—beginning as a mood musician for silent actors, graduating to stunt double performing dangerous scenes, and finally achieving the position of leading man beside Lina Lamont. Throughout it all his motto is "Dignity—always dignity."

This fine comic scene has generated a variety of interpretations. On the most obvious level, the dichotomy presents the familiar Hollywood conflict between publicity image and real self. Don's romantic relationship with Lina is a product of just this sort of publicity fiction, though Lina wants to believe it herself. The ironic juxtaposition also reflects the paradigmatic musical conflict between high art and folk tradition, between classical and vaudeville—a conflict internalized in Kathy Selden's ambivalence toward her own song-and-dance ambitions.[3] One critic emphasizes the different messages addressed via radio/soundtrack as opposed to film/visual track, noting that the soundtrack or radio story is false while the visual film story tells the truth (Mast, *Can't Help Singin'* 264). The sound/image contrast, which Wollen identifies as "the core issue in the film" (55), implies two different audiences as well—the duped audience outside the premiere or over the radio and the privileged (backstage) film audience, of which we are a part. The audience at the premiere becomes a symbol for the dangerous mob, and after the premiere Don must flee their violent adulation.

Rick Altman sees the disjunction of Don Lockwood's words and the film's images as a potential critique of musicals in general: "Is this how it is with the musical as a genre? *Singin' in the Rain* seems to ask. Is the music nothing but window-dressing, nothing but crowd-pleasing rhetoric designed to cover up the inadequacies of the image? Is sound film—of which the musical is the prime symbol—a sham?" (255-57). That this comic scene engenders such interpretative controversies demonstrates the power of cinematic self-referentiality. *Singin' in the Rain* announces early that it will focus on the border regions: the transition between silents and sound, the relation between soundtrack and image track, the line between illusion and reality. *Singin' in the Rain* continues to frame the contrast between illusion and reality along the lines suggested in the opening scene: the conflict between celebrity publicity and genuine personality; the struggle between "dignity" and folk art; the gap between sound and image; and the contrast between duped audience and privileged audience.

The anxiety about the cultural status of popular entertainment is articulated in the argument that Don Lockwood and Kathy Selden have when they meet. Rather than being awed by Don's celebrity, Kathy first thinks that she knows of him from "Most Wanted" posters. When she finds he is the famous movie actor it raises her estimation of him only a little. "If you've seen one [movie] you've seen them all," she says. "Movies are entertaining enough for the masses. But the personalities on the screen just don't impress me. I mean they don't talk; they don't act. They just make a lot of dumb show. . . . At least the stage is a dignified profession. . . . You're nothing but a shadow on films. A shadow." This speech is important in a movie about the movies, and we will see versions of it throughout the years in self-reflective Hollywood films: it identifies Hollywood's concern about the social and aesthetic status of its products. Note how Kathy's attack (as it would be seen by the 1952 audience) criticizes *silent* films as lacking the linguistic grandeur of stage acting. Her speech is one example of how *Singin' in the Rain* distances its critique of film through its setting in the past. But note also how her speech invokes the terms of Don's self-presentation at the premiere: Don claims to have been trained in classical theater, Shakespeare, and Shaw; like Kathy he emphasizes the term "dignity" and seeks to present himself as a member of a "dignified profession" by suggesting a connection between theatrical and film acting. Though Kathy's elitist dismissal of movies understandably angers Don, it invokes the very dichotomies of his tailored publicity speech, except that Kathy groups movies with the undignified. This conflict between high art and popular entertainment is essentially imaginary, since there is no representative of classical art in the picture (as opposed to a musical such as *The Band Wagon*, for example); *Singin' in the Rain* is insistently middlebrow in the art and audience it represents. But the classical/popular conflict shadows the story through these moments of rhetorical invention: the gap between rhetoric and reality reveals Hollywood's contradictory desires to market mass entertainment and to aspire to high cultural status.

The most interesting quality of Kathy's tirade, however, is that she doesn't believe it herself. When she jumps out of the cake and into a dance chorus at the premiere party several minutes later, her pretense is unmasked. The gap between her speech to Don and her real entertainment self duplicates the gap between Don's words and the visual images that reveal his vaudeville background. It seems that Don and Kathy—like so many ambivalent figures in films about Hollywood—are popular entertainers who aspire to greater dignity or gravity. When, at the film's end, Don and Kathy costar in a film musical, they achieve a common ground and surrender their elitist pretensions for an affirmation of popular entertainment.

The endorsement of play, comedy, and music as the primary responsibility of actors is made explicit in the film's next musical number, "Make 'Em Laugh." Cosmo Brown sings and dances in an effort to cheer up Don, who now has lost touch with Kathy (after Kathy trades her dignity for a cinematic gesture in throwing a cake at Don and into Lina Lamont's face). The song could not be clearer about its stand regarding popular culture and the classics. The singer relates how his father advised him to be a comical actor because that is what attracts audiences— making them laugh. To be a serious actor and attempt Shakespeare is to risk pleasing the critics but being destitute. The rollicking number shows Cosmo playing the piano—with his feet and elbows as well as his hands. The dance involves a variety of at-hand props and steps that give the appearance that his body is out of control. Behind the backstage area in which he dances, there stands a photographed set that gives the illusion of an outstretching colonnade. Cosmo's dance takes him right up the set decoration, which thus destroys the illusion of depth it offers. The dance ends with him crashing through a wall. These details are important to recognizing the oddity of this moment in the film: Cosmo Brown is lauding vaudeville, musical comedy, and slapstick to the screen's great dramatic lover. Similarly, he is creating illusion while unmasking it, exactly as these movies do. He creates the illusion of a spontaneous joyful dance, while breaking the illusions of sets and props around him. The song's invocation of Shakespeare, who so often stands for high culture in Hollywood, again demonstrates how the film contrasts an imagined elite culture with the world of movies.

The parallel scenes revealing Don's and Kathy's ambivalences about popular entertainment are followed by contrasting love scenes played on the set. First, Don and Lina enact a love scene before the cameras while snarling at each other; then, Don confesses his love for Kathy with a song on a stage he has filled with scenic effects. The scene with Lina plays on both the ability of an actor to pretend emotions (as we see in Judy Garland's "Lose That Long Face" sequence in *A Star Is Born*) and the gap between sound and image in the filming of a silent picture. Both Don and Kathy brilliantly depict screen lovers as they hiss nasty remarks at one another. In a reversal of the opening scene, the spoken words in this scene depict their true relationship while the visual images present a false show. But at the end of the scene, even Lina is fooled by Don's kiss: "You couldn't kiss me like that and not mean it," she says. "Meet the greatest actor in the world," Don replies. This scene may provide a clue as to why Lina's manipulations of illusion are presented unsympathetically. After all, Lina and Don exhibit the same gap between spoken and pantomimed sentiment in this scene—but Lina gets fooled by the act. Gerald Mast asks the question this way: "Why then is the [false] appearance of Cosmo, Kathy, and Don as performers superior in this film to the appearance of Lina Lamont if all are mere appearances?" (*Singin'* 265). Mast argues that the first three gain a moral superiority by being aware of themselves as performers. This scene suggests that he is right. It is also one of many scenes that reveal cinematic tricks to the audience. In this case the scene educates viewers about how silent pictures were shot: with mood music for the performers, a director shouting commands, and actors speaking lines possibly quite different from what one would imagine. The scene calls attention to the falseness of the emotions depicted on screen. In a memo discussing an earlier production, *Paramount on Parade* (1929), David O. Selznick attests to this common movie knowledge: "You know from experience that often in silent pictures very romantic love scenes were played with the actors talking about a party the night before, or some other totally irrelevant subject" (Behlmer and Thomas 23).

When Don reunites with Kathy, he wants to profess his love for her but claims he needs the proper setting, which turns out to be an artificial stage. He takes her into a huge darkened stage but then fills the empty set with effects: "a beautiful sunset, mist from the distant mountains, colored lights in a garden . . . flooded with moonlight, five thousand kilowatts of stardust, a soft summer breeze" (that is, a lit backdrop, a smoke machine, colored footlights, spotlights, and a wind machine). He puts Kathy on a ladder and asks her to pretend it is a balcony, and then, framed by the wind machine and the smoke machine, he bursts into "You Were Meant for Me." Throughout the song and the dance, these artificial devices remain visible. The screen lover is most comfortable on the set, but here the illusion spells romance, not deception. Since his performance is live, there is no gap between sound and visual image, as in the contrasting earlier scene, nor is there the kind of deception involved in dubbing, where the sound only appears to issue from the lips of a character (an effect played with through the rest of the movie). Similarly, the artificiality in this scene does not create a gap between celebrity self and genuine self: though Don is on a stage, he is singing to an audience of one. Nevertheless, revealing his true emotions requires the trappings of illusion.

Singin' in the Rain shows us the difficulties encountered when Monumental Pictures turns "The Duelling Cavalier" into a talking picture, "The Dancing Cavalier." Once again, the movie provides an education on the technical problems faced by early sound film (microphone placement, extraneous noises, and so forth). When the finished film is previewed, we get a primer in the disasters of early sound technology. But before we discuss the preview of "The Duelling Cavalier," we should recall the reaction to the demonstration of a talking picture at the party following the successful Lockwood-Lamont premiere. One of this movie's many framed films, the demonstration at R.F.'s party simply shows a man talking—slowly and deliberately—"in perfect synchronization" (interestingly, the man comes so close to the camera that his face is distorted—but his voice remains clear). The insider audience at the party is disbelieving: they think someone is hidden behind the screen (in a neat anticipation of Kathy Selden's singing behind the curtain in the movie's final scene). Though they dismiss the technique as a vulgar toy, their original confusion is important to remember. They assume the realistic image of a talking person must be an elaborate magic trick.

The preview of "The Duelling Cavalier" offers a comic compendium of the problems of early talkies. Lina's pearls rattle loudly, her voice shifts into and out of her unrefined accent, Don's staff thunders to the ground with a clunk, and all the voices vary in volume as they move to and from the microphone concealed in Lina's bodice. Finally the entire scene shifts out of synchronization and eventually slows down to a basso crawl. The three-and-a-half-minute episode also reveals the full syntax of film-within-a-film scenes. It begins with a standard framing shot showing the backs of the audience and the movie screen. Then the camera shifts to a close-up of the black-and-white images on the screen, with a telltale red curtain border along the top reminding us that we are watching the framed movie. Seven times the film cuts from "The Duelling Cavalier" to the audience: five of those times to the panicked actors and producers, two times to the audience roaring with laughter. But the laughter is directed not just at the technical follies, but also at the romantic dialogue. The biggest and most scornful laughter follows Don's repeated "I love you." Here *Singin' in the Rain* is alluding to the legendary story of John Gilbert's talkie premiere, in which his repeated "I love you" was met with laughter. Though the legend suggests the problem was Gilbert's high-pitched voice, film historians have demonstrated that there was nothing odd about Gilbert's voice. The real problem was that the histrionics of silent lovers did not translate effectively to the talking pictures.[4] Don senses this in the postmortem discussion of "The Duelling Cavalier," when he realizes the problem was not just technical: "I'm no actor."

Well, what is he then? Don's admission echoes Kathy's original critique of him. As a silent star he passes as a serious actor even though his training is in vaudeville. Thus, Kathy and Cosmo recognize the solution: "Why don't you . . . make a musical!" Indeed, as we saw in the confession-of-love scene, Don Lockwood is more comfortable singing than talking. There is a historical lesson here as well: along with *The Jazz Singer*, many of the earliest talkies were musicals. When voice was brought to film, musicals were the inevitable result. *Singin' in the Rain* captures this connection in an image in the musical montage announcing the coming of sound: at one point, a crooner sings through a megaphone; the megaphone fills the screen in a close-up, so that all we see is a black corridor leading to a mouth; suddenly the outer rim of the megaphone is filled with chorus girls dancing, filmed from above in Busby Berkeley kaleidoscopic style. As Rick Altman phrases it, "When film first learned to speak, it sang instead" (131).

But while Don may have an easier time singing than talking, the musical poses no solution for screechy-voiced Lina. Here the movie (and our heroes) appeal once again to film technology: Kathy dubs Lina's voice, singing and speaking. The dubbing ironically replaces the voice of Don's celebrity lover with that of his genuine lover, so that the illusionary trick puts him closer to his "true" love. But the solution moves the other way on the dignity continuum, by replacing romantic drama with musical comedy.

At this point the movie turns its attention to the mechanics of dubbing. In a wonderful series of images, it depicts the dubbing of "Would You?" The scene begins, appropriately, with a close-up of the microphone. The camera pulls back to reveal Kathy singing behind it, accompanied in a recording studio by an orchestra. As the song continues uninterrupted, the visual track fades to Lina practicing lip-synching by singing over Kathy's voice, which is now present on a record. Then we cut to Lina successfully lip-synching in full costume on the set. The color scene turns to black and white, a sign of the film-within-the-film, confirmed when the camera pulls back to reveal the borders of a screen in the room where dailies are shown. As the song ends in the film-within-the-film, R.F. pronounces his verdict: "Perfect." The scene maintains aural continuity through Debbie Reynolds's soundtrack, while the visuals locate that sound in a series of different locations: the recording studio, the record, the film-within-the-film.

Or is it Debbie Reynolds we hear? Certainly we are invited to assume so. But in one of those fine ironies of which demystifying Hollywood films always seem to be guilty, we actually hear the voice of Betty Royce dubbed for Reynolds (Mast 264). Similarly, the scene that shows Kathy dubbing Lina's dialogue was actually done entirely by Jean Hagen, "using first her 'Lina voice,' then her own cultured speech" (Card 92). These scenes invite us to be skeptical by showing one of Hollywood's most important production techniques—dubbing, or looping. Singin' in the Rain invites us to cheer this technical solution to the movie's problem, but it also suggests that the solution is unfair to Kathy by keeping her talent off screen. Wollen argues that "things can only end happily when, so to speak, a properly 'married print' is produced, in which voice and image are naturally joined together" (55). Thus Kathy is promised a film career of her own after this picture: a star is finally born! This step in the plot is crucial to achieving the resolution of uniting Don and Kathy in love and in a musical career simultaneously, but it also reflects the film's slippery attitude toward the falseness of dubbing (that is, it is hard to condemn Lina and applaud Kathy for conspiring in the same deception).

Singin' in the Rain consistently views musical comedy as the logical conclusion of the development of talking pictures. That point emerges in the lengthy production number "Broadway Melody" and the way it is framed in the film. Don Lockwood is explaining to R.F. a number he wants to add to "The Dancing Cavalier." He gestures toward the blank screen of the rushes room and says, "It goes like this." What follows, though, is not his verbalization of the number, but the full-blown production number shown in full screen (no frame) and in color. The number strings together a variety of Broadway tunes and features Gene Kelly and Cyd Charisse (who plays a dancer) and hundreds of chorus members in an elaborate set with neon signs and its own interior stage (a stage-within-the-screen of sorts). The number is a separately produced musical extravaganza, added to *Singin' in the Rain* much as Don proposes adding it to "The Dancing Cavalier." At the end, an image of Kelly beaming at the camera fades into Kelly gesturing at the blank screen, just as the number began. We, the privileged audience, have seen the number Don has only verbalized to R.F. Though it stems from a plot point and is presented as a musical number by a singer-character, the piece is visible only to the audience, not to R.F., which is consistent with the operetta-style musical. The movie reinforces this point with a joke: "I can't quite visualize it," mutters R.F. "I'll have to see it on film first." Once again, we find that Don is not a very good talker, but the magic of movies crystallizes his words into images for us (the privileged audience), as in the movie's opening scene. Now the musical film eclipses the inadequate words with the truth, which is here, fittingly, a musical comedy spectacle.

The tendency of musicals to make music their subject is epitomized in this movie in the initial performance of the title song "Singin' in the Rain." Feuer categorizes "numbers in which a performer sings and dances as he sings about singing and dancing" as "reflexive songs," and she demonstrates how common they are in musicals (50). "Singin' in the Rain" is surely the most famous, and it has entered popular culture to an extraordinary extent. This particular number belongs to a class of popular songs that preach the power of one's outlook to overcome external obstacles, a significant theme in American popular culture. Thus the rain represents hardship, and Gene Kelly begins the number by dismissing his cab and folding up his umbrella (which he later gives away after using it as a dancing prop). Having fallen in love, Don Lockwood is made oblivious to rain; his smile becomes his umbrella. The lyric's optimism that love conquers all expresses itself in song and dance, but the song is more about singing than being in love. Its self-referentiality is once removed from post-modernist self-reference (as in, say, John Barth's "Lost in the Funhouse," where the narrator describes his struggle to write the story). That is, Kelly does not sing, "I'm singin' and dancin' on a stage," though that is essentially the burden of numbers like "Broadway Melody." Here it is enough that the song identifies and celebrates his musical activity. With its extra-diegetic orchestra and the fake rainstorm (one of Hollywood's oldest and most transparent effects), "Singin' in the Rain" is hardly a demystifying self-reference. Yet it contributes to the more frankly demystifying moments in the film by insisting on singing as the subject of the song. In doing so it captures in miniature the self-referential theme of the movie: a song about singing in a musical about musicals in a Hollywood movie about Hollywood. That the song—like almost all the tunes in *Singin' in the Rain*—is borrowed from an earlier musical is appropriate to the retrospective self-reference of the film, which, according to Mast, "is as much about the coming of musicals to MGM as the conversion of Hollywood to sound" (261). For all these reasons, it makes sense that this song should contribute its title to the picture as a whole (and to the upcoming movie-within-the-movie advertised on the billboard in the film's final shot). Interestingly, the title of the film preceded the plot: *Singin' in the Rain* was conceived simply from "Arthur Freed's wish to make a musical that would use the best of the songs he had written with Nacio Herb Brown. . . . Freed contacted writers Adolph Green and Betty Comden . . . and asked them to come up with a concept, telling them only that the film would be titled *Singin' in the Rain*" (Behlmer and Thomas 310).

The climax of the film, the premiere of "The Dancing Cavalier," takes us full circle to the film's opening, which was the premiere of a successful silent Lockwood and Lamont picture. The final showing solves the problem raised at the film's low point, the ridiculed preview of "The Duelling Cavalier." Directors Kelly and Donen use the same film-within-a-film technique, beginning with a framed shot that shows the backs of the audience and the black-and-white screen they are watching and moving to a shot in which the black-and-white screen is barely framed (here by a black border). Only once do they cut to the (now approving) audience, as we see the concluding number of "The Dancing Cavalier."

The great success of "The Dancing Cavalier" poses a problem for the plot's resolution, and it is Lina Lamont who realizes this, as she argues that R.F. will not tamper with the profitable combination of Lina's fame and Kathy's voice. Indeed, Lina speaks the realistic voice of Hollywood here, and the studio's dedication to an unknown singer who dubbed a star's voice is hardly believable. But it is necessary to the plot, and so the conspiring men—Don, Cosmo, and R.F.—concoct a stratagem to discredit Lina by revealing the fact that Kathy dubbed her voice. This scene is crucial in revealing the problematics of truth and illusion that militate against the comic structure of *Singin' in the Rain*. Lina takes a bow after the successful premiere and insists on exhibiting rather than hiding her speaking voice, telling her co-stars, "Tonight, I'm going to do my own talking." To the audience, Lina's voice and grammar ("Our hard work ain't been in vain") betray her, and some audience members exclaim that that is not the voice in the movie. Then they call on her to sing.

The scene recalls the reception of Gloria Swanson's first talking picture, *The Trespasser* (1929). Swanson was one of the greatest stars of silent pictures, and *The Trespasser* was also a success, but fans wondered if the singing voice was really hers. Since Swanson could not accompany the picture across the country singing at premieres, the studio supplied affidavits and testimony to reviewers to dispel the false rumor that Swanson was dubbed (Swanson 409). Swanson's experience anticipates the audience's skepticism about the demonstration of talking pictures at the party in *Singin' in the Rain*. And the viewers remain skeptical at the premiere of "The Dancing Cavalier." So Lina moves her lips to "Singin' in the Rain" while a live pit orchestra plays and Kathy sings behind the curtain. Don, Cosmo, and R.F. hoist the curtain to reveal Lina's secret voice and thus humiliate her and reveal Kathy as, in Don's words, "the real star of the picture." Aside from the improbability of the dubbing of a voice making one a star, the scene is problematic in other ways. Dubbing was the technical solution that saved Lockwood and Lamont, but now Lina is supposed to lose her career and self-respect when the technique is revealed. Elsewhere, *Singin' in the Rain* reveals technical tricks to celebrate them and show them as still effective, a technique common throughout films about Hollywood. Here, the technique damns Lina. Why is she the villain and outcast in this happy ending?

The plot offers several answers. Lina had acted uncharitably in getting Kathy fired from the Cocoanut Grove and selfishly in blocking her career at Monumental Pictures. She is a classic blocking character, standing in the way of the happy ending by virtue of her faith in the studio publicity that says Don loves her. Lina also appears to be guilty of errors in aesthetic judgment: she *likes* the disastrous preview of "The Duelling Cavalier"; she doesn't understand "what's wrong with [her] voice"; and she can't distinguish between publicity love and real love. These aesthetic crimes reflect her lack of joy in cinematic illusion and—most tellingly for the musical—her lack of musical ability. Still, her negative status in the film is hard to explain, since all the cuts at her lack of refinement run counter to the film's celebration of popular entertainment. These contradictions reflect an unresolved ambivalence about dramatic acting in the world of musical comedy, but they also reflect the difficulty of identifying any value as genuine or real in the multileveled fictionality of films-within-films. The best films about Hollywood always seem to lead us into these sorts of irresolvable contradictions, which arise from the cross purposes of the genre: to unmask Hollywood illusion and to celebrate Hollywood magic. *Singin' in the Rain* is an extreme case of this split tendency. Feuer argues that for all its attention to cinematic technology, *Singin' in the Rain* strives to remain "the product of magic": "Such a technological education, while demystifying in a literal sense, becomes mystifying at the level of audience impact, as we see film technology as a new form of spectacle, a new show" (46). This formulation offers significant truth for the Hollywood-on-Hollywood genre as a whole, though I would not join Feuer in assuming that "remystification" is necessarily an ideological subterfuge or an artistic failing.

Singin' in the Rain invites us to see Kathy and Don in love and in a film together as the real, uncorrupted happy marriage of love and stardom. The ending of the film presents just this resolution. As Kathy returns to Don with tear-stained cheeks at the premiere, he sings "You Are My Lucky Star." The film fades from Don's profile to a match cut of his profile on a billboard advertising "Singin' in the Rain" with Don Lockwood and Kathy Selden. With a chorus echoing "You Are My Lucky Star" in the background, Don and Kathy embrace beneath the billboard and the film ends. This self-referential gesture that alludes to the film we have just seen is an important feature of movies about Hollywood: we see it in the screenplay shots in the 1937 *A Star Is Born* and in the story pitch that concludes *The Player* (1992). But these devices exhibit the limitations of Hollywood self-referentiality, the fact that you can never truly get behind the camera. Here, the titles of the films match, but the actors don't—we have just seen *Singin' in the Rain* with Gene Kelly and Debbie Reynolds. Similarly, our film is a backstage drama about the making of "The Duelling Cavalier" and the *upcoming* creation of "Singin' in the Rain." Still, the film ends with an advertisement of itself, which is fitting for the musical genre's typical self-promotion.

Appropriately, the billboard at the end counters the opening premiere by showing Lockwood-Selden superseding Lockwood-Lamont. Indeed, the ending shows the righting of several of the tensions we identified at the film's outset: the Selden romance ("real life") replaces the Lamont romance (publicity), unabashed musical comedy replaces the pretensions to dignity in silent melodrama, the raising of the curtain behind the lip-synching Lina unites visual image and soundtrack, and perhaps the billboard even looks forward to uniting privileged audience with the "mob" audience within the film (who can now see "Singin' in the Rain"). But these outcomes are not opposed to the world of cinematic illusion. Indeed, the union of one-time stunt double Lockwood and one-time voice double Selden is accomplished through film technology, just as Lockwood's confession of love depends on an artificial set. *Singin' in the Rain* is the first example we will see of a familiar cinematic self-defense: the sheer escapist joy of movie entertainment is posited as a passionate counterbalance to a surprisingly thorough unmasking of illusory effects. The pleasure of the text subverts the realist critique, which the movie presents precisely to discredit. We will see a similar technique in *Sullivan's Travels*, and, recast in terms of audience experience, in *The Purple Rose of Cairo* and *Last Action Hero*.

The musical version of *A Star Is Born* appeared just two years after *Singin' in the Rain*, but it is set in the fifties, not the twenties. Some of the echoes of and contrasts with *Singin' in the Rain* are no doubt intentional. Mast calls *A Star Is Born* a response to *Singin' in the Rain*. He cites the rain puddles Judy Garland dances through in "Lose That Long Face," the opening and closing premiere scenes, and "Born in a Trunk" as Garland's answer to Kelly's "Gotta Dance" (275). I will discuss some additional parallels: the on-stage proposal, the play with recording and dubbing, the dances with at-hand props, and the scenes that reveal the gap between acted and felt emotions. But these echoes and contrasts, whether deliberate or simply a response to the genre, help to demonstrate how the marriage of the cautionary tale and the self-reflective musical creates an anti-musical, what Rick Altman calls "the one film which most effectively contests the genre's clotural conventions while demythologizing stardom, the one film which most poignantly accuses the musical of lying" (265). Certainly if we follow theoreticians of the musical and define the show musical as a film in which the uniting of the couple corresponds with the success of the show, *A Star Is Born* undermines the conventions: the couple splits apart through Norman Maine's suicide and the second half of the picture is virtually devoid of musical numbers. Altman sums it up: *A Star Is Born* "forever banishes the show musical's earlier automatic equation between success in romance and success on the stage" (268). As in the 1937 film, a happy ending of sorts is salvaged by a "show-must-go-on" stoicism on Vicki Lester's part. But this version of the film is even darker than the earlier one in questioning the dynamics of the happy ending and the joyous spirit of the musical.

The plot of the remake is very close to that of the original, with the significant exception I have already noted: Esther Blodgett is mature and talented and only reluctantly interested in screen celebrity. Even the extended musical number in the movie-within-the-movie, "Born in a Trunk," pictures success as the end result of a lifelong struggle, noting how the singer's career began with being born to a show business family. Not only does this change accommodate the shift to a musical, but it also broadens Garland's role. Still, the latter half of the film echoes scene after scene of the original: the humiliating Academy Award scene, the visit to the sanitarium, the pitiful encounter with Libby at Santa Anita, the appearance in night court, the circumstances of Norman Maine's suicide, the mob of fans at the funeral, the admonitory speech to Vicki Lester (here given by her piano player, Danny Maguire, instead of her grandmother), and the dramatic conclusion at a premiere ("This is Mrs. Norman Maine").

Four scenes unique to the musical version of the film display the effect of musical self-referentiality on the Hollywood cautionary tale: the marriage proposal on the soundstage, Oliver Niles's termination of Norman's contract at the party, Vicki's performance of the production number "Somewhere There's a Someone" to Norman at home, and the poignant performance of "Lose That Long Face." The proposal scene clearly echoes Don Lockwood's musical confession of love in *Singin' in the Rain*, but it combines that love scene with the comic play with recording and dubbing that characterized the earlier movie in other scenes. The now successful Vicki Lester is prerecording a song for her next movie. She sings a verse of "What Am I Here For?" accompanied by live orchestra. Norman Maine enters the back of the studio and watches from a stairway. The cuts from Judy Garland singing to James Mason watching invite us to share his gaze, or at least they call attention to Garland as a performer being observed.[5] The song lyrics have their relevance to the developing love between Norman and Vicki as well, as the singer offers to share her life with her beloved. It is almost as if she is proposing to him in song.

When the song reaches the chorus, Vicki runs from the mike to greet Norman. They sit together and talk, but we can't hear them. Sound technicians, however, sneak up a microphone and record their conversation: here we become voyeurs with them—though not quite, because we can't hear what the technicians are eavesdropping on (though we do see them poke one another in the ribs). Then Norman and Vicki go up to a speaker to listen to the playback, only to find their conversation on tape with the chorus in the background. They holler for it to be turned off, but, to their embarrassment, it continues:

> Norman: Will you marry me?
> Vicki: No, thank you.
> Norman: Why not?
> Vicki: Well, you're irresponsible. . . . [sung] You drink too much.
> Norman: Suppose I quit drinking. Suppose I became absolutely dependable on all occasions.
> Vicki: You wouldn't be Norman Maine. I'd be marrying the wrong man. Norman? Darling, would you do all that for me if I said I'd marry you?
> Norman: No, I had a chance to think it over with all that humming and singing—too much to ask.

The playback scene presents us with a complicated soundtrack: the musical playback, the recorded proposal and rejection, Norman and Vicki's embarrassed comments in the present, the orchestra and technicians' laughter and comments. The putatively spontaneous and authentic proposal becomes audible to the film audience only during the playback of a recording that will dub an apparently spontaneous moment in the musical-within-the-musical. This complex framing shows how difficult access to the authentic can be in the context of Hollywood film.

Having refused him live, Vicki accepts him during the playback: "That's much too public a proposal for me to say no to. I accept." They embrace to the cheers of the orchestra and sound technicians. The scene tells us several things about Norman and Vicki. It shows us how intertwined professional and private lives are for them, and it foreshadows how celebrity will conflict with their dreams of domestic happiness. As in the boxing match Wellman used as a backdrop to the 1937 proposal scene, this scene shows the struggle between Vicki and Norman. She puts conditions on their marriage and he refuses them. She turns him down in private, but when their conversation is literally aired she accepts him. The scene is marvelously acted: Garland's facial expressions mix embarrassment with joy as she is forced to listen to herself caught in simultaneous private and public performances, singing what amounts to a proposal and speaking a refusal.

After their marriage, Vicki's career rises as Norman's plummets, in the structure basic to the early cautionary tales. The coup de grace to Norman's career is delivered by Oliver Niles (Charles Bickford) when he tells Norman he must buy out his contract. Both the dialogue in the scene and the structure of the set locate this decision in the context of the financial crisis of the film industry in the fifties. Norman and Vicki are entertaining at home and, in Hollywood fashion, offer a film on their home screen. During the newsreel, Oliver sneaks into another room to watch a fight on television. Norman confronts him, and Oliver tells him the bad news: "They can't afford you anymore, Norman. You're too big a risk." The problem is not the declining grosses of his recent films, because, as the scene explains, that is an industry-wide problem. The difficulty is Norman's drunken unreliability. Cukor sets up the scene so that Oliver and Norman are framed between the television screen and the movie screen (visible through a glass wall). The competition posed by television motivates the scene.[6] When Norman realizes his career is through, he reaches over and shuts the cabinet door to the television. In a following scene, a billboard advertising Norman Maine in "Black Legion" is changed to one advertising Vicki Lester in "Happiness Ahead." The titles reflect the fates of their respective careers, but perhaps they also signal the fifties' infatuation with cheery musicals (usually lifted straight from Broadway). And, of course, "Happiness Ahead" ironically prefigures the couple's future.

As in the original, Norman becomes a househusband while Vicki

works long hours at the studio. Coming home late in her rehearsal costume, she offers to perform her latest number for him. The result is a
wonderfully self-referential parody of a production number, "Somewhere
There's a Someone." She puts the practice record on the turntable and
sings and dances to it. But she adds spoken comments about the number's
intent that mock its grandiosity, and she makes comic use of everyday
furnishings as props and costumes. In the course of the number, she uses
plant leaves, a hassock, a coffee table, several throw pillows, a lampshade,
an animal-skin rug, the telephone, and salt and pepper shakers in a piece
that travels the globe from Paris to China to Africa to Brazil. Norman
mocks along with Vicki the hackneyed use of foreign locations and arbitrary injections of patriotism. Vicki's spoken comments turn her strong
vocal rendition into a parody: "You know I get pretty girlish in this number"; "There's always a harp in a dream sequence, don't be silly"; "Twenty
girls just came out of the floor and there's smoke all over the room." The
most famous moment occurs when she says, "Now here comes a big fat
close-up," and frames her face with her hands. Vicki's marvelously cheerful acknowledgment of how her face becomes an icon (and of how screen
technique differs from stage) became the publicity poster for the movie.
Making a frame of her hands, Garland reminds us of the movie's multiple
frames. The spirit of that moment infuses the whole scene: she is both
celebrating her talent and mocking the genre conventions of the musical.
Having it both ways—the two-edged sword of parody—is the dominant
aesthetic of films about Hollywood. They make fun of the conventions,
the studios, and the town while glorifying and celebrating them. When it
is done right, as it is in this scene, the result is wisdom, not hypocrisy.

The lyrics fit the irony of the scene by describing how the singer
searches the world over for the right "someone." Searching the world for
the perfect mate in her fictional role, Vicki has that someone right at
home (one hears the moral of *The Wizard of Oz* hovering in the background). Similarly, Vicki domesticates her big exotic locale number by
performing it at home for her audience of one and using domestic furnishings as exotic props. Her final prop is the film projector and screen
itself. She turns on their home screen and dances with her screen shadow
in the projector's flickering light. This superb effect captures how her talent is magnified on the screen, while the whole scene epitomizes how she
is caught between home life and screen life. In their moment of ecstatic
embrace at the song's end, the doorbell rings, and it is a messenger who

will call Norman "Mr. Lester" and catalyze his fall into despair.

The rehearsal for "Lose That Long Face" follows Norman's disastrous humiliation at the Academy Awards banquet, where his drunken plea for work upstages Vicki's receiving the Oscar for Best Actress. Norman has reached a low and Vicki is desperate in her attempts to help him and save her marriage. Her most bitter despair, evidenced in a tearful conversation with Oliver Niles, is deliberately juxtaposed with a comical number about wiping the sad look off your face and replacing it with a smile. The scene takes to its logical conclusion the scene in *Singin' in the Rain* where Lockwood and Lamont bicker while filming a love scene. Here Vicki Lester "loses that long face" in an ironic undermining of the optimism of musical comedy.

The number is framed as a rehearsal take, acted on a soundstage with a playback record for accompaniment. Vicki is dressed as a ragamuffin selling newspapers that bear the headline "Bright Future Predicted." She sings and tap-dances through a vaguely turn-of-the-century urban

Vicki Lester (Judy Garland) puts herself on screen in this home performance mocking movie musicals in the 1954 *A Star Is Born*.

scene, exhorting the surrounding townspeople to "lose that long face" and replace it with a smile. She dances through a brief rainstorm, the rain serving as a symbol for glumness, which can be overcome by positive thinking and music, as it does in "Singin' in the Rain," "Over the Rainbow," and, as we will see, "Pennies from Heaven." Through much of the number she dances with two black children, and at one point she relieves a black washerwoman of the basket of laundry she carries on her head. The verses of the song assert, through deliberately silly lyrics, that a smile can banish depression and sorrow. The chorus urges the listener to "lose that long face" by an act of optimistic will. A harmless and lively number, this piece participates in the central tenet of the musical credo—the belief that music brings joy and that the will to be happy can triumph over obstacles and sorrows. But inserting the song here is deliberately ironic: not only does the personal situation of Vicki Lester and Norman Maine belie the song's advice, but the irony raises doubts about the persistent optimism of the musical form and of Hollywood movies in general.

The personal irony is reinforced in the dressing-room scene that follows the first take. At the end of the song, Vicki loses her happy face and retreats for makeup in her dressing room. Throughout the scene, attention to makeup and the mirror reinforces the emphasis on putting a face on and how that superficiality is linked to the art of screen images. Oliver shows up in Vicki's dressing room, having just returned from three months away from the studio. When he asks about Norman, Vicki breaks down in a lengthy and painful speech:

> He's in a sanitarium. He really wants to stop drinking, Oliver. He's trying very hard, I know he is. But— What is it that makes him want to destroy himself? . . . Tell me what it is. . . . You don't know what it's like to watch somebody you love just crumble away bit by bit, day by day, in front of your eyes and stand there helpless. Love isn't enough. I thought it was. I thought I was the answer for Norman. But love isn't enough for him. And I'm afraid of what's beginning to happen to me. Because sometimes: *I hate him!* I hate his promises to stop, and then watching and waiting to see it begin again. I hate to go home to him at night and listen to his lies. My heart goes out to him because he tries. He does try. But I hate him for failing. I

hate me too—'cause I've failed too. I have. I don't know
what's going to happen to us. No matter how much you
love somebody—how do you live out the days?

By the end of this speech, she is, understandably, in tears. She is
forced to fix her own makeup and hurry out to the stage, where she loses
her long face and bursts into smile and song, lip-synching the choric conclusion of the number for close-ups. The speech not only powerfully relates the emotional struggles of living with an alcoholic, it also directly
assaults the central mythology of motion pictures—that love *is* enough.
The story of Vicki Lester's ascent is a paean to the American and Hollywood mythology of desire making dreams come true: "[Your] dream isn't
big enough," Norman says to singer Esther earlier in the film. But the
story of Norman Maine himself shows that "love isn't enough." And "Lose
That Long Face" demonstrates its own inappropriateness. The musical
in particular, and the Hollywood film in general, insist on optimism and
the happy ending; *A Star Is Born* is at war with itself. The focus on alcoholism and depression creates a context in which musical values become
inefficacious, even cavalier.

No one would know that better than the actress Judy Garland. The
beginning of this speech is shot in a mirror with the back of Garland's
head in the left foreground and the medium-shot images of Garland and
Bickford reflected in the mirror. No fifties audience could miss how these
lines about Norman Maine apply to Garland's own self-destructive battle
with depression and addiction.[7] In that context, "I hate me too" takes on
added weight. Hollywood movies about Hollywood always have the potential for this sort of actor self-referentiality. The only false note here (as
in so many stories of Hollywood decline) is the extraordinarily benevolent characterization of the producer and the studio. Here the avuncular
Oliver suggests offering Norman a job to help him out. In real life, MGM
fired Garland for unreliability, and she and producer-husband Sidney Luft
had a difficult time finding a studio to make *A Star Is Born*.

Ultimately, "Lose That Long Face"—the only full number from the
decline portion of the movie—challenges the tyranny of the happy ending
and reveals the contradictions of the genre of films about Hollywood. It
provides a good example of how the intelligent examination of those contradictions can strengthen a film. "Genre" is a problematic term in that it
identifies categories that can overlap. We speak of comedy as a genre,

but also of narrative film and the musical film (as well as the film about Hollywood) as genres. The happy ending creates appropriate structural and thematic closure in comedies; certainly it is one of the defining characteristics of comedy. What we encounter in *A Star Is Born* (both versions) and in the cautionary tale *What Price Hollywood?* is a conflict between the drive for a happy ending (characteristic of comedy) and a plot that moves toward tragedy leavened with elements of satire. Northrop Frye in his famous discussion of comedy observes that "happy endings do not impress us as true but as desirable, and they are brought about by manipulation" (170). Frye even alludes to the "gimmick" as "a Hollywood synonym for *anagnorisis*" (170). But some happy endings in film reflect such blatant manipulation that the conclusion seems at odds with the body of the work, a positive conclusion appended to a film that seems to be moving—structurally and thematically—toward an unhappy ending. Often this occurs when Hollywood adapts a novel or play and alters the unhappy or ambiguous ending. Or it may also occur when an original screenplay is altered by another writer or during shooting or even as a result of previews. All of these familiar phenomena point to how strong is the desire for an upbeat ending in mass entertainment; the medium reconfigures genre. Unhappy endings are a significant box-office risk, as David Selznick's need to defend the original *A Star Is Born* by comparing it to *Anna Karenina* demonstrates (Behlmer 104-5). In *A Star Is Born* and many other films about Hollywood, the forced happy ending also reflects the fundamental contradiction of the genre—that it demystifies and even attacks Hollywood as part of a project that ultimately celebrates it. While the happy endings in *What Price Hollywood?* and *The Star* may seem brief and artificial (and ultimately belied by the spirit of the bulk of the film), the self-parody of "Lose That Long Face" explicitly interrogates the issue of happy endings and the nature of happiness in general.

Yet it is ultimately Vicki Lester's talent, that very quality elided in the original film, that justifies the celebration of song and film in *A Star Is Born*. While the original *A Star Is Born* shows us a star being manufactured, the musical shows a star being discovered. And Norman Maine's condition partakes of the Judy Garland myth in which talent is rendered all the more poignant by its association with a tragically self-destructive character. The artist as mad genius who suffers to bring joy to an unappreciative audience is a recognizable version of the critique as self-justification that is characteristic of the Hollywood-on-Hollywood genre. But while *A Star Is Born* celebrates individual talent, it attacks the faith in music (and entertainment) definitive of the musical comedy and underpinning the affirmations of *Singin' in the Rain*. Still, tragedy and suffering in *A Star Is Born* and *Singin' in the Rain* are restricted to individuals.

The larger issue of the relation between a grim social reality and the persistently optimistic world of the movies forms the subject of our next two films for study: *Sullivan's Travels* and *Pennies from Heaven*. At the beginning of *Sullivan's Travels*, the title character, a successful musical director who wants to abandon musicals, asks: "How can you talk about musicals at a time like this? With the world committing suicide . . . with corpses piling up in the streets, grim death gargling at you around every corner . . . people slaughtered like sheep?" (Henderson 540). The films of the next chapter attempt to answer that question.

3   Let a Smile Be Your Umbrella

Sullivan's Travels (Paramount 1941). Producer: Paul Jones. Director and Screenwriter: Preston Sturges.

Pennies from Heaven (MGM 1981). Producers: Nora Kaye and Herbert Ross. Director: Herbert Ross. Screenwriter: Dennis Potter.

John Sullivan (Joel McCrea) confronts the image of himself as a hobo in preparation for his travels away from the world of Hollywood and comedy in *Sullivan's Travels*.

After the opening credits roll, *Sullivan's Travels* plunges into a vicious fight between two men atop a rushing steam locomotive. To the accompaniment of a melodramatic score, the two struggle until one shoots the other. The wounded man grabs the other by the throat, and they both plunge to their deaths into a lake below. "The End" emerges on the screen beneath a ripple of water. Only then does the camera pull back to show us our location in a screening room, as John L. Sullivan (Joel McCrea) interprets the final scene for a pair of less-than-credulous studio executives. Opening a film with a disguised movie-within-a-movie is the most extreme use of the self-referential technique of the framed movie, particularly since the actual audience identifies wholly with the as-yet-undisclosed diegetic audience. This technique has been used to open a variety of motion pictures, including *Merton of the Movies* (1924 and 1947) and recent examples such as *Hearts of the West* (1975), *Blow Out* (1981), *Romancing the Stone* (1984), *Who Framed Roger Rabbit?* (1988), and *Last Action Hero* (1993). The technique generally signals a thematic focus on illusion; in *Sullivan's Travels* it introduces the theme of moviemaking with a particularly self-conscious concern regarding the problematics of the audience. *Sullivan's Travels* will progress through three movies-within-the-movie; the opening one is significantly labeled "The End."

The movie of which we get a glimpse in this opening scene comes to represent the antithesis of what Preston Sturges implies movies should be. Though Sullivan indicates that he wants to make a socially conscious film in the vein suggested by this excerpt, the framed film is indeed the opposite of the film Sullivan ends up proposing and the film Sturges makes in the process.[1] What looks like the most hackneyed of Hollywood stunts, the struggle aboard a moving train, is for Sullivan an allegory of the battle between capital and labor, a hackneyed conceit of a different sort. Nevertheless, both economic relations and trains will remain important throughout *Sullivan's Travels*. Thus, the opening hook to this picture uses self-referentiality to anticipate the movie's thematic focus on filmmaking and audience, to foreshadow other framed films and other train scenes, and to establish the kind of movie *Sullivan's Travels* will argue against.

The discussion that follows is a superb example of Sturges's comic dialogue, and it is the best statement of a recurrent Hollywood anxiety.

Sullivan: You see? You see the symbolism of it? Capital and

Labor destroy each other. It teaches a lesson, a moral
lesson. . . . It has social significance. It . . .

Hadrian: Who wants to see that kind of stuff? It gives me
the creeps.

Sullivan [to Lebrand]: Tell him how long it played in the
Music Hall.

Lebrand [reluctantly]: It was held over a fifth week.

Hadrian: Who goes to the Music Hall? Communists!

Sullivan: Communists! This picture is an answer to
Communists. . . . It shows we're awake and not dunking our
heads in the sand like a bunch of ostriches! I want this
picture to be a commentary on modern conditions . . . stark
realism . . . the problems that confront the average man.

Lebrand: But with a little sex in it.

Sullivan: A little, but I don't want to stress it. I want this
picture to be a . . . document. I want to hold a mirror up to
life. I want this to be a picture of dignity . . . a true canvas
of the suffering of humanity.

Lebrand: But with a little sex in it.

Sullivan: With a little sex in it.

Hadrian: How about a nice musical?

Sullivan: How can you talk about musicals at a time like
this? With the world committing suicide . . . with corpses
piling up in the street, grim death gargling at you around
every corner . . . people slaughtered like sheep?

Hadrian: Maybe they'd like to forget that.

Sullivan: Then why do they hold this one over for a fifth
week at the Music Hall. . . . For the ushers?

Hadrian: It died in Pittsburgh.

Lebrand: Like a dog.

Sullivan: What do they know in Pittsburgh?

Lebrand: They know what they like.

Sullivan: If they knew what they liked they wouldn't live in
Pittsburgh! That's no argument. If you pander to the
public you'd still be in the horse age.

Hadrian: You think we're not? Look at Hopalong Cassidy,
look at . . .

Sullivan: *You* look at him. We'd still be making Keystone

chases, bathing beauties, custard pie operas.

Lebrand: And a fortune! . . .

Sullivan: I wanted to make you something outstanding,
    something you could be proud of, something that would
    realize the potentialities of film as the sociological and
    artistic medium that it is—with a little sex in it.

[Henderson 540-43]

I have quoted this scene at length because it so richly captures the nuances of Hollywood's debate with itself over the role of motion pictures in society. The central conflict is between movies as entertaining and movies as socially uplifting—the age-old tension between delighting and instructing. The scene reflects an anxiety about popular media that runs throughout film history: we will hear it articulated in *Sunset Boulevard,* *In a Lonely Place,* and *The Player.* But Sturges shows how the debate about what films should do is based upon differing views of the film audience. Sullivan defends the music hall proletariat as representative, while the executives call them Communists. Yet Sullivan dismisses the Pittsburgh audience as ignorant masses because they prefer, as Hadrian suggests, to forget their troubles in the theater. Sullivan argues that filmmakers must lead audiences, not pander to them, and he notes, correctly, that the development of such things as feature films came about against objections that the masses couldn't follow a long story.

The repartee concerning Communism is intriguing in a film about Hollywood as well. *Sullivan's Travels* predates the extreme anti-Communist hysteria of the House Un-American Activities Committee's investigation of Hollywood in 1947. But it follows the skirmishes between Hollywood and Martin Dies's investigation in 1939. Though Sturges was apolitical to an unusual degree for this heavily politicized time (and certainly no radical, as his pictures attest), his screenplay for *If I Were King* (1938) had been accused of being pro-Communist and had to be publicly defended by Paramount.[2] In this brief exchange, Sturges satirizes the ridiculousness of the claims that Hollywood, an essentially conservative cultural institution, was infiltrated by Communists. In particular, Sullivan notes how any kind of social commitment risks being perceived as Communist in sympathy.

The scene also identifies Sullivan as a director with an extremely successful track record for the studio. Lebrand introduces the issue of money explicitly, pointing out that the supposedly primitive early slap-stick comedies were widely popular and lucrative—that is, while movies have progressed in terms of technology and narrative complexity, they have not necessarily become more profitable. The debate about whether movies should reflect social troubles or provide an escape from them is thus predicated upon financial concerns and reveals conflicting attitudes toward the fictitious construct of the audience.

Behind this discussion lies the history—and mythology—of Hollywood's role in American society during the depression (the decade ending just before the making of *Sullivan's Travels*). The familiar myth presents a Hollywood that prospered during the depression by providing Americans with inexpensive escapes from the poverty and social ills that surrounded them. The reality is more complex on both counts—Hollywood's insulation from the effects of the depression and its turn to escapist entertainment. While the coming of talkies delayed the effects of the depression in Hollywood, those effects were causing serious economic crises by 1932, when Warners, Fox, Paramount, and RKO were all los-ing money. By 1933, Fox, Paramount, and RKO were in receivership. So the image of Hollywood unthreatened by depression woes is ultimately misleading. And in the opening years of the thirties, a great many films did succeed that showed gritty pictures of life on the streets rather than escapist fantasies; this was particularly evident in the popularity of gang-ster films. Nevertheless, the very popularity of gangster movies and mov-ies depicting "illicit love" led to increased calls for censorship and resulted in industry self-regulation.[3]

Robert Sklar calls the period 1930-34 "an aberration," however, and argues that the move toward screwball comedies and highbrow epics made from classic novels (after 1934) represents a deliberate turning away from subjects rooted in contemporary life (*Movie-Made* 189). He sees Joseph Breen's enforcement of the Production Code as a response to (not a cause of) a shift in audience taste. Thus the movies from the first half of the decade responded to a vaguely prurient audience desire to see the seamier sides of life, and the movies of the second half of the decade responded to a new audience desire for escape from oppressive social circumstances (an understandable response, given the continuing effects of the depres-sion). This analysis mirrors the competing conceptions of audience in Sturges's dialogue: the conflicting evidence of the music hall audience's interest in a socially conscious film weighed against the producers' accurate suspicion that most audiences eventually seek diversion and escape.

In the lines that follow, the two studio executives question what Sullivan knows about poverty and misery anyway. They suggest that they are the ones who have lived through hardship and penury, and thus they have the authority to assert that audiences want nothing of it, while Sullivan lacks the authority to portray poverty authentically in a film. The argument of the executives invokes the image of the early motion picture founders as impoverished immigrants who hewed out a fortune in the industry they created and thus had a particularly strong stake in depicting the American dream of success in their films. As Neal Gabler shows in *An Empire of Their Own*, there is a great deal of truth in this familiar mythology. The early motion picture producers were largely eastern European immigrants, and they did exercise tremendous control over the content of movies. However, Gabler shows that rather than underestimating audience tastes, the first generation of film producers were anxious to use films to uplift audiences and their own cultural status. Thus they pushed for longer narrative films in the silent era and for sound films with pretensions to high culture (films about classical composers, biographies of historical figures, and films made from classic novels and plays). Still, they remained wary of films that criticized American society or other venerated institutions (as in Louis B. Mayer's obsession about motherhood), and they were hypersensitive, as Sturges's dialogue suggests, to hints of "un-Americanness."

Sullivan accepts the second point of the producers' argument: he agrees that he knows little of poverty and must research it—thus his travels. After he leaves the office, the executives reveal that they know nothing of poverty either; they are of the second Hollywood generation, invoking the rags-to-riches past as a pretense. Their attempt to dissuade Sullivan from making the movie leads to his more elaborate plan to research poverty. Sullivan's plan to impersonate a hobo and gather experience for his socially conscious film provides the structure of the narrative. Four times Sullivan attempts to mingle with the poor, and each time a series of comic (and occasionally slapstick) adventures returns him to Hollywood. On his second excursion, he meets a down-and-out actress hopeful (Veronica Lake, playing an unnamed character) who insists on accompanying him on his subsequent travels. Finally, when they recoil in disgust from examining a garbage can for food, they return to Hollywood voluntarily. Sullivan decides his experiment is over, but he vows to distribute a stack of five-dollar bills to the homeless population he has been encountering: "I'll go down tonight and give them some money and that'll end it." Instead, his scheme begins his real travels. A bum knocks him out and robs him, but when the bum is killed by a train he is identified as Sullivan because Sullivan's identification card is in the shoes the bum stole. Meanwhile, Sullivan, in a dazed state, fights with a railroad security guard and is arrested, tried, and sentenced to six years in prison.

Now presumed dead by Hollywood and suffering from temporary amnesia, Sullivan begins his sentence as "Richard Roe." He works on a chain gang under a cruel warden and begins to despair. One night the chain gang is invited into a neighboring black church to join the congregation for a movie showing. The film is a Disney cartoon, and the inmates laugh uproariously at the characters' antics. Eventually, Sullivan joins them in laughter. After this cathartic experience, he hits upon a scheme to make his identity known. He confesses to the murder of Sullivan and gets his picture in the paper. Identified by friends and studio executives, he is sprung from prison (because "they don't sentence picture directors to six years for an argument with a yard bull"). But when he returns to Hollywood, he no longer wishes to make his socially conscious film, "O Brother, Where Art Thou?" Instead he insists on making a comedy because the ability to laugh is "all some people have."

Sturges may have drawn this plot from his similar experience in the thirties, when he joined William Wyler and John Huston touring hobo jungles for research purposes (Jacobs 248). The mixing of genres in the film may also owe something to the 1933 Rodgers and Hart musical *Hallelujah, I'm a Bum* (starring Al Jolson), which was "the only musical in Hollywood's history that was about and dealt directly with the depression" (Hirschhorn 72)—that is, until the 1981 *Pennies from Heaven*. The plot of *Sullivan's Travels* is extraordinarily suggestive in its treatment of the impulse toward comedy and the battle over Hollywood's social role. The film can be seen as Sturges's defense of his penchant for comedy, and some critics have attacked it as a cheap argument for dodging artistic responsibility. Charles Higham and Joel Greenberg call it "a cynical piece of self-justification if ever there was one" (158). Penelope Houston says of the ending that "as a comedy director's apologia this is notably unconvincing" (134). And in an article that Ray Cywinski cites as "the most important negative appraisal of Sturges's work," Siegfried Kracauer sees *Sullivan's Travels* as the "turning point of Sturges's career" leading to a decline into political conformism and complacency (Cywinski 94).

But the paradox of film self-referentiality is important to take into account here. Sullivan makes films such as "Ants in Your Pants of 1939," and he is moved by a Disney cartoon (Sturges had hoped to use a Chaplin film in this scene but couldn't get permission [Jacobs 257; Henderson 532]). Sturges, however, makes a more complex film. While *Sullivan's Travels* is certainly a comedy (and even strains to include a romance because "there's always a girl in the picture," as Sullivan mentions), it contains much that is serious, both in its depiction of poverty and in Sullivan's chain-gang experiences. Only the surrogate death of the thieving hobo (and Sullivan's significant confession to murdering himself) allows the tragedy to return to comedy. *Sullivan's Travels* appears to endorse escapist entertainment over socially conscious films, but it actually makes a subtler distinction: it argues against didactic message films (particularly of an allegorical nature) in favor of films that use humor, wit, and satire to examine social problems. Sturges, though a satirist, is hardly a radical, but it would be a mistake to see this film (or his others) as strictly escapist. In his travels, Sullivan learns not only respect for comedy, but also respect for his audience.[4]

The broadest comedy in the film occurs in the first half—the series of abortive attempts to escape from Hollywood to the world of real life. Public relations men turn Sullivan's quest into a stunt and follow him in a "land yacht." Hitching a ride with a child inventor in a homemade vehicle, Sullivan leads the land yacht on a cross-country chase. Slapstick scenes like these (or the comedy of Sullivan's getting arrested for stealing his own car) stress the impossibility of his quest. As a wealthy film director, Sullivan can't escape the world of the movies. The boundary between Hollywood and the real world is impassable, for even dressed as a hobo on a freight train, Sullivan carries the ubiquitous film world inside him. Indeed, when he accidentally runs into the land yacht at a Las Vegas coffee shop, Sullivan takes it as an omen that he shouldn't try to leave the confines of his artificial life. Sturges seems to be criticizing Hollywood's insularity and narcissism, a particularly paradoxical angle to take in a film about Hollywood. Of course, the criticism also applies to those who naively believe that they can sample reality for filmic inspiration. The failed travels point to a recurrent problem: if Hollywood gets locked into its own world of crazy illusion, mansions, limousines, butlers, and swimming pools, how can it remain in touch with its middle-American audience?

It is tempting, but mistaken, I think, to identify Sullivan too closely with Sturges.[5] Doing so misses the way in which the film spoofs Sullivan, and, more importantly, the way in which the film delivers a more intelligent and sympathetic picture of poverty than Sullivan can. Critics have differed in how they react to the depiction of the poor and homeless in *Sullivan's Travels*, but it is clear that Sturges (unlike Sullivan) attempts, in the context of his comedy, a serious portrayal of the extent of poverty. Many critics find the portrayal of poverty in this film genuinely moving. Houston, however, sees the poor in this movie as sentimentalized (134), and Higham and Greenberg see the artificiality of the poverty scenes as the film's great "unintentional irony" (158).

But Sturges is more conscious of the difficulties of what he is attempting than these analyses allow. That is, the film's portrayal of poverty is of a piece with its satire of Hollywood artificiality, not naively in opposition to it. The poverty scenes are preceded by an important cautionary scene that uses comedy to warn against the dangers of condescension. When Sullivan prepares for his first trip, we see him trying on ragged jackets in front of a mirror, aided by a valet. The mirror shot calls attention to Sullivan's putting on of a false image for the sake of his movie. Then his butler enters and assumes, disapprovingly, that Sullivan is dressing for a masquerade party: "I have never been sympathetic to the caricaturing of the poor and needy, sir." Sullivan explains that caricature is not his goal, but the scene alerts us to the pitfalls inherent in Sturges's project. When the butler learns of Sullivan's expedition, his disapproval mounts, and he delivers an eloquent speech on poverty and how the privileged fail to understand it: "The subject [of poverty] is not an interesting one. The poor know all about poverty, and only the morbid rich would find the topic glamorous. . . . Rich people and theorists, who are usually rich people, think of poverty in the negative, as the lack of riches. . . . But it isn't, sir. Poverty is not the lack of anything, but a positive plague, virulent in itself, contagious as cholera, with filth, criminality, vice, and despair as only a few of its symptoms. It is to be stayed away from, even for purposes of study; it is to be shunned." The butler's speech offers another dig at moralizing filmmakers who use poverty for entertainment value, even if the intent is to edify. But it is also a warning that this film itself must heed—not to glamorize poverty or to believe naively that the conditions of hopelessness can be remedied simply by money. Though Sullivan is taken aback by the butler's speech, he dismisses it comically. And later he will try to assuage his conscience with the publicity stunt of handing out five-dollar bills. The speech clarifies the distance between Sturges and Sullivan, and it prepares the viewer for how the film will treat the serious issues of poverty and homelessness.

Sullivan's third trip (this time accompanied by his actress friend dressed as a boy) provides the first demonstration of the extent of suffering among the poor. The butler drops Sullivan and his companion at the railroad yards, where dozens of hobos await the train. The bums stare at Sullivan and friend, and two eventually scorn them in a freight car when Sullivan attempts a political conversation. As the train passes and the men attempt to board, Sturges uses a series of crane shots to show the vast numbers of homeless people riding the rails; the sheer numbers give impact to the sequence of shots of various individuals hopping onto freight cars, throwing their ragged bundles before them.

Sullivan's fourth trip is a six-and-a-half-minute montage without dialogue, designed wholly to picture the effects of homelessness. A scene without dialogue is unusual in Sturges, and this sequence is extraordinary. Backed by music, the camera follows Sullivan and his companion through a nighttime hobo jungle. Some men are shaving; others tend fires or coffeepots; others are half asleep. In the flickering light, various of the figures turn and stare at Sullivan and his friend as they pass. The sequence cuts to a soup line, shot from above to emphasize the numbers but also to show an out-of-place publicity photographer snapping Sullivan in line. We follow Sullivan and his companion through a night of sleeping in a vermin-infested alley, to community showers at a hostel, followed by a sermon delivered to a large crowd enduring it in return for dinner and a night on the floor. The camera pans the rows of impoverished men and women, showing a variety of physiognomies and attitudes (some intent, others asleep or halfway there). Through it all, Sullivan and his companion stand out; they just don't look like they belong. This effect is accomplished not by rendering the homeless masses grotesque, but by lighting and photographing McCrea and Lake so that they still appear glamorous (and, often, simply illuminated). Whether they are shown fighting off bedbugs or toting sandwich boards, they appear comically out of place in this otherwise somber sequence. When they find themselves scouring a garbage can for food, they flee back to civilization. The montage ends, and a jump cut takes us rudely to a public relations agent promoting Sullivan's humane expedition to the press. Again the distinction between the film and Sullivan is clear: his four travels have taught him little. Indeed, the crowning glory of what has now become a publicity stunt will be his distribution of two thousand dollars in five-dollar bills.

This scene is clearly the turning point of the film, and, once again, Sturges shoots it with a musical background and no dialogue. By now, we read this style as a signal for seriousness.[6] It is useful to consider the three "silent" sequences together: the opening film-within-the-film, the progress through poverty of Sullivan's fourth trip, and the distribution of largesse. This third scene has the same dark and allegorical quality of the opening film-within-the-film; it is quite different from the euphoric distribution of gifts in *Christmas in July* (though the wide-eyed disbelief of the recipients is similar). A high-angle shot of Sullivan's feet walking through back alleys opens the sequence; the camera returns several times to this shot. We see Sullivan distributing the five-dollar bills, but the camera focuses on the recipients, not Sullivan. A bearded tramp begins to follow him, and the sequence takes on a noir feel. The noise of a train begins and increases in volume through the scene. The bearded tramp pounces on Sullivan from behind and takes his money, leaving him unconscious in the trainyard. The tramp runs across a maze of tracks until he trips and falls; he drops the money onto the rails. As a train approaches, the tramp stuffs his pockets with the bills. Sturges crosscuts from the tramp in full shot to a point-of-view shot from the train showing the headlight illuminating the track. Finally, with the train upon him, the tramp panics and is run over. Like the opening framed film, this scene presents a struggle to the death on the train tracks, but here the symbolic economic base is more clearly represented. Indeed, the pathetic image of a deprived man risking his life to grab piles of five-dollar bills provides a more gripping and less ponderous allegory than the opening struggle between "Labor and Capital." The bearded tramp seems to bear out Sullivan's butler's analysis of poverty as a positive plague, and the onrushing train, so often a presence in this film, can stand for progress or history or simply the uncaring machinery of society. Grabbing for money while death threatens—this image applies equally to the farthest reaches of the American Dream, from success to desperation.

The tramp's death and Sullivan's later arrest for striking a railroad guard threaten to turn the comedy toward tragedy. But the mistaken identity by which the tramp is seen as Sullivan while Sullivan suffers temporary amnesia prepares the comic conclusion. Mistaken identity and convenient amnesia are the stuff of comedy. But more importantly, the tramp's death has a surrogate function: he is like a sacrificial victim whose death allows the ultimate comic resolution, a plot element that Northrop Frye calls the "point of ritual death" (179). Sullivan's prison experience as Richard Roe allows him a symbolic rebirth: the Hollywood director dressed as a bum and distributing cash is reborn as a nameless prisoner forced to behave on a chain gang for the chance to see a Disney cartoon. Sullivan's butler had identified his travels as a kind of "dress-up," the light masquerades of the privileged. Now Sullivan is stripped of his clothes and identity and assigned new ones. He had wanted to get closer to the dispossessed; now he is literally chained to them. Sullivan ironically gets his experience.

The climax of the prison sequence—and of the film—is the film-within-the-film in the black church, the third framed film in *Sullivan's Travels*. But to understand this scene, we need to see it in the context of the film's overall self-referentiality. The opening film-within-the-film was shown full screen with the audience obscured, not even implied. A serious political allegory, this first film represents the antithesis of Hollywood's values and, the film comes to argue, the antithesis of the values of the audience. Thus it is appropriate that this excerpt includes "The End" and that it is shown without a real audience; indeed, it makes us the audience and then ironically pulls back to reveal an insider's argument about what audiences want. The framed film that occurs in the middle of *Sullivan's Travels* is in many ways the opposite of this first self-referential moment. This framed film Sullivan attends with two older women for whom he has been performing chores during his travels. The sequence never shows us what is on the screen; it focuses entirely (and unflatteringly) on the audience—as if to show us that Sullivan is now trapped on the wrong side of the screen.[7] Sullivan is dressed up in a suit belonging to the deceased husband of one of the women; he sits uncomfortably between them. Like many in the audience, he appears to be on a formal date. Kids in the row behind them noisily munch popcorn; another child blows a penny whistle; a baby cries; a drunk hiccups. Somber music plays beneath the brief scene, and as the camera leaves the theater it lingers on the triple-feature bill as if to emphasize the length of Sullivan's trial. This scene can be interpreted as evidence of Sturges's contempt for his audience, a "small, genial contempt" Houston identifies in all his films (131). Yet the scene educates Sullivan about the context of the moviegoing experience. It reminds him that a movie is a social experience as well as an artistic statement, an experience linked to eating, drinking, and romance.

Much of the rather clichéd comedy in this scene comes from the widow's proprietary and romantic interest in Sullivan. The cheap comedy here gives way to the more developed love interest supplied by Veronica Lake's character. The unnamed character is a young woman trying unsuccessfully to break into an acting career; it is as if she had wandered in from *What Price Hollywood?* When she takes pity on the penniless Sullivan and buys him breakfast, the film seems to be reversing the Svengali stereotype of the-birth-of-a-star movies. But the reversal of the "meet" is temporary. Once Sullivan reveals who he is and offers an introduction to director Ernst Lubitsch, the familiar pattern is reasserted. But Lake's character is important in Sullivan's education because she has experienced disappointment and failure, and done so in Hollywood, the dreamland Sullivan seems unable to escape. Moreover, she is, as the film makes explicit, the required love interest, the necessary element that takes a serious plot and puts "a little sex in it." That chorus in the opening dialogue and Sullivan's remark that "there's always a girl in the picture" define Lake's role in the context of the film's self-referentiality. She provides the tongue-in-cheek sexual element needed to make this film a screwball comedy with a fittingly romantic resolution. The scenes where the couple banter and tussle around Sullivan's swimming pool could be from many an escapist depression-era film. And the plot whereby a chance meeting in a coffee shop elevates a broke and luckless starlet into the life of a wealthy and handsome director partakes of the rise-to-wealth comedy of such Sturges films as *Easy Living* and *Christmas in July*. That Sullivan is married (albeit unhappily) provides the required obstacle to their romance, and the elaborate intrigues of the resolution (in which his wife, assuming him to be dead, marries his business manager and thus frees him to join with Lake's character when he is resurrected) complete the comic subplot. My point is that Lake's entire role is cast in self-conscious terms that heighten our awareness of the comic conventions competing with the intimations of tragedy in the plot.

The film's elaborate self-consciousness prepares for the remarkable scene in the church, in which the chained prisoners are led in to watch a picture show with the rural black congregation. The first framed film is shown in the private confines of a studio screening room; the second is shown in a very public, middle-American, small-town theater; the third is shown in a church. The setting implies the religious function of filmgoing, particularly with regard to comedy. In *Comic Faith,* literary critic Robert Polhemus argues that comedy serves essentially religious functions: "to honor creation; to provide hope; to reconcile people to their harsh fates; to smooth over social enmity and to defend culture by authoritative moral sanction against selfish and destructive behavior; to make people feel that they are important and part of a 'chosen' group; to institutionalize ways of getting rid of guilt; to allow people to identify with righteousness and let loose wrathful indignation and hostility in good conscience; to assure them of the possibility of future well-being; to lift them out of themselves and free the spirit" (5). Polhemus's listing of religious and comic functions helps explain why Sturges's series of framed films concludes with a cartoon in a church. And not only can we see how this list applies to the prisoners watching Pluto's antics (reconciling them to harsh fates and freeing their spirits), but we can also see the applications to Sturges's overall project (getting rid of guilt and letting loose indignation in good conscience). But if film comedy serves a religious function, it is important to remember that such a religious function must then take place in a highly commercial context. That the viewers are prisoners comments on the ways in which audiences can be imprisoned by what they are shown, which is, in turn, a product of how they are conceived of in Hollywood (Wineapple 155). But if this audience is imprisoned, it is also liberated.

The climactic church scene risks sentimentality throughout, but does not, I think, succumb to it. Sturges stakes Sullivan's conversion and the statement of his own comic credo on this scene. Like Sullivan's travels in disguise, this scene is framed with instructions in how to view it. The preacher (Jess Lee Brooks) addresses his congregation. Announcing a picture show as a sheet is lowered to serve as a screen, the preacher exhorts the congregation to "share our pleasure with some neighbors less fortunate than ourselves." He warns them not to make the guests feel awkward, because "we is all equal in the sight of God." These warnings might apply to the film's treatment of the black congregation itself or to the unemployed drifters in earlier scenes. In any case, Sturges finds a compelling tone here, and the church scene is dignified, even somber. None of the buffoonish comedy that so often characterized the presentation of blacks in film (and unfortunately characterized the cook [Charles Moore] aboard the land yacht earlier) is present.[8] The congregation sings "Go

Down, Moses," and the intoning of "Let my people go!" informs the scene. The texts of the Exodus have been important in black churches and liberation theology in general; here the familiar parallel drawn between black Americans and the Israelites in bondage suggests a broad affinity of the oppressed.

During the singing of the hymn, Sturges cuts to an external shot of the clapboard church, illuminated against the rising fogs of the swamplands. With the hymn now distant and softer, the guarded prisoners march in the foreground in silhouette, the jingling of their chains mingling with the choruses of "Let my people go." From the inside of the church, Sturges shows the prisoners entering by twos, heads bowed and hats in hands. An extended shot lingers on their manacled ankles. The film, Disney's *Playful Pluto* (1934), begins. The cartoon enacts a theme certainly resonant with prisoners: frustration. Pluto gets caught in dresser drawers and stuck on flypaper in the brief clip we see. But where the first framed film showed the screen entirely and the second the audience entirely, this film-within-the-film cuts back and forth. The prisoners and parishioners begin to laugh uproariously, and the camera focuses on their laughing faces. Sullivan remains aloof and unlaughing and then breaks into laughter unwillingly. The framed film scene contains only one spoken line: Sullivan asking in disbelief, "Am I laughing?" Then he joins in the all-out hilarity. Sturges cuts again to the shot of the church from outside, and now the distant laughter mingles with organ music on the soundtrack, reinforcing the religious nature of the comic catharsis.

"If ever a plot needed a twist, it's this one." So Sullivan muses the next day, while planning how to make his identity known. Thus, the scheme that follows and ends in Sullivan's being sprung from prison is identified as a movie ploy, a comic plot twist. But, significantly, it is only after losing himself in laughter at the cartoon that Sullivan comes up with the idea of confessing to his own murder. The plot device reinforces Sullivan's change: as prisoner Richard Roe he is forced to identify with the audience and with the oppressed, and doing so reveals to him the power of laughter. He frees himself by symbolically killing his old self. The freed Sullivan then renounces his plans to make a socially conscious film. He gives three reasons, though most critics cite only the third, the importance of making people laugh because "it isn't much, but it's better than nothing in this cockeyed caravan." The other two reasons he gives are that he still doesn't know enough about suffering and that he is just *too* happy (this said with a significant look to his new love). These two reasons fit together in an important way: Sullivan accepts his isolation from suffering (rather than exploiting his prison experience melodramatically), and, metacritically, he accepts his stake in the happy ending as a movie character in love. Love and happiness are the ingredients of comic endings, and just as Lake's character works throughout the film to remind us that we are watching a movie, so too does the two characters' implied union underscore the filmic imperative of the happy ending. Their faces are center screen, circled by a montage of laughing faces, as "The End" appears on screen for the second time. We have traveled from the first "The End," with its conventional assertion of tragedy as a higher and more realistic art, to a second ending that affirms comedy in form and function.

Our social conscience reminds us, as the glow of the movie fades, that Sullivan's chain-gang companions still languish in prison under a brutal warden and that the ranks of the hungry and homeless have not diminished. Can we really believe that comedy somehow frees them of their chains? This question divides viewers and critics of Sturges. Sturges seems to imply that film cannot hope to do more, that the alternatives to comedy are turgid moralizing and uninformed condescension. In concluding thus, the film supports Hollywood; it endorses the perspective of the producers in the opening scene who challenge Sullivan's new project. And yet, the film's self-reference complicates this message, first because *Sullivan's Travels* manages a good bit of satire at Hollywood's and Sullivan's expense, and second because the very questioning that this film inspires reflects its comic seriousness. Sturges is the master of the happy ending with a wink, a happy ending so comically contrived as to remind us that its proper realm is the conventional. Sturges's position involves a partial disavowal of the potential for film as a medium of political or social criticism, and that disavowal implies assumptions about genre, about the superiority of the comic, the conventional, and the entertaining—at least within the medium of motion pictures. It is a disavowal likely to make many uncomfortable: are there not films that successfully provide the social criticism Sturges says is deadly to entertainment? On the other hand, what is appealing about the conclusion of *Sullivan's Travels* is the honesty with which the film recognizes its dependence on just such disavowals. That is, only a rejection of the trenchant political drama makes the endorsement of comedy in times of social crisis viable. Sturges realizes that something must be sacrificed for his comic faith.

In an unproduced screenplay, "Song of Joy" (1935), Sturges wrote a strongly self-conscious spoof of Hollywood. Its very premise is self-refer-ential. Sturges was asked to write a musical comedy for the European singer Marta Eggerth, and to rush it because of her need to return to Europe for an opera engagement. He wrote a comedy about a studio trying to produce a film on short notice for a European opera star. In "Song of Joy," studio executives worry that films of Hollywood tend to be unprofitable and reflect poorly on the trade: "I wouldn't put a dime in a Hollywood story. . . . What are you trying to do . . . give the industry a black eye?" (qtd. in Jacobs 168).[9] In real life, Universal expressed the same worries and canceled the film. A letter from Eddie Sutherland to Univer-sal head Carl Laemmle Sr. complains of Sturges's screenplay: "I am sure that making fun of producers, writers, etc. is not entertainment. . . . This seems to me a DANGEROUS EXPENSIVE experiment. . . . it attempts to point out specifically that we are all inefficient in our jobs" (qtd. in Henderson 513). So Sturges learned from experience the limits of satire in a popular medium, and, indeed, he uses comic conventions to stretch those limits (notably in *Hail the Conquering Hero!* [1943], a wartime film that remarkably spoofs motherhood and features a would-be soldier ex-cused from service who later claims to be a war hero). Similarly, Sturges simultaneously practices and satirizes happy endings. In *Sullivan's Trav-els*, he makes fun of message films intent on realistically depicting pov-erty and suffering, but in the process he makes a film that emphasizes rather than hides the gap between the world of luxury so much a part of depression-era films and the poverty and malaise rampant in American society.

The film's self-referentiality is underscored by Sturges's placing him-self in one scene and his producer in another (both uncredited). Sturges appears, appropriately, on a movie set, in the background of a brief scene that shows Lake's character pursuing her film career after Sullivan's ap-parent death. The producer, Paul Jones, whose job was to watch over Sturges in production, appears as the moving eyes of the portrait of the widow's deceased husband in a scene of Sullivan's second travel. These light touches comically exploit the metacritical possibilities of the movie about movies. And it is not surprising that in the making of *Sullivan's Travels* Sturges suffered criticisms similar to those Sullivan receives from his bosses. Studio executive Buddy DeSylva encouraged Sturges to cut scenes of poverty and the opening film-within-the-film, telling him to "soft pedal the misery" (Jacobs 259). On the other side, some reviewers and critics, notably Bosley Crowther of the *New York Times* and Andre Bazin, felt the film was not ironic enough and criticized the ending.[10]

Indeed, Sturges tries to have it both ways (as is often the case in the Hollywood-on-Hollywood genre). He defends himself as a comic film-maker, but makes a socially conscious comedy. The film's resolution gives comfort to the Hollywood status quo by endorsing the happy ending and the escapist function of film, but the film mixes genres more than elevating one above the other. The border between film world and the suffering of the poor is ostensibly shown to be impermeable, but the latter part of the film depends upon Sullivan and the motion picture being able to cross that boundary. Sturges presents escapist fantasy and comedy as valuable artistic functions (thus endorsing the myth of depression-era film-making), but in doing so he insists on showing misery coexisting with comic euphoria. Diane Jacobs sees the ending not as overly ironic, but as boldly juxtaposing the laughter of comedy with the inescapable injustices of life (261).

This sort of juxtaposition, which seems to work toward a unified comic resolution in *Sullivan's Travels,* functions more disruptively and ironically in *Pennies from Heaven,* an MGM musical made forty years after *Sullivan's Travels* and long after the heyday of the musical. I have suggested that *A Star Is Born* can profitably be seen as an "anti-musical." In a different way—but more blatantly—*Pennies from Heaven* is a musical that undermines musicals. It implicitly raises the objections of Sullivan when he claims that musicals are incongruous in a time of suffering and privation. Consider the plot of *Pennies from Heaven.* Set in "Chicago, 1934," the film follows a sheet-music traveling salesman, Arthur Parker (Steve Martin). Arthur feels oppressed by his circumstances: he longs to give up his job and open a record store, and he wishes for financial success and romance. He feels his wife, Joan (Jessica Harper), denies him sexual pleasure as well as her inheritance, which she refuses to loan him to start his record store. On a sales trip through his territory, Arthur seduces a young schoolteacher, Eileen Everson (Bernadette Peters). When he returns to Chicago, Joan senses she is losing him and loans him the money and gives in to his sexual demands. Meanwhile, Eileen discovers she is pregnant and loses her job. Arthur visits her and comforts her by giving her a fake address. During the same trip, a homeless accordion player, whom Arthur had briefly befriended, kills a blind girl in an alley-

way. Circumstantial evidence points to Arthur, and his wife ends up con-
firming his strange behavior after a trip to Galena. Arthur's record store
goes under. Eileen becomes a prostitute to survive and to finance an abor-
tion. When Arthur accidentally encounters Eileen, their romance rekindles
and he leaves his wife for her. But now Arthur is wanted for murder, and
after a few weeks on the road with Eileen, he is arrested. He is tried and
convicted and (apparently) hanged. Now there's a plot for a musical comedy!

More specifically, turning this plot into a musical comedy combines
the apparently antithetical genres discussed in the opening of *Sullivan's
Travels:* realistic depiction of depression life and uplifting comedy and
song. While *Sullivan's Travels* mixes different genres with an eye toward
creating a seriocomic unity, *Pennies from Heaven* maximizes the jarring
effects of ironic juxtaposition. Into the narrative outlined above, *Pennies
from Heaven* inserts fourteen elaborate song-and-dance numbers. "Inserts"
is, I think, the appropriate term, because, in contrast to *A Star Is Born,*
the songs in *Pennies from Heaven* are blatantly disruptive of the narrative and make no attempt to cover up their artificiality. Though Arthur as
a hawker of songs presumably has some musical talents, none of the
characters who sing and dance are performers per se (indeed, many
clearly are not—a loan officer in a bank, a group of salesmen at a bar, a
classroom of schoolchildren). The songs are all prerecorded numbers by
other musicians to which the principals lip-synch. *Singin' in the Rain* revealed how dubbing a number works, but those dubbed numbers successfully created the illusion that the principal character was actually singing.
Here, there are even numbers where Steve Martin lip-synchs to a female
voice, or Bernadette Peters lip-synchs to Betty Boop. In Feuer's analysis
of the film, she observes that "the idea that one spontaneously, naturally
sings is exposed [as ludicrous] through this technique" (128). The full-
blown production numbers also suddenly introduce huge choruses of singers and dancers in costume and are often shot with Busby Berkeley–style
camera work.

Herein lies the sense in which *Pennies from Heaven* is a movie about
Hollywood. Though the plot has ostensibly nothing to do with Hollywood
or the movies, the musical numbers that animate it are clearly drawn
from the tradition of movie musicals, as the climactic scene in a movie
theater screening Fred Astaire and Ginger Rogers in *Follow the Fleet*
shows. Including *Pennies from Heaven* in this study may be a stretch, but

it shows the pervasiveness of Hollywood, the way the images derived from the screen can infiltrate lives anywhere in America. The movie also ends with one of the most complex and effective uses of the framed screen as a self-reference.

In one sense, the songs in *Pennies from Heaven* reflect Arthur's imagination: as a salesman of sheet music and records, Arthur believes passionately in the idealized world of the song lyrics: "They tell the truth—songs do." Deliberately set off from the remorselessly depressing narrative, the musical numbers comment in a variety of ways on that narrative. Dennis Potter's explanation of the numbers in his script is revealing: "The movie steps sideways into another convention. The [characters] are now characters in a musical picture. . . . The action regularly zooms off to the other side of the rainbow—to the land of song, or dream, or of Arthur's inner life. . . . Then the movie is a genuine period musical, lovingly recreating, as well as obliquely commenting upon the marvelous old musical-picture zest, style, panache, dream" (4-5). The most common relation between musical number and non-musical narrative in *Pennies from Heaven* is blatant ironic reversal. Early in the picture, Arthur goes to a bank to apply for a loan to open his record store. A scowling loan officer tells him he needs collateral—like his wife's savings account. Arthur tries to speak the American Dream rhetoric so common in the movies of the thirties and forties: he points to his head as collateral and argues, "It was salesmanship that made this country great, and it'll be salesmanship that'll keep us great." The loan officer turns him down and asks him to leave. Then suddenly the music starts, and Arthur and the loan officer kiss and begin to sing "Yes, Yes." As they dance through the elegant deco bank set, other employees and customers join the chorus. Singing the lead, Arthur marches past a line of tellers who hand him bags of money. The silver coins spill out over him and a fade-out transforms the set. Suddenly forty dancers are twirling on a giant silver dollar, choreographed into three concentric circles shot from above. Then the dancers form a chorus line, high-stepping on a mirrored floor that reflects them. Arthur reappears in tails, gloves, spats, and a tie with a sparkling dollar sign on it. Finally, a hundred-dollar bill fills the screen and Arthur's face replaces Ben Franklin's. When the song fades out, Arthur is back on the road in his normal clothes—and very depressed.

This exuberant number represents the most common relation between song and narrative in the movie. The songs are jubilant affairs framed by misery; they break out in ironic opposition to the depressing circumstances of the narrative and they end by deflation. This pattern is even clearer in Eileen's first number. She is reading "Rapunzel" to her elementary school class, and when she grows dewy eyed in describing Rapunzel's suitor, the class giggles. She shouts "Quiet!" and that forms the ironic cue for music. Suddenly she is wearing a silver lamé low-cut gown and waving a baton; the children's desks are transformed into miniature white grand pianos; the children are decked in white as well. They perform "Love Is Good for Anything That Ails You." After one chorus on the pianos, the students man a jazz combo, playing trumpets, saxes, trombones, violins, a string bass, and drums (all white). Then, as suddenly, they are tap-dancing atop their pianos. These scene changes, as in the bank number, show clearly that these are cinematic musical numbers that would be impossible on stage. At the end of the number, the children are back in their desks, clothed normally, and laughing. An angry principal enters and administers discipline. Once again the song contrasts with the reality and is deflated by the voice of unsympathetic authority. As in the bank scene, the content of the musical number represents a kind of wish fulfillment. Money and love, the respective themes of these two numbers, are the dream ingredients throughout the movie. Songs such as these represent and satirize the escapist films of the depression that expressed desires for wealth and romance.

Sometimes, however, the songs reinforce the diegetic narrative rather than forming a direct contrast to the action. When Arthur's wife questions his fidelity through the song "It's a Sin to Tell a Lie," she is voicing her feelings exactly. Similarly, when Eileen sings "I Want to Be Bad," she is expressing her innermost desires to experience life to the fullest. Both of these functions have parallels in traditional musicals. That is, songs in musicals often represent an idealized world that the characters in the narrative long to enter, or songs may serve to express feelings a character has trouble articulating in speech (as in Don Lockwood's confession of love to Kathy Selden in *Singin' in the Rain*).[11] But *Pennies from Heaven* exaggerates both relationships, through the grimness of the reality against which the songs are contrasted and through the frankness with which submerged feelings are articulated.

The most vivid example of the latter technique, whereby a song reveals the true but hidden dynamics of a situation, occurs when the pregnant and unemployed Eileen ventures into a rough bar to pick up some money. She is timid and out of place, and the bartender urges her to leave. But a local swell, Tom (Christopher Walken), takes her aside, buys her a drink, and essentially preys on her desperation. While Eileen struggles to accommodate herself to trading sex for cash, Tom bursts into "Let's Misbehave." On one level, the song straightforwardly expresses his proposition. But on another, the context turns a gleeful transgression into a grim financial transaction. The call of one lover to another to violate social convention in the name of passion becomes a calculating exploitation whereby a working married man can pick up a girl in desperate straits for five dollars. Appropriately, this revealing song becomes a striptease, as Tom tap-dances on a pool table and begins to undress to burlesque-hall music. Finally he strips off his undershirt atop the bar to reveal a giant red heart with "Lulu" (Eileen's assumed name) tattooed across his chest. The gender reversal of the male striptease illustrates the film's critique of the exploitation of women during the depression. The lyrics expose the terms of the veiled negotiation in this particularly poignant intersection of love and money. But the playful mood of the music contrasts with the somber mood of the narrative. Eileen is near tears throughout the scene as she mounts the courage to carry through with her intention, and after the dance Tom warns her, "You're not a tease are you . . . 'cause I'll cut your face." The scene shows the dark successor to flapper mores (the song refers to 1928) as sexual license degrades to sexual transactions driven by economic necessity in the face of the depression.

Two songs focus explicitly on the struggle to be happy in the face of daunting circumstances: the title song and "Life Is Just a Bowl of Cherries." The latter song is performed at a low point for both Arthur and Eileen. Eileen has just entered a life of prostitution, while Arthur has failed in the record business and lost all his wife's inheritance. Though they are apart, the musical number joins them, along with Joan, to make an unlikely trio (in fact, these three are never together in the diegetic narrative). This trio, dressed in sailor suits with Arthur strumming a ukelele, sings the optimist's credo, "Life Is Just a Bowl of Cherries," a song that argues that, since you can't take your earnings with you when you die, you might as well not work so hard—just "live and laugh." This depression-era carpe diem captures the desperation behind the insistently jaunty lyrics of songs extolling optimism. The light number seems as if it is meant to provide consolation, to be a sort of moral instruction against worry in a time of trouble. *Pennies from Heaven* recontextualizes depression feel-good mov-

ies and musicals to expose their relation to social conditions. This formulation may sound a bit academic, but the movie so remorselessly exposes
the gap between lyric and narrative as to disconcert the audience. This
effect is the movie's strength, but it may have a good deal to do with its
unpopularity and mixed critical reception. Though Pauline Kael lauded
the film's irony and Brechtian qualities in the *New Yorker,* Janet Maslin
in the *New York Times* came closer to popular sentiment when she called
Pennies from Heaven "the most adventurous movie of the moment [but]
far less involving than it might have been" (24 January 1982). Commer-
cial-oriented *Variety* was much more blunt. Its capsule review was "Makes
no cents," and it dubbed the movie "one of the most hopelessly esoteric
big-budget Hollywood pictures ever made [with] virtually no artistic pay-
off. . . . In short, it's 'Penny Gate'" (3 December 1981).

The title song is performed early in the film by a homeless accordion player (Vernel Bagneris) for whom Arthur buys a meal. When Arthur
offers him his own plate of food in addition (he is too lovesick over Eileen
to eat), the grateful accordion player bursts into song in the diner. The
introduction to the song, with its invocation of a primitive world in which
everything was free, poses a version of the fortunate fall in which our
world, where we must endure hardship to appreciate riches, is ultimately
superior to carefree prelapsarian freedom. As in the song "Singin' in the
Rain," rain stands for the difficulties of life, but here it is not love that
makes us oblivious to the weather but hope that we are "paying" for a
better day by suffering now. The staging of the musical number reifies the
financial metaphor of the song. At the beginning of the chorus, the side of
the diner slides open and the accordion player walks out into the rain.
The diner that now forms a background to him is deliberately staged to
suggest Edward Hopper's *Nighthawks* (1942). Soaked with rain, the homeless singer approaches various diners; they are all frozen in attitudes of
despair. As a violin in the background music picks up the theme, the scene
changes, and the accordion player begins to dance in what is now a shower
of coins (pennies, presumably, though they look more like gold pieces).
Now the background to the dancer becomes a wall-sized collage of depression-era photographs: people sleeping on the street, signs for the NRA,
a street urchin in ragged dress. Though the lyrics of the song are happy,
this rendition by Arthur Tracy is slow and sad. More than any other piece
in the film, this song is about the relationship of hard times to optimism;
it takes on the same subject the film treats. Its virtuosity suggests that

escapist entertainment carries with it its own poignant subtext, if we only know how to interpret the region between optimism and desperation.

Throughout the film, Arthur's character changes little. He is driven by desires for success and sex, and his character maddeningly mixes charming naïveté in believing in the idealized world of songs and cowardly selfishness in his treatment of Joan and Eileen. The unpleasantness of his character may have something to do with the unpopularity of the film (along with its uncomfortable mixing of genres). But the character of Eileen is considerably more developed. When she falls for the traveling salesman, her complacent life is disrupted forever. Though Arthur betrays her, Eileen remains grateful for being shaken out of her complacency. "When you made love to me, I saw things differently," she confesses late in the film to Arthur. "I had to see something else, something more. I want nice things." This speech shows sexual desire turning into commodity desire, in which the longing to break social conventions regarding physical passion broadens into a frustration with the narrowness of life's horizons and the bleak prospects of poverty. The film places her lament into a context that explicitly speculates on the limitations imposed on women. Eileen doesn't want to become like her mother, who "worked her fingers to the bone" for "a life at the stove and the washtub," ending with her death at forty-five. Eileen's tribulations make her wise and philosophical, not bitter. While Eileen certainly does not believe that "life is just a bowl of cherries," she accepts the song's precept that life's finitude requires the exercise of desire and creativity with great urgency: "We've only got one life, Arthur." This she says as she goes out to turn a trick to pay the rent.

Arthur and Eileen, living together on the lam, are at their lowest point. So what do these depression-sufferers turn to? They go to the movies, and, as *Sullivan's Travels* might predict, they go to a musical—Astaire and Rogers in *Follow the Fleet*. The scene begins with another set that evokes a Hopper painting: this time a virtually exact copy of *New York Movie* (1939). As in the painting, we see the interior of a theater with a sliver of black-and-white screen visible on the left, backs of seats in the middle of the shot, and a red-curtained entryway on the right with an usherette in blue beside it. The middle of Hopper's painting is occupied by the wall that divides the viewing area from the lit entryway. The usherette looks sad and distant amidst the theater elegance, and the painting suggests the same urban loneliness more famously evoked in *Nighthawks*.

The scene that follows crosscuts between Arthur and Eileen in the audience and Astaire and Rogers on the screen (though the black-and-white images of the screen are also visible behind the audience on a mirrored back wall). Arthur and Eileen have a tearful conversation that ends in forced optimism: "There's gotta be something on the other side of the rainbow," Arthur states. "There always is," Eileen responds. Then we cut to the black-and-white full screen as Astaire sings "Let's Face the Music and Dance," again presenting musical comedy itself as the alternative to "troubles ahead." When the scene cuts back to Arthur and Eileen, Arthur is mouthing the words, then singing along. Throughout the whole scene, of course, the soundtrack of the movie-within-the-movie provides aural continuity. As the vocal part of the song ends, Astaire and Rogers begin to dance, but now Arthur and Eileen are dancing too—on the stage in front of the screen. Clearly offset by color against black and white, they mirror Astaire and Rogers perfectly. Along with the mirror at the back of the theater, this action reveals how viewers in the audience imaginatively identify with the performers on stage. And, of course, this identification or mirroring suggests the escapist function of film: from their tawdry neon-lit hotel room paid for with "Lulu's" prostitution, Arthur and Eileen are transported to an elegant formal dress benefit at sea. The chorus of men wearing top hats and sporting canes appears, and when the camera in the film-within-the-film shifts back to Fred and Ginger they have become Arthur and Eileen. Now in black and white and part of the full-screen film-within-the-film, Arthur and Eileen finish Fred and Ginger's dance. The scene shows vividly the power of movies as a medium of imaginative escape. But as a self-referential gesture, it forces us to question the larger film, *Pennies from Heaven*. Is that film endorsing the escape offered by movies and songs, the imaginative identification that puts Eileen and Arthur into the dancing shoes of Ginger and Fred? Or is the movie once again ironically framing movie as well as song to demystify that identification?[12]

The end of the number implies the latter. The rising canes of the chorus dancers become jail bars, foreshadowing Arthur's future. Then the film cuts to Arthur and Eileen exiting the theater into the pouring rain. Arthur is distraught: "It's always the same. . . . You come out of the movies, the goddamn world has changed." But Eileen begins to sing "Singin' in the Rain" and to laugh, while in the background a newsboy hawks a paper with the headline "Music Salesman Sought in Blind Girl's Murder."

The melody of "Pennies from Heaven" emerges on the soundtrack. By compressing the juxtaposition of narrative reality and musical fantasy, the movie questions the escapist function of depression-style films. But as this scene shows, it also celebrates that power of imaginative transport. Like *Sullivan's Travels*, *Pennies from Heaven* endorses the courage to laugh in the face of despair, while it refuses to accept that sad subjects should not be presented. But unlike *Sullivan's Travels*, the contrast between musical comedy and grim realism is repeatedly disarming; nothing in the film allows a graceful union of the competing discourses. *Sullivan's Travels* would lead us to think that a movie that places suffering and comedy side by side is forced to choose one or the other for the ending, but *Pennies from Heaven* continues, disruptively, to try to have it both ways.

In a rapid sequence, Arthur is arrested and convicted, Eileen moves into a Dickensian apartment across from the jail, and we cut to Arthur invited to speak his last words on the scaffold. What follows is a veritable catalog of expressions of depression optimism. For his last words, Arthur

The ultimate in audience identification: Film viewers Arthur (Steve Martin) and Eileen (Bernadette Peters) enter an Astaire-Rogers musical dance on screen in a movie-within-a-movie in *Pennies From Heaven*.

speaks the lyrics of "Pennies from Heaven." As he moves to the chorus he begins to sing (Martin's own voice is used here, and with a limited accompaniment); the screen frames his face on the right and a noose on the left. It is hard to imagine a more ironic setting for this heavenly pay-back song.

The next scene begins, incongruously, with Arthur running (over what appears pretty baldly as a soundstage) to Eileen's apartment. Like us, she is surprised to see him. He "explains": "Whoever said you could stop a dream? We couldn't have gone through all that without a happy ending. Songs aren't like that are they?" As they embrace, background music begins and then breaks out into "The Glory of Love" as the film cuts to an enormous chorus in sepia tones. Finally, Arthur and Eileen sing the song as a duet; they are lit as silhouettes and the background theme of "Pennies from Heaven" takes over; the shot fades to a rainbow against storm clouds and then pans above to blue skies and sunshine as Arthur's voice asserts, "I'm Arthur and I love you"; the vocal version of "Pennies from Heaven" introduces the final credits. Love and money, happy endings, blue skies over the rainbow, raindrops transformed into the bless-ings of coins: sometimes too much is just enough. The wild mixing of the clichés of depression optimism exhibits a self-consciousness similar to Sturges's comically extreme happy endings, but the exaggeration under-cuts the affirmation. Like *Sullivan's Travels*, this film insists on having it both ways, in mocking happy endings and pulling the audience's heartstrings with just such an ending, but the film that has preceded the hyperbolic ending makes the authenticity of such an ending impossible. Where *Sullivan's Travels* uses the trope of education to take Sullivan from an ideological position alien to Sturges toward one congruent with him, *Pennies from Heaven* uses subversive juxtaposition to make the comic resolution demanded by the genre ineffectual.

The result is even more disconcerting than in *Sullivan's Travels*. Both movies differ from the framed movies they show as typical of Holly-wood. And both movies stop short of indicting the escapist and comic function of films, in part by creating comedies that include the horrors we are told comedies irresponsibly offer escape from. These films seem to argue that the excesses of Hollywood escapism, and the view that the entertainment function is cinema's highest calling, are valid if one views them with awareness and a critical eye. But if we bring the critical aware-ness of *Sullivan's Travels* and *Pennies from Heaven* to our movie viewing, can we ever enter the screen world with the abandon of Arthur and Eileen? The self-canceling aesthetic of *Pennies from Heaven* is surely related to its box-office failure, as is its attempt to revive an ailing genre through a nostalgic parody that subverts nostalgia and the genre itself. That box-office failure reminds us of the uncertainties about audience that inform Sullivan's opening discussion with his producers, and it looks forward to *The Player*, which hints at how audiences write their own films. *Sullivan's Travels*—a comedy about a director of musicals—and the three actual self-referential musicals we have examined express, in different ways, the limitations of an artistic medium defined in terms of popularity and mass appeal. They translate the devil's bargain of stardom to a broader social canvas in which the relationship to audience is frighteningly reciprocal. The films discussed in the next chapter turn their attention to the audience that is for the most part only implied in these films; they examine the other side of the coin paid for admission to the theater, the way in which Hollywood, at its most mythically successful, shapes the lives of its most loyal fans.

4 Screen Passages

The Purple Rose of Cairo (Orion 1985). Producer: Robert Greenhut. Director and Screenwriter: Woody Allen.

Last Action Hero (Columbia 1993). Producers: Steve Roth and John McTiernan. Director: John McTiernan. Screenwriters: Shane Black and David Arnott. Story by Zak Penn and Adam Leff.

Movie character Tom Baxter (Jeff Daniels) introduces Cecilia (Mia Farrow) to life on the other side of the screen as she enters the movie-within-the-movie in *Purple Rose of Cairo*.

In J.B. Priestley's 1933 novel *Albert Goes Through,* Albert Limpley, a British clerk and inveterate moviegoer, attends the premiere of the new feature starring his favorite actress, Felicity Storm. Limpley has a bad cold, but he doesn't want to miss the show, so he takes some strong medicine offered by his landlady. His fever and the medicine make him delirious, and he hallucinates entering the movie screen, "going through," or what I call a screen passage. Paired with his beloved heroine, Limpley wanders from one genre film to another (through various literary "dissolves"). He travels from an espionage adventure set in the Russian Revolution to a saga of the wild West, to a Chicagoland gangster story, and finally to a musical farce set in a British estate. In each environment, the bemused hero bumbles about, gradually learning the highly stylized lingo and finding that he must endure exhausting physical trials to save Felicity Storm. As each potential embrace is interrupted by new trials, Albert grows less enamored of Felicity and rebels more against his heroic role. The book reaches a climax as all the different genre villains gang up against him, and he shouts, "You're not real, Felicity Storm. . . . You're just a silly fake" (64). As they attack him, he wakes in the office of the theater manager. Albert learns from his delusions and resolves to court a woman from his office (who had oddly appeared in his filmic hallucinations). The novel ends with them engaged. Priestley's little novel mocks movie clichés and star worship. It offers a happy ending in which the moviegoer sacrifices his dangerous fantasies for a real-life romance.

Priestley's story of a frustrated young man entering the world of movies in a dream state echoes an earlier film, Buster Keaton's *Sherlock Jr.* (1924). In *Sherlock Jr.,* Keaton plays a projectionist who longs to be a detective. Early in the silent film, he is foiled by a rival for a young woman's love. The rival has stolen the girl's father's watch, pawned it, bought the girl a better gift than Keaton's character can afford, and then framed him for the robbery. The girl's father banishes him from the house, and he returns distraught to his job at the movie theater. Falling asleep while screening "Hearts and Pearls or the Lounge Lizard's Lost Love," the would-be detective goes into a dream. In the dream, the girl, her father, and the rival all become characters in the movie. Keaton's character rushes from the projection booth and, after two failed tries, jumps into the screen. In the screen world he becomes "Sherlock Jr.," hired by the father to find missing pearls. Through elaborate comic machinations, Sherlock Jr. recovers the pearls and exposes the villain. He is united in an embrace with the young woman he desires. When he wakes from his dream, he discovers that the woman has figured out that his rival stole the watch. She conveys her father's apologies, and they resume their courtship.

These works exploit the familiar metaphor of movies as dreams—in the sense of both visual fantasies and aspirations. To step from the everyday world into the magic of the life represented in motion pictures—to "go through," or penetrate the two-dimensional screen—is a fictive conceit that allows Keaton and Priestley to examine the gap between movie fantasy and audience reality. Though the works interpret the relation between fantasy and romance differently (Albert learns to discard the world of fantasy for the rewards of reality; Keaton's character draws courage from the wish fulfillment of the fantasy world), both works exploit the social dynamics of Hollywood ideality and audience identification. Hollywood fiction becomes imaginative criticism when it recognizes that the screen looks both ways: it projects images and it reflects the projected fantasies of individual viewers.

This trope of passage through the screen, a passage that allows imaginative contact between the real-life world of an audience member and the fictional realm of movie characters, appears as the central conceit in two important films of the last decade, Woody Allen's *The Purple Rose of Cairo* and John McTiernan's *Last Action Hero*. Allen's film is set in the depression and focuses on Cecilia (Mia Farrow), who works as a waitress and struggles to support her out-of-work and abusive husband, Monk (Danny Aiello). Cecilia's passion is attending the movies, where she particularly enjoys seeing the glamour and romance her life lacks. When the film begins, a movie entitled "The Purple Rose of Cairo" is playing at the local theater. Cecilia loves it and attends several showings. With each of Cecilia's viewings, we see different segments of this black-and-white, elegant comedy. At her fifth viewing, a character in the film, Tom Baxter (Jeff Daniels), notices her and steps off the screen to court this devoted fan. The rest of the audience is aghast as the other film characters panic and discuss what to do about Tom's absence. The film keeps running with its cast suspended in dramatic limbo, while the producer and the actor who played Tom Baxter, Gil Shepherd (Jeff Daniels), come to the New Jersey town where the boundary of the screen has been violated. Desperate to avoid a career-damaging scandal, Gil woos Cecilia away from Tom. Rejected by Cecilia, Tom returns to the screen, but when Cecilia prepares to escape to Hollywood with Gil, she finds he has left her already. Desolate, she goes to the movies, and in the final scene, we see her smiling through her tears at Fred Astaire and Ginger Rogers dancing to "Cheek to Cheek," a scene that explicitly recalls the conclusion of *Pennies from Heaven*.

Last Action Hero uses a remarkably similar premise, and critics noted the obvious debt to *Purple Rose* (as well as the debt of both to *Sherlock Jr.*). *Last Action Hero* is set in the present and follows a young teenage boy, Danny Madigan (Austin O'Brien), through his New York City neighborhood. Danny loves movies too, especially action pictures, and especially action pictures starring Arnold Schwarzenegger as Jack Slater (Schwarzenegger plays "himself" as well as Slater in the film). The film opens inside the dramatic conclusion of such a film, and only as the credits of the internal film roll do we see Danny in the audience. Danny is a regular at this theater and has become friends with the kindly projectionist, Nick (Robert Prosky). Nick invites him to watch a personal preview screening of the new Jack Slater movie at midnight. When the excited Danny turns up at twelve, Nick gives him a magic ticket given him years ago by Houdini. The agency of this magic ticket allows Danny to enter the film, "Jack Slater IV," in the middle of a daring car chase. Jack Slater doesn't know who Danny is or how he got there, and unlike Tom Baxter of *Purple Rose*, Jack doesn't know he exists in a movie. Danny tries to prove it to him but doesn't succeed until much later, when, pursuing a criminal, they must follow the criminal out of the movie and back into Danny's world. Jack finds his hero role tougher to sustain in the "real world" and is crushed by learning that he is fictional. Nevertheless, Jack and Danny pursue the criminal, Benedict (Charles Dance), through the real world and kill him in a miraculous—and very cinematic—finale. But, unlike in the movies, Jack is seriously wounded and Danny must use his magic ticket to rush him back to the action-film world, where all injuries to good guys are flesh wounds. They succeed, and Danny and Jack have an emotional parting as Jack persuades Danny he must return to the real world, where he can sustain Jack through his faith in him—and help his single mother (Mercedes Ruehl) survive the mean streets of contemporary New York.

The parallels between these films are many and significant. Both focus on an alienated hero who finds refuge in the movies. Cecilia lacks romance and glamour and finds escape from her abusive husband and grinding poverty in the romantic comedies of the wealthy. Danny lacks a father and fears the violence of his society: Jack Slater serves as a paternal figure capable of protecting him, and, more importantly, Jack's world is one in which crime is consistently defeated by the heroism of the police. Both films show us lengthy segments of the films-within-the-films, both show us the "real" character passing into the film and the film character passing into the "real world," and both provide comic encounters between actor and character (portrayed, of course, by the same person). Both films end with order restored: the fictional characters back in the movies and the "real" characters reluctantly choosing real life. Indeed, both movies present tempered cautionary tales in which excessive investment in filmgoing is depicted as harmful, while movies are still celebrated for the imaginative alternative they offer to the struggles of everyday life. However, the reputations of the directors and the nature of the marketing of the two films would suggest that they were aimed at different audiences (Allen's movies appeal to well-educated adults and his films often play "art houses"; *Last Action Hero* was a "summer movie" and its promotional tie-ins were aimed at adolescents). Nevertheless, the similarity of the films extends to their ideological stances toward Hollywood and the movie audience.

Both films invite consideration of film or a film genre as a "world," a universe that one can enter and live in, if one follows the generic rules. This metaphor of the artwork as world is familiar and has been applied to novels as well as films. But in these movies, the trope of film as world is responsible for much of the humor and satire, satire that depends on both the predictability and the unrealistic nature of the movie genres satirized. In this respect, these movies hark back to another early Hollywood novel, Elmer Rice's *A Voyage to Purilia* (1930). Rice's novel is a science fiction satire in which two voyagers from Earth explore the planet of Purilia (that is, childishness). We soon realize, though the characters do not, that Purilia is not Hollywood per se, but the world depicted in Hollywood movies. The whole planet is bathed in a pink haze, a musical soundtrack is always audible, a voice-over narrator (a "megaphonic presence") introduces characters and locales. There are no toilet facilities since the residents never need them. Most of the residents are venerated mothers, virgin daughters, heroic millionaires seeking the hands of the virgins, or evil men seeking to foil the heroes. Purilia reveals the racism of Hollywood: all the black people are Pullman porters, musicians, or maids, and they are always cheerful except when running in a panic from ghosts. As in these films, the humor tends toward the obvious, but the premise is essentially the same. In *Purple Rose* and *Last Action Hero*, however, the exploring characters are aware of being in the movie world. Since they are experienced viewers, they know the genre constraints and are less alien to the world they've entered than are the explorers of Purilia. All three works rely upon audience awareness of genre clichés.

This satire of genre constraints is the most obvious source of humor in both movies. The satire echoes Tzvetan Todorov's argument about verisimilitude and genre—the argument that realism, or verisimilitude, has meaning only within the context of a given genre. What is believable in one genre may seem out of place or disruptive in another generic context. And yet the humor of these films is based not simply on generic predictability, but, as in *A Voyage to Purilia*, on the realization that certain genre rules are inherently unrealistic and thus comic and absurd when framed by the context of the "real world," which in these works is the framing film outside the film-within-a-film. That the so-called real world is by necessity just another film convention is the central contradiction of both films. In *Last Action Hero*, genre humor appears within the framed film with such devices as the extreme stereotype of the angry black police lieutenant, the exaggeration of the number of weapons carried by heroes and villains, and the fact that Jack Slater routinely fires into his closet to kill the terrorists who are always hiding there ("It costs me a fortune in closet doors," he complains). Danny's attempts to convince Jack that he is a movie character depend on the same comic premise: he anticipates Jack's trademark quips, and he complains about the absurdity of everyone's having a phone number that begins with "555." Most of the genre humor in *Purple Rose* occurs when Tom Baxter tries to survive in the "real world." He is surprised when kisses do not end in fade-outs; he finds his stage money won't buy dinner; and his romantic sentiments about love only amuse a couple of prostitutes who pick him up. When he fights for Cecilia's honor, his hair and makeup are unmussed by the rough altercation. Jack Slater, in *Last Action Hero*, has the opposite experience (but one illustrative of the same contrast between movies and real life): when he breaks the windshield of a real car it surprisingly hurts. Similarly, he finds that, in the "real world," cars don't always explode when you shoot them, guns need to be reloaded, vacant automobiles do not come equipped with keys, and so forth. Both films handle this humor cleverly, though it is hard to escape its rather obvious quality. The humor reminds us that films, while vividly realistic (particularly in their appeal to the visual sense), require a willing suspension of disbelief. And audiences are extremely willing to make that suspension, as these films demonstrate. Thomas Schatz explains that "the viewer's negotiation of a genre film . . . involves weighing the film's variations against the genre's preordained, value-laden narrative system" (10). Viewers learn well the rules of various genres, so that film-viewing creates pleasure through fulfilling carefully nurtured expectations or by exaggerating them, as in more blatantly parodic films such as *Blazing Saddles* (1974) or *Naked Gun* (1988) or earlier parodies such as the "Abbott and Costello Meet . . . " series.

While the genre comedy of these films is by nature predictable, the attitude toward film-viewing and the concept of audience is not. The fictional premise of screen passage scrambles genre contexts (an effect, incidentally, widely blamed for the box-office failure of *Last Action Hero*).[1] The premise also allows these films to theorize the relationship of film and spectator in allegorical terms. In other words, these self-referential films offer a cinematic take on a subject generally the province of film critics. Recall the "Face the Music" scene in *Pennies from Heaven*, where Arthur and Eileen dance with the screen images in the movie theater. Arthur's reactions to the film suggest a continuum of audience responses: he begins in rapt attention, face illuminated by the reflected light of the screen, a spectator; during the song he mouths the words, singing along, now identifying with the characters or at least participating as a chorus; then he and Eileen dance in front of the screen, suggesting imitative identification with the characters; finally, they enter the screen and become the characters, the extreme of "identification." Film theory struggles with this dual nature of movie-viewing: voyeuristic spectatorship and character identification. Often those extremes are theorized in psychoanalytic terms, but I don't think we need necessarily rehearse spectator theories to map the processes suggested in these films. Theories of spectatorship have important gender implications as well, and we will turn to these shortly. Suffice it to say here that films allow viewers to be *both* spectators and imaginative participants, and they allow identifications to shift: one may move from being a voyeur to identifying with a central character to identifying with another character. Novels allow observation and identification as well, but the visual emphasis of film in general seems to accentuate the former while the wish-fulfillment content of commercial films heightens the latter.

Since movies depend on their audiences, they are in an odd but privileged place to critique them. As in all Hollywood-on-Hollywood films, there are limits to self-criticism, and these extend to criticism of audience identification and fantasy. Indeed, Woody Allen was urged to change the ending of *Purple Rose*, on the assumption that a happier ending would translate to millions more in grosses (Lax 27). A filmmaker who lacked the extraordinary artistic control Allen has over his pictures would probably not have been able to preserve the movie's ending (in which the real world disappoints bitterly). Recall that Preston Sturges (one of the very few writer-directors of his time) was encouraged to "softpedal the misery" in *Sullivan's Travels* (Jacobs 259). But commercial films also have a privileged vantage point from which to examine audience dynamics: unlike film theorists, they have a wide audience, and that audience may be positioned in complex ways with respect to the audience depicted within the film.

Cecilia and Danny are obsessed spectators. This characterization is the salient point about them, and it is established early. *Purple Rose* opens with Cecilia gazing at a movie poster; *Last Action Hero* opens with Danny at the movies. Both films quickly show us that film fanaticism encroaches on these characters' work and school lives: Cecilia chats about film stars and movie plots to the detriment of her waitressing job (eventually she is fired for inattention); Danny skips school to attend repeat showings of Jack Slater films. Cecilia and Danny are portrayed sympathetically, yet they are further defined by the happiness or completion they lack. Cecilia is shown imprisoned in a violent and apparently loveless marriage, mired in poverty and laboring in unfulfilling jobs (she takes in laundry to supplement her restaurant work while Monk gambles their money away). Danny's situation is somewhat more subtle. He has a concerned mother who works nights and worries about leaving him alone in a rough neighborhood. On the first night of the film, a burglar breaks into their apartment and handcuffs Danny to the bathtub. The film does not dwell on the absence of a father, but the plot development underscores that issue as the Danny-Jack relationship develops. The burglary early in the movie, as well as suggestively sinister shots of New York streets, clarifies by contrast what Danny looks for in action films.

The renewed popularity of ferocious crime-saving heroes in the eighties and nineties addresses American middle-class insecurities about violent crime by offering imaginative (and simplistic) resolutions to complex

social problems.[2] Ironically, the violence of action films is broadly perceived as contributing to a climate of violence, especially in young males,
who constitute a significant portion of these movies' audience. Though
Last Action Hero touches on this irony (particularly in its panning of
theater marquees displaying violent titles), it is easy to see why Danny
takes comfort in Jack Slater films. Early on he announces his confidence
in the resolution of such films, telling Nick, "Jack Slater can't lose—never
has, never will!" Cecilia's comfort in films comes, as we have noted, from
the elegant and exotic vicarious life they provide. The framed film, "Purple
Rose," opens with the words "I'm bored," spoken by a tuxedo-clad sophis-
ticate at a white grand piano in a New York City penthouse. The film
follows with travels to Egypt and a return to Broadway nightlife.

In delineating the contrast between film content and viewers' lives,
these movies open the way for a cautionary tale about obsessive
spectatorship. But that cautionary tale is tempered (as cautionary tales
in self-referential films generally are) by the myth of utopian spectatorship,
that is, the view that movies satisfy—and perform a social service—by
providing an imaginative escape from daily hardships into a fantasy, an
idealized world. As we have seen, this view is argued by the producers at
the outset of *Sullivan's Travels* and apparently endorsed by Sullivan at
the end. These two screen-passage films offer both messages. They demonstrate that turning to movies for the satisfaction of desire poses the
danger of increasing one's alienation from the circumstances in which
one lives, but they also demonstrate that the escape offered by movies is
magical, wonderful, and deserving of celebration. Little is novel about
this ambivalent analysis of film-viewing. What is interesting is how the
films negotiate the contradictory moralistic impulses shaping their narratives. Those contradictions are most evident in the moments of self-
referentiality, the moments in which the audience's consciousness of watching a film about film is most heightened.

That we can perceive such contradictions in Hollywood-on-Hollywood films is a function of our position as audience to a film that presents
a fictional audience. Jane Feuer, in her discussion of backstage musicals,
provides the best analysis of the relationship between the film audience
and the internal, or what I call the "filmed," audience. She points out how
certain shots position the film audience alongside the "filmed" audience:
shots where the film-within-a-film fills the screen and shots where that
image is framed by limited theater surroundings (a curtain border and

perhaps also the backs of some of the "filmed" audience). Other shots grant a privileged view not accessible to members of the diegetic "filmed" audience: backstage shots in movies about stage musicals and shots of the audience from the apparent point of view of the stage or screen. Most of Feuer's discussion of the manipulation of these two kinds of shots focuses on films of *stage* musicals. She argues convincingly that these shots are combined in a syntax that "makes of the movie audience a live audience," thus restoring the shared experience of live theater (26). Feuer also notes that the combination of the two kinds of shots grants a "doubled identification": "We feel a sense of participation in the creation of the entertainment (from sharing the perspective of the performers) and, at the same time, we feel part of the live audience in the theater" (30).

But, I would argue, in films about films that depict the movie audience, this privileged view creates distance from the "filmed" audience just as it creates identification with performers. That is, because frontal shots of Cecilia or Danny or Arthur watching a film allow us to criticize their apparently naïve or obsessive viewing, we are offered a dual subjective position that allows us to watch what the "filmed" audience watches but not wholly identify with them. We are fittingly distanced from identifying with an audience in a film that cautions against excessive audience identification. As in movies like *A Star Is Born*, where we view the mob of fans at the funeral with disgust, we are invited to fantasize ourselves as a superior audience. Only on reflection may it occur to the viewer of these films that the critique of the internal audiences might apply to him or her. We are allowed to have it both ways, in part because Danny and Cecilia are presented as atypical: Danny watches the preview of "Slater IV" alone, and Cecilia's fellow audience members are mostly outraged by the actor's walking off the screen. But these movies are richer and more complex than a banal message about being a moderate rather than obsessive viewer might suggest.

Recurrent images of Cecilia as filmgoer—*Cecilia watching*— frame *The Purple Rose of Cairo*, with the most powerful and extended image of the heroine as enraptured spectator coming at the conclusion of the film. Mary Ann Doane cites this image at the beginning of her study *The Desire to Desire: The Woman's Film of the 1940s*. For Doane, Cecilia's spectatorship is emblematic of the "peculiar susceptibility to the image—to the cinematic spectacle in general—attributed to the woman in our culture" (1). She argues that for the situation of the film to work, the enraptured spectator must be female. *Last Action Hero* suggests a revision of this paradigm: the enraptured spectator must be female or a child. And Allen's earlier pictures *Play It Again, Sam* and *Zelig* interestingly suggest models of *male* excessive identification. In any case, Allen's setting of *Purple Rose* in the 1930s certainly reinforces the myths of the female film-viewer. Though later studies showed that men and women attended movies in equal numbers, the film industry apparently assumed a predominantly female audience early on, and fan magazines unequivocally assumed such an audience. But how well does Cecilia fit the model of "the female spectator who, in the popular imagination, repeatedly 'gives in' to [the cinema's] fascination" (Doane 2)?

Certainly as an obsessive movie-viewer, Cecilia fits the stereotype. But in her active desire for the male character, Tom Baxter, a desire so strong it draws him off the screen, Cecilia appears to subvert Laura Mulvey's famous paradigm whereby women are the subjects of the male gaze and not, as constructed by films, desiring agents themselves (Doane 19). Doane points out that the very image of the excessively zealous female spectator appears to contradict the gendered theories of the gaze, creating "seemingly insurmountable difficulties in conceptualizing the female gaze" (7). She would argue, however, that Cecilia's desire becomes mediated—becomes an envy of masculine voyeuristic desire—rather than being pure sexual longing. Indeed, one could argue that Cecilia wishes to usurp the place of the nightclub singer that Tom falls for in the internal movie: "You're Tom Baxter—you wind up with Kitty Haynes, the nightclub singer!" As a chanteuse, Kitty Haynes (in the internal movie) is a comic example of the woman on display for the male gaze.

But this ingenious analysis misses the way in which Cecilia's agency drives the film. She is unquestionably the central character in an era (the 1980s) in which films featuring top-billed women are exceedingly rare, and the plot follows her actions and decisions: leaving her husband twice, going dancing with Tom, and accepting Gil's proposal to go to Hollywood. On the other hand, these actions are reactive, and the tragedy of the film is how thoroughly Cecilia remains under the sway of masculine imperatives. Her cheating, abusing husband predicts that she will come back to him—and he is right. He tells her that real life is harsher than the movies and even harsher than her marriage to him—and he is right. When Gil jilts her, she must haul her bags back into the movie theater, where, having been defeated as an active agent, she returns to her role as a passive spectator. But this seems to be precisely Allen's point: Cecilia finds, in film, images that console and enrich her in a world that is fundamentally cruel and unfair.

We encounter again the paradox of *Sullivan's Travels:* the framing film is quite unlike the framed film. In *Purple Rose* both films have the same name. But while the color *Purple Rose* celebrates the sophisticated escapist comedy of the black-and-white "Purple Rose," it is itself a more somber and less idealistic movie. The color *Purple Rose* blatantly defies realism in having characters walk off the screen and confront their actors, but it remains naturalistic in its presentation of Cecilia as imprisoned by destructive social circumstances. One critic argues that the legendary purple rose that Tom Baxter searches for in Egypt (in the framed film) is "an emblem of film. Because film provides only illusions, however, the rose is mythical" (Yacowar 247). Ironically, Baxter searches for the purple rose in the black-and-white film, while the characters who live in color seek their heightened experiences also in the black-and-white films. Seen in the light of Woody Allen's struggle with an audience that prefers his comedies to his more serious films, *The Purple Rose of Cairo* interestingly frames an urbane comedy in the context of a more bittersweet, even sad, movie.[3]

If *Purple Rose* examines the stereotype of female passivity and "susceptibility to the image," *Last Action Hero* engages the macho myths of the action-adventure genre. Pairing these films invites consideration of how movies perpetuate a dichotomy of female passivity versus male activity. *Last Action Hero* establishes that Danny is drawn to Jack Slater films for compensatory reasons—because he lacks a father and because he seeks law and order in his chaotic and often lawless environment. This compensation in turn suggests a familiar analysis of the popularity of action-hero films: that films showing the simple triumph by force of good over evil respond to anxieties about the intractability of evil and the decline of American military might. While the first screen passage in *Purple Rose* involves a character's walking off the screen and into real life, *Last Action Hero* begins the other way, with Danny catapulted from passive spectatorship into the heart of action, the middle of a death-defying car chase. Once the villains in this scene have been dispatched—with a half dozen exploding vehicles, bullet-ridden bodies, and one villain impaled on an ice cream cone—Danny is integrated into the movie as Jack Slater's partner. When the police lieutenant orders Jack to work with

Danny, Jack responds, "Death would be better." Danny recognizes the classic reluctance of the buddy film and argues, "We're perfect material for a buddy movie—I'll teach you to be vulnerable, and you'll teach me to be brave." *Last Action Hero* spends much more time than *Purple Rose* parodying the genre within the framed movie, but it is not clear whether such self-conscious attention to genre clichés amounts to a critique. Indeed, the movie uses its self-consciousness as a license for excess, comically multiplying the chases, explosions, and other violent stunts that characterize the action genre. Perhaps the failure of the movie to attract and please the traditional adventure-genre audience is evidence of the success of the parody.

A clearer criticism of the masculine excess of the genre emerges in some scenes within the "real" New York City world. Danny takes Jack to his home and introduces him as "Arnold Braunschweiger," a double for Schwarzenegger. The movie then cuts away to Benedict, the ruthless villain of the internal film, who now finds himself in the real New York City. He wanders through the streets, shocked by hookers and vagrants and surprised by the violent titles on movie marquees. He murders a garage mechanic, and there is no response. He shouts out in disbelief, "I just shot somebody. I did it on purpose." But nobody cares. The film cuts back to Danny's apartment, where Jack has spent the night talking to Danny's mother, and he says, "I never just talked to a woman before. It's neat." When Danny wakes up, Jack assumes a fatherly role, admonishing him not to worry his mother and showing concern when Danny's mother says Danny has no friends. Danny is repelled by this family tableau. "You turned him into a wimp," he exclaims to his mother. To top it off, Jack shows an interest in classical music. This lightly comic scene suggests how inapplicable the macho action stereotype is to real life. Indeed, most of the real world scenes (except the problematic finale) emphasize the incongruity of the action hero on real streets. While Danny complains that "this world stinks," the film clearly shows that action heroes offer no solution to real-world problems, but it stops far short of critiquing the fantasy as harmful. Rather, *Last Action Hero* poses the film world as an abstract ideal worthy of faith: "I'll be here where you can always find me," Jack tells Danny before he returns him to the real world at the film's end. "But I need you to believe in me. I need you to take care of your mother for me." In a comically self-aggrandizing moment, the villain Benedict says, "If God were a villain—he'd be me!" In Jack Slater's final speech, film heroes seem elevated like gods themselves, worthy of our belief as they act out our desires on an Olympian level.

Released in 1993 and filmed the preceding year, *Last Action Hero* appeared at the height of debate over the social effects of movie and television violence. In 1992, Michael Medved's *Hollywood vs. America* provided the most publicized attack on violent entertainment and the industry that sponsored it. Medved's analysis of contemporary film is disturbingly literal—he evinces virtually no awareness of the function of fantasy and vicarious experience in popular entertainment and asserts an unquestioned link between screen violence and violent crime. That audiences might have complex reasons for viewing behavior they do not wish to emulate or experience firsthand eludes Medved's simplistic analysis. Nevertheless, the book's popularity testifies to how widespread the public discussion of cinematic violence had become. Medved's book follows and makes use of national public opinion polls from 1989 to 1991 condemning film violence; he relies heavily on studies such as the book-length *Watching America: What Television Tells Us about Our Lives*, by S. Robert Lichter, Linda S. Lichter, and Stanley Rothman (Prentice Hall 1991) and the 1990 conference "The Impact of the Media on Children and the Family." Interestingly, Medved cites Arnold Schwarzenegger films as exemplars of a "cruel new notion of comedy" in which sadistic violence becomes a source of humor. *Last Action Hero* makes fun of what Medved calls Schwarzenegger's "murderous *bon mots*," but the film also makes light of the predictability and excessiveness of action-adventure-genre violence. Even while the film makes fictional violence "real" by immersing the boy from the "real world" in the cinematic fiction, it highlights the ridiculousness of filmic violence. Once again, the parodic circle (in which part of the fiction film must stand for extra-cinematic reality) allows the movie to eat its cake and have it too, to make fun of the action genre's trivialization of violence and celebrate the genre just the same (while significantly stopping short of declaring it harmless).

Both *Last Action Hero* and *The Purple Rose of Cairo* parody the clichés of film genres, explore the compensatory relation of film-viewer to film, question the limits of traditional gender roles, and contrast the neatness of art to the messiness of life. On each point, the films display ambivalence: the clichés are mocked as unrealistic yet celebrated as a source of pleasure; film-viewing is seen as dangerous but revitalizing; gender roles are criticized but seen as intractable; and the ideality of fiction is both celebrated for its utopian possibilities and criticized for its harmful potential. The moments of screen passage—when the films focus on the mixing of antithetical worlds—reveal these contradictions most sharply. In the most self-reflexive parts of these very self-referential films, the duality of the filmmaker's position as critic and celebrant is heightened. And as one might imagine, the self-referential contradictions reach their zenith in the conclusions, where the filmmakers are forced to negotiate the tensions of the happy ending.

The opening of *Last Action Hero* is one of the most dramatic and unusual instances of the movie-within-a-movie. As in *Sullivan's Travels,* we essentially begin within the framed movie, only to pull back later with a "reality cut." But the brief opening shot gives us a clue that we are in a movie theater. It shows the screen at an angle so that the screened image is full screen at the right but only partially filling the screen at the left. As a police car on screen approaches, the angled screen itself zooms toward the viewer and fills the screen (no longer angled) at the moment the police car slams on its brakes. We are then plunged into the climactic showdown scene of "Jack Slater III" for more than six minutes, until the movie

Movie character Jack Slater (Arnold Schwarzenegger) makes a surprising appearance in the film of *Hamlet,* at least in the imagination of the young Slater fan watching this film-within-a-film in English class in *Last Action Hero.*

blurs and Danny shouts, "Focus!" Then we cut to a more conventional framing shot showing Danny in a virtually empty theater watching the now blurry movie.

Even more radical in playing with viewer expectations is the fact that *Last Action Hero* never provides opening credits or titles of any kind (the only credits shown in the beginning of the film are the closing credits of the framed film). Along with the zoom effect of the opening shot, this technique draws us into Danny's viewing experience, as if to give us a briefly unmediated taste of the genre that will be heavily mediated by parody and framing throughout the rest of the picture. When we pull back from the movie, the effect, as it is so often, is disenchantment: a bum is sleeping in the theater, the concessionaire is barely conscious, the projectionist is snoring away, the street outside is crowded and dirty. Later we will learn that the blurring of the picture hid from us (though not from Danny, who has seen the picture several times) the death of Jack Slater's son, whom Jack had apparently earlier saved from the evil super-villain, Ripper (Tom Noonan).

Shortly after this scene, we encounter another framed movie, this time in an English classroom. The teacher (Joan Plowright) introduces Hamlet as one of the "first action heroes." Using Olivier's film *of Hamlet,* she tries to interest her late-twentieth-century students in Shakespeare. Of Olivier, she notes resignedly, "Some of you may have seen him in the Polaroid commercials or as Zeus in *Clash of the Titans.*" Casting Plowright, Olivier's widow, in the role of the schoolteacher exhibits a self-referential humor that, the very joke itself warns us, is likely to elude the younger audience targeted by the film. This movie-within-the-movie is handled very differently from the first one. It begins with the black-and-white screen showing Claudius praying, and then cuts to Danny, a reasonably alert viewer. The film cuts back to the screen, now occupied by Olivier as Hamlet, and then returns to Danny, now clearly getting interested since Hamlet brandishes a dagger. The camera shows his heightened interest by zooming in. We cut back to Hamlet preparing to lower the knife and then to a close-up of Danny, growing frustrated and urging Hamlet, "Don't talk about it—just do it!" The camera zooms in to Danny's eyes and then back to the black-and-white screen, now occupied by Jack Slater lighting a cigar (with a color flame) and saying, "You killed my father—big mistake!" The onscreen scene becomes a trailer or preview of coming attractions where various violent scenes of Hamlet slaughtering or blowing up adversaries are accompanied by the voice-over "Something is rotten in the state of Denmark, and Hamlet is taking out the trash." As brightly colored flames roil over the black-and-white set, the voice continues, "No one's going to tell this sweet prince good night." The onscreen explosions then cut directly to an animated explosion in a Roadrunner cartoon. The camera pulls back to reveal Danny as the viewer, now at home after school.

The scene makes fun of the attempt to make *Hamlet* relevant by presenting him as an action hero, and it also demonstrates vividly the gap often present between the media experiences of children and their schoolroom experiences. The Roadrunner cartoon, as much as the Jack Slater movies, shapes the modern student's narrative expectations. Danny's verbalization "Just do it!" echoes the popular Nike commercials as well and illustrates how audience response can be conditioned by other media. We should notice, however, that this scene presents a resistant spectator, a viewer so resistant to the film content as to be capable of transforming it imaginatively, reshaping the content according to the expectations of his preferred genre. Later we see that Danny talks to the screen in Slater pictures, too—usually to console himself with the pleasurable predictability of the genre ("Boy, are you gonna pay!" Danny says to the movie villain Vivaldi [Anthony Quinn]). While the opening film sequence draws us virtually unmediated into the action film, the cuts and transformations of the *Hamlet* scene emphasize audience distance and then a kind of imaginative reinvestment. The scene is a useful warning against overly simplistic paradigms of audience response; at the very least, it suggests that individuals may respond to different kinds of movies very differently with regard to such characteristics as identification. We may transform or "misread" the characters with whom we identify. The scene also illustrates the naturalizing effect of film-viewing, the way in which a viewer translates film content into something more familiar or comfortable. Thus, even a film that challenges audience expectations and familiar genre patterns may be naturalized, read by the audience as if it were more conventionally patterned.

When Danny attends his personal preview of "Jack Slater IV," his entrance into the film is preceded by the introduction of the magic ticket, perhaps the hokiest aspect of the whole conceit. The projectionist, Nick, dresses up in his old usher's uniform and talks about working the theater back in the days when it included live entertainment. His hero then was Houdini, and he had dreamed of being a magician. That dream was never realized, but he views his job as projectionist as related: "It's not much, but it's still showbiz." Magic is one of the hoariest metaphors for film (along with dream). Woody Allen, himself an amateur magician, frequently uses this metaphor as well. The invocation of magic by *Last Action Hero* connects this contemporary film to the early days of film, the days when movies shared billing with vaudeville acts and magicians and when the illusion of moving pictures was considered a magical novelty. It reminds us that much of the appeal of action films lies in the "special effects," a kind of visual sleight of hand that creates the dramatic illusions of daring feats, tremendous explosions, and so forth. As the producer in *Sullivan's Travels* suggests, the early appeal of motion pictures is more consistent with later cinematic pleasures than we care to admit. The magic ticket also shifts some of the responsibility for the screen passage away from Danny; it is not just his obsessiveness that breaks the boundary but the intervention of a magic ticket that "does what it wants to do." In *Purple Rose* the initial passage is voluntary and willful; in *Last Action Hero* the cinematic world seems to overpower the spectator (the movie even hurls dynamite into the theater, thus luring Danny into the screen world).

Though Danny is an unwilling guest of the cinematic world he seemed to manipulate so easily in English class, he comes to relish being in the picture. As we have seen, he becomes Jack Slater's partner, and he uses information he gleaned from his brief period in the audience to help solve the case. The participation of the spectator alters the narrative, and it does so most dramatically when the villain uses the stolen magic ticket to escape Jack's pursuit by fleeing into the real world. Scenes like this one remind us of how stories of screen passage work as allegories for the active role of the viewer in the construction of meaning and conversely as allegories of the role of narratives in the social construction of meaning that shapes how a viewer interprets a film. Figuratively speaking, the construction of meaning is a two-way screen passage: audience members complete the meanings initially constructed in an individual film, but films as a whole pass into the consciousness of viewers and shape how they watch and interpret. If we can enter films and change them, we also must recognize that films enter and alter us as well.

When the villain passes through the screen, Jack and Danny follow, emerging into the deserted theater. They find themselves face down in the theater, with the image of the room they had just occupied frozen on the screen. Jack looks at the screen and says, "We're still here," the illusion briefly effective enough to convince him that he remains in his familiar environment. But Danny urges him to look around, and he sees the huge, empty theater with the villain escaping at the far end. When Jack and Danny exit the theater, Jack is shocked: it is nighttime and rainy, and the myriad flashing marquees convince him he is in New York. Stunned and disappointed when exiting a theater: we have already seen this late in *Pennies from Heaven;* it is the coded symbol for the disillusioning force of reality when juxtaposed with immersion in the film world. All of Jack's comic discoveries about the limitations of his powers in the real world, combined with Danny's choric reminders that this world is "different," serve the same disillusioning function. One can think of *The Purple Rose of Cairo* as a full-length version of such tropes of disillusionment, and that movie is filled with a variety of such disillusioning cuts (such as the jump cut from the first showing of the framed "Purple Rose" to Cecilia daydreaming at work). Eric Lax discusses Woody Allen's several attempts to convey the feeling of rude awakening that comes with entering the harsh sunlight from the darkened movie theater. He explains how such a scene was planned in *Crimes and Misdemeanors* but was eventually shot in rain rather than sunlight because bright sunlight is so difficult for photography (28). As we have seen, however, rain is just as effective as sunlight as a symbol of disillusionment.

The painful contrast of movie fantasy and reality is more clearly central in *The Purple Rose of Cairo.* The contrast is articulated every time Cecilia goes to the movies or talks about them. After her first viewing of *Purple Rose* she tells her sister that, in the movie, "the people were so beautiful. They spoke so cleverly and they did such romantic things." Allen introduces the central theme of the painful contrast between imaginative fantasy and reality in the opening sequence of the film. The movie begins with credits on a dark screen and Fred Astaire singing "Cheek to Cheek" on the soundtrack. The music continues as we share Cecilia's gaze as she examines the poster for "Purple Rose." The camera, mimicking her eye movement, scans the poster carefully, pausing at the sphinx and palm trees, the men in tuxedos holding champagne glasses. Then we cut from Cecilia's gaze to Cecilia's face *"staring dreamily at the now offscreen movie poster"* (Allen, *Three Films* 321). She is awakened from her revery by the loud clunk of a letter falling from the marquee; the clunk coincides with an abrupt stop to the music. The theater manager posting "The Purple Rose of Cairo" on the marquee warns Cecilia, "Oh, Cecilia, be careful. Are you all right?" Allen's use of the movie music, subjective shots of Cecilia's gaze surveying the poster, the falling letter, and the manager's warning all establish the movie's dual pattern of involving us in Cecilia's perspective and her cinematic fantasies and pulling away from them. The movie will include Cecilia's gaze but will not be consumed by it; the movie will include the framed movie of the same title but will present much more than that. That the movie opens with a warning to be careful underscores its function as a cautionary tale about overidentification with film characters.

Allen's modulation of perspective—from sharing Cecilia's view to a position where we can be sympathetically critical of it—is apparent in the first viewing of the framed "Purple Rose." Unlike the wholly involving opening of *Last Action Hero*, Allen's treatment repeatedly reminds the viewer that the audience is as important as the film being viewed. Six minutes into the movie (at about the very point that *Last Action Hero* cuts away from the internal film to reality), Cecilia returns to her local theater to attend the opening of "The Purple Rose of Cairo." In those opening six minutes we have seen her at her job and met her husband; we have a context for her viewing. At night, the theater we saw in the opening shots is transformed, its vivid lights flashing in the darkness as a vivacious crowd buys tickets. The film shows us the lively audience from the perspective of the screen: as the lights dim, the crowd becomes quiet and a projector beam is illuminated over their heads. Reverse angle takes us to the classic framing shot: the black-and-white opening credits of the framed movie surrounded by the red curtain and a shot of the backs of the audience. Then the framed screen occupies the entire screen. This shot is followed by a reverse-angle shot of Cecilia rapt with attention. Through a three-and-a-half-minute scene, Allen cuts back and forth among these three kinds of shots: framed screen, full-screen internal movie, frontal shots of Cecilia or other audience members. The syntax is very precise. A couple of times, audience laughter at a joke in the internal movie serves as the cue for cutting from the internal movie to the audience. Twice Allen uses fade-outs to take us not only from Cecilia as viewer to the images viewed on screen but also to indicate a jump to a later point in the internal movie. The effect of Allen's editing is to keep us conscious of the act of viewing and to hammer home the contrast between the glamorous urban sophistication on screen and the impoverished lives of Cecilia and her fellow audience members.

The scene where Tom Baxter steps off screen is brilliantly managed. In the midst of a speech we have heard before, Tom's gaze wanders toward the audience and he becomes distracted. He stops his speech and addresses Cecilia directly: "My God, you must really love this picture. . . . You've been here . . . all day and I've seen you twice before." Tom walks off the screen, transforming into full color as he does so. The other performers break their roles and gasp, as do members of the audience, one of whom faints. As the audience continues to watch the screen intently, the remaining actors complain to the theater manager and then bicker comically about which one of them is the central character and what the movie is about. The dialogue of the abandoned characters borrows from Pirandello in conception, and, indeed, they seem like theater performers except that they have no life outside of the performance—"Don't turn the projector off. . . . It gets black and we disappear," one of them says. When a later audience comes in and watches the altered film, they complain: "They sit around and talk . . . and nothing happens," says one. "I want what happened in the movie last week to happen this week. Otherwise, what's life about?" questions another.

These scenes have great fun with the existential status of imaginative creations, but they also stress the variety of audience responses: different characters interpret the movie differently according to their roles in it; some audience members find the altered movie amusing while others are insulted or bored by it. The variety of responses reminds us that we cannot treat "audience" as a unitary, easily knowable entity. Meanwhile, Cecilia finds herself in the odd position of being wooed by a fictional character to whom she must explain the harsh realities of depression life: "Right now the country's not in great shape," she says.

The Purple Rose of Cairo and *Last Action Hero* both play with the conceit of a fictional character loose in the real world, a situation that suggests metaphorically the role of fictional narrative in everyday life. Late in the movie, Cecilia confesses, "I'm confused. I'm married. I just met a wonderful new man. He's fictional, but you can't have everything." Tom Baxter's fictionality as a character in a romance renders him flawless if naive: "Tom's perfect," Cecilia tells the actor who portrays him. The actor responds, "But he's not real. What good is perfect, if a man's not real?" This question is central to the analysis of escapist fantasy in both films: what good are imaginary solutions to the problems and complexities of everyday life? It is the question central to *Sullivan's Travels* and *Pennies from Heaven*, and in these two screen-passage movies it is answered with varying degrees of ambivalence by filmmakers committed to illusion but wary of its dangers. A fascination with storytelling as an uncomplicated good is juxtaposed with a moralistic fear that engagement in imaginative fictions can have an alienating, even disastrous effect.

In *Last Action Hero*, Nick greets Jack with enthusiasm, "This is a wonderful moment for me, Mr. Slater. I've never met a fictional character before." But Jack is stricken by the discovery that he is fictional, particularly because the continuing violent struggles of his action-hero life (and the trauma of his son's death) are rendered all the more unjust when they are viewed as devices to entertain others. Here we see a commentary on the social function of movies, particularly violent ones. Imagining the characters as real temporarily shifts our understanding of the cathartic value of violent fantasies and suggests what critics of violent films have argued—that imaginary violence creates real harm. The comment also raises the Pirandello-like theme of the moviemaker (or writer or actor) as a kind of god, giving life to a character.

This metaphor-made-real appears in both movies when the character encounters the actor who portrays him. These scenes involve special effects (doubles and split screens) to allow the same actor to portray both parts. Jack Slater's encounter with the actor who portrays his character, Arnold Schwarzenegger, occurs at the world premiere of "Jack Slater IV," which Slater attends to stop Benedict and the Ripper from assassinating Schwarzenegger as part of a plot to destroy Slater. The premiere scene is a staple of Hollywood-on-Hollywood films and has a life of its own from the days of radio and television coverage of such events. McTiernan uses the scene in a Hitchcockian manner as the public locus for the climactic struggle of hero and villain; the self-referential comedy gives the whole sequence an absurdist tone. The premiere is filled with celebrity cameos where actors (such as Chevy Chase, Damon Wayans, Quincy Jones, Jim Belushi, and even Schwarzenegger's wife, Maria Shriver) portray themselves. Such star-studded galas have been a common feature in Hollywood-on-Hollywood films, from early examples such as James Cruze's *Hollywood* (1923), Robert Florey's *Hollywood Boulevard* (1936), and the Doris Day musical *It's a Great Feeling* (1949) to contemporary films such as *The Player*.

The film mocks celebrity publicity through its characterization of the real Arnold Schwarzenegger, who brags that in his new movie "we only kill forty-eight people, compared to the last one, where we killed 119" and cannot resist touting his new restaurant, Planet Hollywood (a franchise that captures in its name the ubiquity of Hollywood imagery in everyday life). To add to the reflexive comedy, the real Ripper, having been brought to life by Benedict and the magic ticket, shows up in costume, as does the actor who portrays him (also played by Tom Noonan), causing the actor's agent much confusion. Spotting the Ripper preparing to kill Schwarzenegger, Slater pulls his gun but is wrestled to the ground by the real Schwarzenegger. Character wrestling with actor aptly represents the antagonistic relationship assumed in both films to exist between actor and screen representation. Schwarzenegger assumes that Slater is just a particularly good celebrity look-alike (whom he would like to hire for shopping center appearances). Slater responds bitterly, "I don't really like you. . . . You've brought me nothing but pain." This antagonism may suggest (ironically) the way in which actors often feel constricted by the public image created by the roles they portray. The metaphor of bringing a character to life suggests the actor as creative force, while the converse sense of limitation and being trapped expressed by the characters reflects the way film freezes a single performance as chosen and manipulated by director and producer.

This paradox of acting as creative and imprisoning emerges in the exchange between character and actor in *The Purple Rose of Cairo*. Tom and Gil meet at an empty carousel in an amusement park, an appropriate setting for two whose livelihood depends on filling theater seats. "I took you from the printed page, and I made you live," Gil asserts. Tom agrees, "So I'm living [and] I want my freedom." The character asserts will by disobeying his creator. But is the actor the real creator? Even starstruck Cecilia doubts that, asking Gil, "Well, didn't the man who wrote the movie [create the character]?" Gil agrees that this is technically true but takes credit for "fleshing out" Tom Baxter. In another scene, Tom connects the writer with God, a concept he is unfamiliar with until Cecilia introduces him to it. She defines God as "uh, the, the reason for everything—the world, the universe." "Oh, I think I know what you mean," responds Tom, "the two men who wrote 'The Purple Rose of Cairo'—Irving Sachs and R.H. Levine, they're writers who collaborate on films."

Aside from the existential comedy of playing with the artist-as-God conception, these scenes remind us of the collaborative and ambiguous nature of cinematic creation. Few movies are written and directed by one person, let alone an individual with the creative control of Woody Allen. Thus it is important to remember that the plots and characters generally result from writers, actors, and directors working together under the supervision and control of businesspeople. In a highly mediated way, the audience (as it is perceived and articulated by producers) shapes its own narratives and creates its own heroes. *The Player* explores this premise explicitly. And while it may be true that Gil Shepherd brings Tom Baxter to life, what we see in the movie is that Cecilia draws the character through the screen with the intensity of her emotional investment. In *Last Action Hero* this relationship is termed "belief," as Jack twice urges Danny to believe in him: once when he rescues him from his precarious perch on a gargoyle many stories above the New York streets, and later when they part for their respective worlds. In the Planet Hollywood on which we live, screen images are communally created and walk among us.

In both films, the real characters must choose the "real world" over their in-screen existence. In *The Purple Rose of Cairo* this choice is powerfully dramatized as the choice between two glamorous lovers offering Cecilia two different escapes from her drab existence. Tom's passion for Cecilia brings him to life; Gil seems genuinely moved by Cecilia's devotion to his acting career. The star and his image both reciprocate the adoration of a fan—clearly a wish-fulfillment fantasy for Cecilia. Tom offers Cecilia his total devotion and his fictional perfection; Gil offers to take her to Hollywood for a life of glamour (and *his* money is real). The confrontation occurs at the end of Tom and Cecilia's night on the town. Tom has taken her on a date in the world of his film. Though she discovers that the champagne is ginger ale, Cecilia has the time of her life: "My whole life I've wondered what it would be like to be this side of the screen." As Cecilia and Tom embrace in black and white, Gil enters the theater and breaks their cinematic clutch. Both Gil and Tom express their love for the understandably befuddled Cecilia, who responds, "Last week I was unloved—now two people love me. And it's the same two people."

Cecilia and Tom come off screen and join Gil in the theater while the rest of the internal movie cast look on from the screen in black and white. They have been transformed into an audience and offer advice and wry comments on the scene that Cecilia, Tom, and Gil act out. The elder actress encourages Cecilia to "go with the real guy, honey; we're limited." The ingenue advises, "Go with Tom; he's got no flaws." In this

moment of role reversal, Cecilia is transformed into the heroine of a romance and movingly acts out her choice of the real world as the onscreen
audience of actors looks on intently. Of course, Cecilia must choose the
real world, but her reasons are interestingly contradictory. Cecilia dismisses Tom to his movie world, consoling him by saying, "In your world
things have a way of working out right. See, I'm a real person. No matter
how tempted I am, I have to choose the real world." Yet in choosing Gil,
Cecilia is opting for a movie-like romance: she will be with a handsome
actor who claims to have fallen in love with her at first glance (just like in
the movies) and who offers to spirit her from her drab existence to a life of
excitement in Hollywood. What could be more in the spirit of a fan-magazine fantasy? As Sam Girgus points out, "Ironically, the real world to Gil
the actor is Hollywood, the epitome of the unreal" (85).

Cecilia knowingly chooses the world in which things don't necessarily work out, and thus we should not be surprised when Gil leaves for
Hollywood without her. She learns of Gil's departure from the theater
manager whose opening words in the movie warned her to be careful.
Once again, he is on a ladder attending to the marquee, but this time he is
taking down the sign for "The Purple Rose of Cairo." Allen's framing film
has lasted for the run of the internal movie. Cecilia shows up that night for
the opening of the new film, and we once again hear Astaire singing "Cheek
to Cheek." The crushed Cecilia entering the darkened movie theater with
her suitcase and ukelele in tow offers a wonderful image of the viewer
awaiting imaginative transport by the movies. The final scene cuts back
and forth from the Astaire-Rogers dance number to Cecilia's face, ending
as that face breaks into a smile and is brightened by a whiter light reflected off the screen. The ostensibly unhappy ending deftly merges real-
life disappointment and screen consolation. As in *Pennies from Heaven*,
Fred Astaire musicals seem to epitomize the idealized existence offered
by Hollywood. The movie that began with Cecilia's gaze scanning a movie
poster ends with a reverse-angle shot of her face illuminated by reflected
movie light. Though it provides a cautionary tale about the harshness of
real life—in words spoken by Monk as Cecilia leaves him, "Go. See what's
out there. It ain't the movies! It's real life!"—*The Purple Rose of Cairo* also
endorses the escapist power of movie fictions and borrows a moment
from an elegant musical for its own conclusion.

A happy ending joining Cecilia with either Tom or Gil would be clearly
untrue to the film's insistence on realistically depicting Cecilia's trapped

existence. But an ending that wholly undercut the imaginative power of films would be untrue to the world of film, of which this movie is necessarily a part, and it would be untrue to Woody Allen, whose work as a filmmaker is consistently a tribute to the history of film. Allen even filmed some of *Purple Rose* in a theater that he had attended regularly as a child (Lax 35).[4]

Last Action Hero exhibits less compunction about using the unequivocally happy ending. It too exploits a cyclical structure and echoes its opening scene. When the Ripper holds Danny captive atop the building in which "Jack Slater IV" is premiering, we reprise the conclusion of "Jack Slater III," with which the movie began. Danny, who resembles Jack's son, stands in the murdered son's place. Yet the reversals of this scene contradict the movie's premise that the real world lacks the happy endings and triumphs of the good guys characteristic of the film world. In the movie "Jack Slater III," the son (unbelievably) dies; in the "real world" of *Last Action Hero,* Danny is thrown off the roof but catches hold of a gargoyle and is miraculously rescued by Jack, who electrocutes the Ripper and goes on to track down and kill the evil Benedict—"No sequel for you!" Benedict has brought other movie villains to life to work for him in the "real world" because "here in this world bad guys can win." But of course he does not win in *Last Action Hero* either. The contradiction points to the original paradox that the real world in these films is simply another filmic convention. *Last Action Hero* is as much an action film as a parody of one. The problem is that this happy ending undercuts the points the film has made about the violence and ambiguity of the world Danny wants to escape.

But while the miraculous rescues of the climax of *Last Action Hero* may evidence less integrity than the ending of *The Purple Rose of Cairo, Last Action Hero* provides a coda that cleverly explores the very contradictions it sets in motion. When Jack dispatches Benedict, Jack is gravely wounded. The dying Benedict drops the magic ticket off the rooftop and it lands in front of a theater showing a revival of Bergman's *The Seventh Seal.* The ticket brings the hooded figure of Death (Ian McKellan) to life. His sickle splits the screen and the theater audience flees in terror. Finally he tracks down Jack and Danny in the original movie house, where Danny hopes to transport Jack back to the movie world because there his injury would be just a flesh wound. Death approaches Jack, but only out of curiosity, saying, "He's not on any of my lists"—because he is a fictional character. Death holds the ticket in this wonderfully suggestive scene, which reminds us that film has been seen from its earliest days as a kind of animation that triumphs over death. The persistence of the filmed image that outlasts the actors and directors who create it, as well as the propensity for comic, happy endings, are ways in which movies cheat death. "I don't do fiction—not my field," Death admits. The figure of Death does note that Danny *is* on his lists, but for much later, thus reinforcing the separation of worlds and underscoring who belongs in which. Using Death's advice (and thus profiting from real-world sensibilities), Danny locates the other half of the magic ticket and Jack is saved in a whirl of projectors and beams of light, with Nick shouting, "Three cheers for Houdini!" In this hodgepodge ending, it is difficult to discern how effectively *Last Action Hero* thematizes its own contradictions. Often, the very act of ending a film brings the conflict between genres into high relief. Action film, self-referential parody, and family melodrama all demand different resolutions, and the incoherence of the ending (or endings) testifies ironically to the ambition of the conception.

In *The Purple Rose of Cairo*, however, there is a kind of death for fictional characters, the darkness of the end of the film. Recall the actor who begs the theater manager, "Don't turn the projector off . . . it gets black and we disappear. . . . You don't understand what it's like to disappear, to be nothing, to be annihilated." This image turns the tables again by implying that the ideal world of the cinema is dependent on the audience's devotion and belief; it is essentially a projection, a mass fantasy. That cycle of dependence is articulated in the final scene of *Last Action Hero*, where Danny and Jack have their tearful parting: "I'll be here where you can always find me," Jack offers. "But I need you to be out there to believe in me." Both of these scenes suggest a mawkish view of the cinema as a grand life-enhancing fantasy that perfectly serves the needs of its consumers. As such, it is a faith that seems curiously out of place in the context of movies about the dangers of audience overidentification. Cecilia's explanation of God to Tom may offer a perspective on the claims made for movies in these films. Life without God, Cecilia explains to Tom, would "be like a movie with no point, and no happy ending." Allen hints that movies, fictions, provide a contemporary faith. Like religion, they offer imaginative triumphs over hardship and death and give a narrative shape and meaning to existence.[5] These are large claims for romances, musicals, and action movies, but the films under discussion here only make sense if those claims are taken seriously. Allen's choice of Astaire's "Cheek to Cheek" allows the line "I'm in heaven" to function as background for the fade-out from Gil Shepherd aboard an airplane to Cecilia at a movie theater. Nevertheless, Allen's inclusion of producers and exhibitors and his play with the worthlessness of screen money remind us of the economic base of this commercial faith. Cecilia is a dreamer, but she is also a consumer.

Screen passages allow for complex interrogations of how film-viewing works. Though both of these films shape that interrogation around a simplistic contrast of reality and filmic illusion, they explore in a more nuanced way the dynamics of viewership. They show moviegoers seeking solace and wish fulfillment in the fictions of movies, and they show the danger of overidentification leading to naïveté and disillusionment. But by showing how film images and audience desires interpenetrate, they complicate the easy critique of excessive identification that they initiate. If the screen offers a passageway to another world, it also becomes a mirror that tells us our own desires, their seductive beauty and their unattainability. But the magic of these films assumes a tighter reciprocity between audience and motion picture content than could really exist. Movies are imperfect mirrors, and the process of manufacturing dreams in a "dream factory" brings all the corruptions and foibles of the business world into creative collision with the artistic.

The fascinating story of the promotion, critical reception, and ultimate failure of *Last Action Hero* demonstrates not only the familiar subordination of artistry to business but also the simple fact that corporate assumptions about audience behavior are often wrong. *Last Action Hero* was enormously expensive to produce; the *Nation* reported pointedly that "its reputed cost was roughly half the annual budget of the National Endowment of the Arts" (Klawans 116). It exceeded its budget and required much-publicized last-minute rewrites (from an uncredited William Goldman, brought in as the fifth writer) and eleventh-hour retakes. *Business Week* referred to it as the "first $60 million commercial," noting that it was Sony's "most ambitious attempt at cross-marketing and product tie-ins since it bought Columbia Pictures in 1989" (Grover 56). The film featured Sony recording artists on the soundtrack, a Sony disc player and cellular phone in the film, and tie-ins with video game and amusement park attractions as well as the usual children's toys.

The *Los Angeles Times* reported a disastrous preview or test screening of the film. Columbia denied it had taken place and threatened (and then backed down from) sanctions against the *Times*. When *Variety* panned the film, Columbia executives tried to strong-arm the editors. And to promote the New York opening of the film, Columbia raised a seventy-five-foot inflated Arnold Schwarzenegger balloon on Times Square; unfortunately the dynamite he brandished in his hand was considered a tasteless reference to the World Trade Center bombing that had occurred just three days before.[6] Appropriately, the movie was dubbed the biggest bomb of the year, and most reviews were devastating and sarcastic. Richard Corliss called it "the industry's all-time costliest inside joke" (67). Both *Newsweek* and the *New Yorker* used the term "deconstructionist" to characterize the film, and Stuart Klawans in the *Nation* called it "self-reflexive in the full late capitalist, postmodernist sense" (116). Anthony Lane, writing in the *New Yorker*, offered one of the few positive reviews, lauding it as cheerfully comic and "a Hollywood thriller that owns up to its artifice" (94). Woody Allen commented of *Purple Rose* that it was an example of films that were "not popular, yet . . . not so esoteric that they're art films exactly" (Lax 197). That characterization applies all the more vividly to *Last Action Hero*, caught in the financial machinations of the megahit yet hampered by the ambiguity of self-reflexive nuances. "This is a confused piece of work," wrote Lane, "deeply in love with what it mocks, and troubled by aspects of cinema that it can never laugh off" (97). That perceptive formulation applies to the best films of the Hollywood-on-Hollywood genre.

5 No Business Like

Stand-In (United Artists 1937). Producer: Walter Wanger. Director: Tay Garnett. Screenwriters: Gene Towne and Graham Baker. Based on a story by Clarence Budington Kelland.

The Bad and the Beautiful (MGM 1952). Producer: John Houseman. Director: Vincente Minnelli. Screenwriter: Charles Schnee. Based on a story by George Bradshaw.

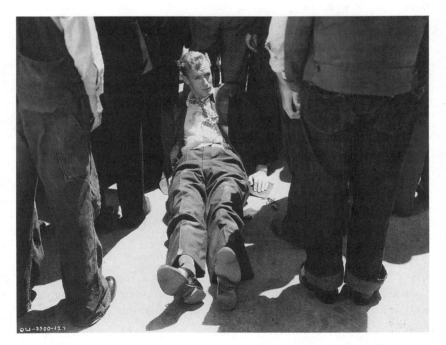

The stand-in takes a seat: New York executive Atterbury Dodd (Leslie Howard) is knocked down by angry studio workers in *Stand-In.* When he gets up, he will champion the workers' cause and save the studio.

S how business," "dream factory," "entertainment industry"—the terms are so familiar and hackneyed that we are likely to forget how blatantly they call attention to the economic base of movie artistry. That these terms are also oxymorons emphasizes the ever-present conflict in Hollywood creations, the conflict between art and business. While this conflict is not unique to film, it is exaggerated or foregrounded by various dynamics of the movie industry: the high cost of film technology, the historical development of film production in the context of film distribution, and the collaborative nature of filmmaking. All of these factors have made the business end of filmmaking more prominent in the shaping of creative processes than is the case in other arts. Yet films about Hollywood have been more prone to reveal the private lives of stars or the film techniques behind the cameras than to reveal the business dealings essential to studio existence. The two films under discussion here—*Stand-In* (1937) and *The Bad and the Beautiful* (1952)—are exceptions. In extraordinarily different ways, they focus on film production and finance, taking the viewer behind the scenes, not only to the world of cameras and key lights, but to the world of business deals and accounting ledgers.

The contrast between these films is instructive. *Stand-In* is a modest comedy, fast-paced and often silly. *The Bad and the Beautiful* aspires to tragedy, as stressed by a melodramatic score and a variety of allusions to *Citizen Kane*. In this sense, these films exemplify a general trend in films about Hollywood, from comedy (which dominated in the thirties and forties) to bitter exposés (which dominated in the fifties and sixties).[1] For all its madcap silliness, *Stand-In* is a rich and provocative film, touching on the relations between Hollywood studios and New York financial control, on the struggles between labor and management, and on financial conspiracies to bankrupt studios for essentially hostile takeovers. *The Bad and the Beautiful* is more simply a study in egotism and how it manifests itself in film production. Both films provide a skeletal outline of Hollywood management depicting representative figures (often stereotypes) of presidents, producers, directors, actors, writers, extras, and technicians. Both films position themselves critically toward Hollywood, although, as we have come to expect, they discover ways to affirm Hollywood in the process. *Stand-In* shows the corrupting influence of Hollywood in a poorly run studio rife with back-stabbing conspiracies; but it also shows Hollywood restoring the main character's humanity and vitality. *The Bad and the Beautiful* shows its ambivalence explicitly by focusing on a producer who "makes" the careers of the people he betrays, while his business and artistic flair take him from "Genius Boy" to pariah.

The plot of *Stand-In* is predicated on the Wall Street takeovers of Hollywood studios that occurred during the depression. It opens with a shot of Wall Street and then cuts indoors to a banking firm whose executives are debating whether or not to accept an offer to sell Colossal Studios. Colossal is a Poverty Row studio that hasn't been turning a profit, but young hotshot Atterbury Dodd (Leslie Howard) advises the elderly bank trustees not to sell it. He stakes his reputation on his mathematical calculations that show Colossal should turn a profit. His bosses send him to Hollywood to investigate. In Hollywood, a radio commentator gives us (but not Dodd) the inside scoop: Colossal's star actress, Thelma Cheri (Marla Shelton), and émigré director Koslofski (Alan Mowbray) are running up costs on producer Douglas Quintain's (Humphrey Bogart) feature, "Sex and Satan." Thelma and Koslofski are doing so in conspiracy with a rival producer, Ivor Nassau (C. Henry Gordon), who wants to acquire Colossal for its physical plant. Into this mess stumbles the comically prim Atterbury Dodd. A publicity man, Potts (Jack Carson), tries to divert Atterbury with women and parties, but he retreats to the boarding house where Lester Plum (Joan Blondell), the sympathetic stand-in for Thelma Cheri, lives. Lester befriends Atterbury and teaches him about Hollywood; she also tries to teach him about love and passion. Eventually, Atterbury comes to understand the fraud that Thelma Cheri and Koslofsky are engaged in. He teams up with Douglas Quintain to save the picture, but for Douglas to edit "Sex and Satan" satisfactorily he must circumvent Thelma's contractual power over the final cut. To accomplish this end, Atterbury gets Thelma drunk and is photographed with her in a compromising position. He then fires her, invoking the morals clause of her contract. But when the escapade hits the papers, Atterbury's New York firm sells Colossal and Ivor Nassau takes control. Atterbury engineers a mini-rebellion with the newly fired Colossal workers: they toss Ivor Nassau over the studio wall and seize the studio for the forty-eight hours Douglas needs to reedit the picture. They succeed and the sale is voided. The picture will presumably restore Colossal's fortunes as well as the jobs of the workers. Atterbury becomes engaged to Lester, and, more remarkably, Douglas proposes to Thelma (with whom he has always been in love), but only on condition she abandon acting to be his wife.

The plot is dizzying, and the caricatures—from math-obsessed

Atterbury Dodd to the temperamental foreign director Koslofski—are painted broadly. But the giddy comedy of *Stand-In* is consistently concerned with aligning people with their genuine natures and putting moviemaking in the hands of the creative and visionary. The theme of Wall Street control of studio production draws upon actual events of the early 1930s, when attempts to introduce cost-efficiency management techniques into Hollywood studios generally proved short lived and ineffective. Chicago businessman Harley C. Clarke, for example, tried unsuccessfully to apply management techniques used in public utilities to Fox in 1931. John Hertz of the Wall Street firm Lehman Brothers similarly proved disastrous during his tenure at Paramount from 1931 to 1933. He was succeeded by another businessman without movie experience, John Otterson, who was equally unsuccessful (Balio 23-24). The popular notion, however, that Wall Street firms influenced film content is apparently without foundation. Wall Street and Hollywood were both interested in achieving profit by making popular motion pictures, and the management of production soon returned to Hollywood although ultimate budgetary authority remained in New York. The conspiracy theme in *Stand-In* no doubt draws on William Fox's contention (elaborated in Upton Sinclair's book) that Wall Street bankers conspired to wrest his studio from him.[2]

The conclusion of *Stand-In*, which depicts an angry mob of laid-off workers, veers close to mentioning the virtually forbidden Hollywood topic—movie industry unions. The film obliquely reflects the increasing public awareness in the mid-thirties of labor disputes in the film industry. And while it hardly endorses unions, it offers a faint paean to the everyday worker in a highly conflicted and paradoxical climactic speech. To this financial plot of rescuing a studio in distress and thus saving the workers' jobs is wedded a more disturbing romantic plot involving both the masculinization of Atterbury Dodd and the brutal taming of Thelma Cheri (the latter echoing the vilification of Lina Lamont in *Singin' in the Rain*).

These two plot patterns—saving the studio and uniting the romantic couples—meet in the complementary metamorphoses that result from the collision of Wall Street and Hollywood: bloodless Atterbury Dodd is humanized by Hollywood, and the studio and its denizens are revitalized by their contact with his cheerful naïveté. When we first meet Atterbury he is dictating a speech about the virtues of mathematics, "a science more important than food and drink." He asserts that "when one is in business, one is forced to ignore human factors." Even his aged Wall Street boss, Pettypacker, knows the folly of this outlook and lectures him on how movies are the collaborative result of various idiosyncratic and talented people working together. One of the contradictions of the film is how it demonstrates this point while nevertheless presenting a studio full of corrupt and talentless individuals.

Atterbury's arrival is presented through an economical montage of Hollywood sights, which establishes Atterbury as the amazed easterner encountering a brash and vulgar culture. Riding in the Colossal limousine, he gapes in astonishment at palm trees, a tropical billboard for the Cocoanut Grove, a hawker selling maps to the stars' homes, and restaurants shaped like hats, windmills, airplanes, and puppy dogs, or built entirely of oyster shells. When the limo pulls to a stop at a traffic light he catches a glimpse of W.C. Fields obliging an autograph seeker. The cutting back and forth from Atterbury's wide-eyed look to the Los Angeles curiosities suggests point-of-view shots, but director Tay Garnett varies the strict use of point of view by tracking rapidly in on each icon to emphasize Atterbury's astonishment. A similar montage is used in the original *A Star Is Born* (released in the same year) but to opposite effect, since Esther is finally seeing the famous landmarks she has dreamt about. Atterbury the befuddled easterner is closer to Aldous Huxley's British hero, Jeremy Pordage, in *After Many a Summer Dies the Swan* (1939), who is also particularly fascinated by the restaurants shaped like animals (which he dubs "zoomorphs"). *Stand-In* emphasizes that the Hollywood that Atterbury Dodd is entering is a crazy world bound by different rules than those to which he is accustomed.

Stand-In presents a Hollywood hierarchy ranging from the New York financial bosses to the lowly stand-in herself. The "cute meet" that brings Atterbury Dodd and Lester Plum together unites top and bottom of the hierarchy when Lester hitches a ride in Atterbury's company limousine. This ride is the first of a series of stand-ins, or scenes where one character acts as surrogate for another (here Lester shares the space officially allotted to Atterbury alone). She explains to him what being a stand-in involves (as it becomes clear that he knows absolutely nothing of the film industry—not even the names of the stars). He explains that he is a stand-in of sorts, too, in that he represents his company's stockholders. Throughout the film, Atterbury's appeal to stockholder interests functions as a way of distancing his actions from his personal desires, even though he is forced to admit that his job hangs on his success with Colossal. Deferred desire is ultimately the understanding of Hollywood machinations that emerges from *Stand-In;* again and again, we see the folly of such deferrals. Ironically, it is the literal stand-in, Lester Plum, who consistently cuts through the deferrals to tell the truth about her desires and those of others.

In short order, director Garnett exposes Atterbury Dodd and the audience to a studio corrupted. We see producers and publicity men interrupting everything but their drinking to follow the horse races on the radio; a director constantly lying down while waiting for his exorbitant demands to be met; a private home liberally furnished with studio property; an overbearing stage mother auditioning her saccharine daughter in a hotel room; the publicity agent plying Atterbury with hired women and a compliant Thelma Cheri; and a cynical and embittered Douglas Quintain skulking about the studio with a Scottie dog under his arm. "That's Hollywood!" is the refrain used to explain the bizarre, wasteful, or tasteless to the increasingly appalled efficiency expert, Atterbury. Despite Douglas's cynicism, he is the one who offers Atterbury an educational tour of the studio and outlines how the three thousand workers contribute to the finished product. The moral Atterbury draws from this tour is not what Douglas intends: "In these walls, three thousand units just to manufacture motion pictures . . . cogs in a machine!" David O. Selznick would later similarly describe directors at Warner Brothers in this era as "purely cog[s] in the machine" (Balio 79). Though the film works to humanize Atterbury's mechanistic view of the workers, it still exhibits the familiar Hollywood pride in its mechanical base, a pride that extends to showing the workings of a special-effects scene. In amazement, Atterbury witnesses a ski slope on a treadmill, a snowbank and tree revolving on pulleys, and a blizzard created with soap flakes and a fan, with Lester sweating out her stand-in role in a snowsuit under the bright lights. Despite Atterbury's exaggerated ignorance, this scene invites the audience to share his perspective in being educated about filmmaking techniques.

The Hollywood satire extends outside the studio to the classic boarding house populated by extras, bit actors, and has-beens left over from the silents. But, as in *What Price Hollywood?* and *A Star Is Born,* the boarding house is a supportive community of Hollywood outsiders still uncorrupted by success. It is to this redemptive milieu that Atterbury Dodd flees from the excesses of the studio suite and Potts's overtures. Though he shares the bath with a trained seal, he also shares a hall with the lively Lester, who offers her services as his secretary.

Lester Plum proves to be an adept secretary, but her primary function in the film is to reform Atterbury's bloodless character. In a key speech, she upbraids him for having "figures in your blood instead of red corpuscles." She asks him if he has ever hit a man, loved a woman, gotten drunk and been thrown out, ever been wicked or desired to be wicked. He responds negatively to each question (and in the course of the film he experiences each of these things). Atterbury is moved by Lester's speech and stiffly resolves to "not tether my emotions. I will give life the opportunity to make me the kind of person I might have been." Strengthened by this resolution, he asks Lester to teach him to dance. This initiates a series of scenes in which Atterbury engages in increasingly intimate physicality, dancing and then fighting, both of which function as precursors to love.

The dance instruction scene exhibits a mediated eroticism. Atterbury plays a record and asks Lester to "just do it by yourself first." "You mind if I use a stand-in?" she asks, propping his hat on a ruler and outlining the dance steps. As she dances alone, Atterbury hurriedly follows her, making chalk outlines of the steps and asserting with enthusiasm the importance of mathematics to rhythm and dance. Finally they dance together until Atterbury announces that he will use his newfound skill to accept Thelma Cheri's invitation to a dinner dance. Once again, Lester finds herself as Thelma's stand-in. In her frustration, she refers to Atterbury as "you vacuum you," and a fade-out and audio-match cut take us to the dance party at Koslofski's, where Atterbury is laboriously counting tango steps to Thelma's compliments. At the elegant party he praises the virtues of mathematics to the incredulous guests. But when he confronts Koslofski about all the studio property furnishing his house, Koslofski punches him, and Atterbury leaves in anger. Standing outside the Hollywood mansion, he hears the silence of the crowd turn to laughter, muted somewhat by his distance from the party. He returns to the party for his efficiency-expert notebook (on which he had been listing Koslofsky's studio property) and finds that his role as honored guest has been transformed to that of scapegoat (always a fine line in celebrations). Potts is mocking his mathematics speech and his labored dancing; Atterbury, the outsider, is forced to confront the Hollywood image of himself.

The Hollywood party is a classic set piece, which generally serves

as an occasion for the newly rich to flaunt their wealth and for business to
be conducted in earnest. Leo Rosten calls Hollywood parties "a business
investment" and "a barometer of prestige" (184). Behlmer and Thomas
quote a studio boss in the film *The Best Things in Life Are Free* who
argues, "In Hollywood that's what parties are for—to talk business" (300).[3]
We have seen how Esther Blodgett in *A Star Is Born* works as a waitress
at a Hollywood party in order to be noticed and how Margaret Elliot
listens to her last story pitch at the very business-oriented party she
stumbles into in *The Star. The Player* goes even further in demonstrating
how social occasions can turn into subtle jockeyings for power. Here in
Stand-In, the whole affair is part of the deliberate effort to distract
Atterbury Dodd from his job as efficiency expert. When that pretense
fails, the party reverts to a true celebration, from which Atterbury is forcibly excluded.

Atterbury returns from Thelma to her stand-in, whom he hears crying next door in his boarding house. Seeing his black eye, the angry Lester
offers to teach him jujitsu. She pulls back his tux jacket and flips him. He
lands in a heap, exclaiming, "You're wonderful, Miss Plum." In this scene,
fighting functions as surrogate lovemaking, just as dancing had in the
earlier scene. Lester makes the connection explicit: "I taught you how to
tango and look what happened." Continuing to be his teacher, she throws
him again, and he falls for her—or so it seems. "Let me do it to you," he
exclaims provocatively, and the musical soundtrack and the soft-focus
close-up of Lester telegraph the erotic content. Lester senses it, the audience is cued to it, but Atterbury remains oblivious. "Don't you know what
to do?" coos Lester, anticipating a kiss now that she is finally in his arms.
He flips her hard against the wall, and she collapses in tears as he con-
gratulates himself on mastering the technique. These comic scenes do
more than mock Atterbury's obtuseness, however. They show a succes-
sion of sublimations of his love for Lester, a love the audience knows is
essential to a successful resolution of the comedy's problems. His sublimations go from watching Lester dance with his hat and a ruler to dancing with the vapid Thelma to being struck by Koslofski to being flipped by
and flipping Lester. Atterbury has ironically noted earlier how his future
"depends on 'Sex and Satan'"; now we sense the truth that Hollywood
will teach him "wickedness" and introduce him to sexuality, which, in turn,
will enable him to save the studio. This odd causal sequence amounts to
a mediated version of the traditional defense of Hollywood: the dreams

on the screen enable viewers to live off screen, through modeled behaviors (as when one falls in love, "just like in the movies") or through vicarious wish fulfillment.

The first screening of the finished print of "Sex and Satan" is filmed in the standard framing style. An establishing shot shows the framed screen with the backs of the elite studio audience; the movie cuts to a shot where the framed picture fills the screen; and, a few moments later, when "The End" appears, the movie cuts back to the framed-screen shot. This familiar syntax keeps us conscious of the fact that the film is being screened for spectators whose reactions are more important than the film itself. It also informs us that the snippet we see stands for the film as a whole. And the film is truly horrible: assorted shots of jungle animals with spliced-in shots of Thelma Cheri emoting in a scanty outfit of leaves with a cougar headpiece; a dying man in a pith helmet croaking out, "Good-bye, little . . . jungle . . . goddess"; and Thelma exclaiming "Congo, he's dead!" to her gorilla companion. The title echoes Gilbert and Garbo's *Flesh and the Devil*, but Behlmer and Thomas suggest parallels with Dorothy Lamour vehicles (138). The animal scenes recall Tarzan epics as well. Though they have intentionally made a bad picture, neither Koslofski nor Thelma Cheri seem to sense how bad. Thelma's failure to understand the picture's poor quality (which is immediately apparent to her stand-in, Lester) discredits her in much the same way that Lina Lamont's reaction to "The Duelling Cavalier" aesthetically discredits her in *Singin' in the Rain*. Douglas Quintain pronounces the picture "a turkey" and advises Atterbury to "junk it and forget it." By this point, it seems that Atterbury senses that Thelma is no good. Nevertheless, he fires Douglas because Thelma and Koslofski falsely blame his drunkenness for the failure of the film.

Atterbury still doesn't trust his judgment (or Lester's), and he proposes a preview, which he defines formally as "a procedure by which we might gauge the merits of 'Sex and Satan.'" The results are predictably disastrous: "Two hundred and fifteen cards and all of them like the gorilla better than [Thelma Cheri]." The failed screenings of "Sex and Satan" form the crisis that leads to two crucial speeches in the oddly bifurcated plot. Lester's defense of the studio workers to Atterbury is predictable enough: "I'm thinking of the people who'll go out on their ear if you close this studio: Pop Jones at the Commissary, Miss Cooley up in wardrobe, carpenters, prop men, electricians—three thousand people you call units, units who happen to have homes and families and kids and rent to pay and doctors' bills." This speech provides the penultimate moment in Atterbury's education; eventually he will adopt just this perspective in his rallying speech to the workers.

But Douglas's vicious verbal assault on Thelma is less clearly functional in the plot (and thus more revealing of the film's contradictions): "I'm the guy that dragged you out from behind a cigarette tray and put you up on a billboard; the chump that shoved you down an unsuspecting public's throat, made you the biggest star in the business until they got wise to the fact that your hips were doing the acting and not your face. . . . The whole thing is so rotten it makes me retch. But it's not your fault, girlie, it's mine. Yeah, mine. For putting a dumb, little, small-town dame in a spot where a million fans treated her like royalty. I made you an applause addict. I had no right to expect you to kick over a habit like that. . . . They've got a name for people [like me] who peddle shopworn merchandise to the suckers." His anger is understandable since she (with Koslofski) has betrayed him, but the plot function of that betrayal and the subsequent leveling of Thelma seem gratuitous. The brief scene introduces themes that are important to the Hollywood-on-Hollywood genre but that *Stand-In* never fully develops: the corrupting influence of fame, the gap between fame and talent, the loss of self-respect in making films you know are inferior. But all of these themes are encrypted in a scapegoating of Thelma that is fueled by a virulent misogyny.

Perhaps the scene is simply a concession to Bogart's tough-guy image—it is his strongest scene in the picture. But I think it also reflects an anxiety built into the male-female relationships of the studio system, in which the biggest stars were female and all the other powerful figures (director, producer, production chief) were male.[4] Sometimes this gender distribution manifests itself in paternalism, other times in the politics of the casting couch. But here, as in *Singin' in the Rain,* the female star must be deposed and humbled for the comic resolutions to occur. In *Singin' in the Rain,* voice double Kathy Selden literally takes the place of the star for whom she has been a vocal stand-in. In *Stand-In,* both Lester Plum and Thelma Cheri find happiness in marriage, not stardom. That is, Douglas Quintain marries the humbled Thelma on the condition she resign from acting, and Lester marries Atterbury with no hints that her film career will return to the stardom she knew as a child actor. Both films are structured to parallel the righting of the studio with the righting of the romantic relationships, but *Stand-In,* like Bette Davis's *The Star,* explicitly equates marital happiness with escaping show business, at least for the women. In this respect, *Stand-In* echoes the gender politics of cautionary films such as *A Star Is Born*, where the price for fame is explicitly domestic unhappiness.[5] The comic resolution necessitates stripping the female stars of their power.

The Bad and the Beautiful develops the image of the misogynistic producer more fully. Like Jonathan Shields in that picture, Douglas Quintain seems happiest when partnered with men. When he and Atterbury plot to save the studio, Douglas exclaims: "Hey honey, if you could cook, I'd marry you!" The male bonding and the scapegoating of women suggest the paternalistic role of the studio in protecting—and tempering the power of—female stars.

The plot to save the studio involves two elements: reediting the film to make it successful and recapturing the sold studio from the clutches of Ivor Nassau. Douglas plans to save the film by trimming down Thelma's part and making the gorilla a star, thus converting Thelma into a sort of stand-in for the gorilla, who becomes the new lead. This device is a familiar one in comedies about Hollywood: turning a failed melodrama into a successful (if not wholly intentional) comedy, a hook that goes back to *Merton of the Movies* (1924). As in the later *Singin' in the Rain*, the exclusive contract of the ditzy star presents an obstacle. Atterbury's stratagem—to involve Thelma in a scandal—is meant to show how he has been humanized by Hollywood; he becomes capable of playing dirty pool for a good cause and shows that he can drink with the best of them. But the plan is another instance of cruelty to women—not only to the unsympathetic Thelma (who loses a contract that gave her a power traditionally reserved for men in Hollywood), but also to Lester, who, left out of the plan, assumes Atterbury has abandoned her for Thelma's charms (note the similarity with the plan the men hatch in *Singin' in the Rain*, in which Kathy Selden is left in the dark even though she stands to benefit). In getting drunk and thrown out of a Hollywood nightclub, Atterbury fulfills two more of Lester's criteria for humanity, but, as in the dance scene, he does it with the star, not the stand-in.

Eventually, of course, the relationship with Lester is rectified when Atterbury fights to save the studio and the workers' jobs. This conclusion is the most remarkable example of how *Stand-In* reflects its historical context. In the finale, the workers will trample Atterbury, jeer him, and hit him with a tomato; then they will rally behind him to forcibly evict Ivor

Nassau from the studio he has acquired and hold the studio grounds by force for forty-eight hours to preserve their livelihoods. The first reference to "forty-eight hours" clues us in to the social context of this fascinating conclusion: on a radio that Ivor has turned on for race results we hear a news item that reports, "Sitdowners in the steel strike have defied all attempts to oust them for the last forty-eight hours." The item presumably inspires Atterbury's plan in which he bizarrely rallies workers to an illegal occupation of their studio, but it also situates the scene in the context of the labor struggles of the country as a whole.

Such labor struggles were finally reaching the notoriously open-shop Hollywood in the years in which *Stand-In* was written and produced.[6] In 1933, the Screen Writers Guild was revitalized and the Screen Actors Guild was formed. Early in 1936 the International Alliance of Theatrical Stage Employees and Motion Picture Operators (IATSE) secured a closed-shop agreement for technicians with the studios. And months before the release of *Stand-In* in November 1937, national interest was aroused at the prospect of a strike by the Screen Actors Guild. That strike was averted, though the craft workers did not succeed in winning a satisfactory agreement. In short, the unionization of studio employees and the extreme anti-union stance of studios were much in the news in 1937. So when Atterbury Dodd addresses a mob of angry workers by admitting, "I'm capital and you're labor," *Stand-In* comes as close to dealing directly with union issues within the movie industry as any contemporary Hollywood film.

I have mentioned the irony of making Atterbury Dodd, the capitalist, into the organizer of the workers. Atterbury's argument for saving the studio is equally perverse. He begins by appealing to the personal humanity of the stockholders, whose interests he represents. He finds a worker who owns some stock and asserts that the other stockholders are similar individuals, working people across the country whose personal savings are at stake. Of course, the appeal to stockholder interest is the traditional way in which a business justifies actions that may be harmful to communities or workers. And in humanizing the stockholders as humble individuals, Atterbury falsifies the situation. Indeed, the role of Wall Street in Hollywood production resulted directly from banks and their trustees' holding huge volumes of shares, not from individual stockholders and their actions. Nevertheless, humanizing the stockholders is the way in which Atterbury progresses, under the tutelage of Douglas and Lester, to recognizing the workers as individuals instead of "units." In this sense, the transformation of Atterbury Dodd is typical of Hollywood's treatment of social problems: only by framing issues in terms of individual personalities can justice be attained. This reasoning dominates Atterbury's climactic moralizing speech about his own "modification of viewpoint." He tells Douglas, "It seems to me that the only thing that matters is that a man must be true to himself. . . . It's not a question of who's right and who's wrong; it's simply a question of what's inside a person." Such extreme relativism serves to eliminate conflict between individuals who have come to stand for social interest groups that are less easily reconciled. There are dramatic as well as political motivations for such an approach, but it is importantly not an approach capable of recognizing the function of labor unions. The one consolation Atterbury offers to the workers is the possibility of their becoming stockholders: "I will convince the stockholders that we are entitled to an interest in this business that we have saved." Though this is an admirably progressive proposal (especially given the suspicion of worker interests in Hollywood), it further attempts to erase the distinction between capital and labor by which Atterbury reluctantly identified himself earlier. What is fascinating about the scene is how the imagery of worker rebellion (a mob of milling and angry laborers) is transformed into a comic resolution that preserves the studio and enshrines the banker as hero.

Here the themes of the picture come together: Atterbury Dodd's interest in saving the studio with his need to become a man and a lover. Atterbury's repeatedly stated beliefs—"The science of mathematics is more important than food and drink" and the workers are "units . . . cogs in a machine"—give way simultaneously, as in saving the studio he becomes a man. The transformation is signaled by physical changes in Atterbury: he is trampled by the crowd; he loses his glasses and sees in multiple vision; he is struck by a tomato. After losing his glasses, Atterbury cuts through the soundstages to reach the studio gates before the mob of exiting workers. The comic excursion of the half-blind Atterbury Dodd recapitulates his education in the crazy ways of Hollywood. He bumps into the wall, falls on the artificial ski slope, bangs into an artificial tree, and falls through a false floor, all to the accompaniment of a comic chase-scene soundtrack. In his desperate race, he is literally tripping on the illusions of moviemaking; only when he passes through those stages can he see with new eyes. He finds the voice to stir the crowd, he punches Potts ("You ever hit a man?" Lester had asked earlier), and he hurls a tomato at

Koslofski. When he slips into a manhole, the workers help him out, enacting his symbolic rebirth. He ejects Ivor Nassau by force from his office, using the jujitsu Lester has taught him. Last on his list of things to do is propose to Lester ("You ever loved a woman?" she had also asked).

In the midst of his awkward proposal he quotes the line that had so often irritated him in the past: "That's Hollywood." *Stand-In* resolves the other two refrains (about mathematics and cogs) through Atterbury Dodd's education in the ways of Hollywood. But, true to the limits of self-reflexive criticism, the film never really resolves the absurdities excused by the repeated "That's Hollywood." Indeed, Atterbury's speech to the workers invokes a Hollywood ending to the complex problems the film has hinted at: "There's no trouble here that a good picture won't cure." When Atterbury voices his plan of seizing the studio to Douglas Quintain, Douglas warns: "Don't forget that in Hollywood, when you turn the other cheek—they kick it." Douglas's attitude echoes language used by the Screen Actors Guild in a brief presented in 1933 to the National Recovery Administration: "Every dishonest practice known to an industry . . . has been resorted to by the producers against the actors" (Balio 153).[7] In spite of Douglas's sanguine warning, the film endorses Atterbury's meliorism. Atterbury's formulation affirms the restorative power of Hollywood so central to its self-mythologizing: "There's no trouble here that a good picture won't cure." It's a sentiment that points ahead to the faith of the audience manifested in Arthur's dancing along with Fred Astaire in *Pennies from Heaven* and Cecilia's returning to the theater at the end of *The Purple Rose of Cairo*. It is the faith that underlies the Disney cartoon in *Sullivan's Travels* and the making of "The Dancing Cavalier" in *Singin' in the Rain* and Esther Blodgett's final success in *A Star Is Born*. That Hollywood offers a palliative to worldly wrongs is especially ironic in films that locate those wrongs within Hollywood. And, indeed, that is what distinguishes the faith in movies expressed in *Stand-In* from the faith expressed in films like *The Purple Rose of Cairo* and *Pennies from Heaven*: *Stand-In* never loses sight of the bottom line.

Fifteen years later *The Bad and the Beautiful* reverses the optimistic collective spirit of the conclusion of *Stand-In*. This detailed anatomy of studio relationships shows filmmaking as a collaborative effort undertaken by competing (and often ruthless) individuals. The movies, of course, are not the first medium in which egotism can be seen as the motivation for artistic and business success. But the image of Hollywood as a working environment demanding a particularly driven temperament is a powerful one. The image recurs in Hollywood literature—most famously in Fitzgerald's *The Last Tycoon* (1941) and Budd Schulberg's *What Makes Sammy Run?* (1941). The ruthless producer is not, however, a familiar figure in film until the 1950s (recall the avuncular producers in *What Price Hollywood?* and *A Star Is Born*). Indeed, the figure of the driven, egotistical self-promoter in films of Hollywood before the fifties is restricted primarily to caricatures of press agents. *The Bad and the Beautiful* in 1952 introduced the tyrannical but brilliant producer to the screen. In the same year, screenwriter Robert Carson published a Hollywood novel, *The Magic Lantern*, which has interesting parallels with *The Bad and the Beautiful* in that it too narrates the story of the movie-producing son of a ruthless, first-generation, movie-mogul father whose career ended in disgrace. David Selznick is clearly one model for these portraits (and Budd Schulberg's father also was a first-generation movie producer). *The Bad and the Beautiful* brings to the screen a stereotype already familiar in the Hollywood novel.

The rise and fall of Jonathan Shields (Kirk Douglas) is told through three flashback narrations by people who knew him, a technique clearly borrowed from *Citizen Kane* (*Kane* is also "quoted" in the shot that tracks through the gate of the Lorrison estate). Director Fred Amiel (Barry Sullivan) recounts how he and Jonathan worked their way up the Hollywood ladder, making B movies for studio chief Harry Pebbel (Walter Pidgeon). Eventually the two men earn the chance to produce a serious movie, using a treatment Fred has adapted from a novel he has always longed to film. But in making the deal Jonathan opts to use a more established director, and Fred quits in bitter anger. He goes on to become a great director apart from Jonathan, his good friendship with him severed permanently.

Actress Georgia Lorrison (Lana Turner) recounts how Jonathan Shields made her a star—teaching her how to act for the camera and breaking her of her alcoholism and her failure-ridden allegiance to the memory of her famous father, an actor who died of drink. Jonathan guides her through her first starring role and woos her in the process, only to drop her on the night of the picture's successful premiere. Georgia never speaks to Jonathan again, though her career flourishes at another studio.

Professor and novelist James Lee Bartlow (Dick Powell) relates how Jonathan Shields tempted him to become a screenwriter and then helped him learn the craft. He also tells of how Jonathan arranged an affair between a prominent actor and James Lee's wife, Rosemary (Gloria Grahame), in order to distract her from distracting James Lee from his writing. Rosemary and the actor, a Latin lover named Victor "Gaucho" Ribera (Gilbert Roland), perish in a plane wreck. When James Lee discovers that Jonathan had arranged the affair he splits with him. Later he wins a Pulitzer Prize for the novel in which he memorializes his wife.

Jonathan Shields has a strong and successful career in spite of his alienating people in this manner, but eventually his ego gets the better of him. He takes over direction of a film after a dispute with still another stereotyped foreign director, Von Ellstein (Ivan Triesault). He botches the film, and, when his pride will not allow him to release it, he loses his studio. The three characters who hate him are brought together a few years later by Harry Pebbel, who is trying to help Jonathan rekindle his career with a new production. To do so he needs the help of the people he has alienated; their flashback narrations explain their refusal. At the end of the film, Harry calls Jonathan and tells him of their rejection. The final scene, however, shows the three central characters listening in on Harry and Jonathan's conversation in a manner that implies he may persuade them yet.

The fundamental contradiction of the film is embodied in the character of Jonathan Shields—and in the title of the movie. A working draft of the script was titled "Tribute to a Bad Man" (Behlmer 327), and Charles Schnee's screenplay was based on two short stories by George Bradshaw, "Of Good and Evil" and "Memorial to a Bad Man." All these titles suggest the story's obsession with moral evaluation of Shields, and they imply that the qualities that make him a great producer also make him a "bad" or "evil" man. This combination implicates the industry itself by suggesting that the cost of success is dehumanization and disloyalty. Works of beauty arise from immoral and faithless acts, from the bad. Is this condition a result of the nature of the motion picture business? Since *The Bad and the Beautiful*, like *Stand-In*, prefers to treat systemic problems in terms of idiosyncratic individuals, the movie can never really answer that question. But by placing Shields in a studio context that is drawn with remarkable fullness for a Hollywood insider movie, *The Bad and the Beautiful* raises the question in provocative ways.

As in *Stand-In*, *The Bad and the Beautiful* shows quite a range of the studio hierarchy, from producers Shields and Pebbel to directors, actors, and a writer. Briefer portraits are sketched of publicity men, accountants, agents, and wardrobe designers. In focusing on Jonathan Shields, *The Bad and the Beautiful* gives the fullest treatment of the role of the producer before Robert Altman's *The Player*. The function of the producer is frequently unclear to people outside Hollywood, and *The Bad and the Beautiful* is surprisingly detailed in depicting it. The film shows Jonathan developing and choosing stories to serve as the basis for films, assembling and negotiating for talent (directors, writers, and actors), and developing that talent both in technical and psychological terms. As in *Stand-In,* the movie briefly shows the producer involved in screening and editing versions of the film being considered for release, though this important function (sometimes ceded to the director) is not given much attention. The film presents an image of the producer as a worker who assembles and manages a variety of studio professionals. But though the film is informative in this regard, it is hardly neutral. It supports Raymond Chandler's characterization of picture-making in his article "Writers in Hollywood" as "an endless contention of tawdry egos" (71). And though it unquestionably presents Jonathan Shields as a success in bringing those egos together to produce good motion pictures (referring to "the Shields touch" and "Jonathan's magic"), the movie also supports the conception of the producer as one who can manage but cannot do, as illustrated by his directing failure.

In its portrait of Hollywood, *The Bad and the Beautiful* offers the requisite party scene, packed with Hollywood insiders talking business while the real power brokers play poker in the back room. The film also dramatizes another crucial Hollywood social occasion—the funeral. The first scene in the retrospective narration is the funeral of Jonathan Shields's famous father. The scene participates in a tradition of Hollywood funerals as comically garish shows of support, a kind of dramatic last act for the inveterate performer. Evelyn Waugh's novel *The Loved One* (1948) and the movie later based on it satirize the falsity of such occasions. Monroe Stahr's star-studded funeral in *The Last Tycoon* and Henry Greener's ill-attended funeral in *The Day of the Locust* demonstrate the stakes in the Hollywood funeral. So does the formal funeral in *The Bad and the Beautiful,* which builds to a punch line: all the mourners except Jonathan are paid extras. Jonathan later explains to Fred Amiel, in an echo of *The Great Gatsby:* "He lived in a crowd; I couldn't let him be buried alone." It is possible to see Jonathan Shields's entire career as an extension of this scene—paying to avenge his father's abandonment by Hollywood.

Jonathan's ambitions distinguish him from Harry Pebbel in that Jonathan (like Selznick, on whom he is partially modeled) has pretensions to artistry; he is interested in making pictures that aspire to high culture. Harry, on the other hand, is a master of the B picture. One of those pictures, represented by a movie poster visible in his office, was entitled "Money Talks," and Harry's motto is "Give me pictures that end with a kiss and black ink on the books." This distinction is important in the criticism the film implicitly levels at Jonathan Shields: he is not one who subsumes art to money but rather one who shapes (and perhaps distorts) artistry out of a hunger for cultural recognition. Jonathan wants to "ram the name of Shields down their throats," and his pictures begin with the Shields shield (recalling the sign that opens David O. Selznick pictures and contrasting with Irving Thalberg, who didn't even want his name on his pictures).

With each of the three principal narrators, we see a scene of Jonathan teaching them about filmmaking—and we see a less savory scene of Jonathan manipulating them psychologically. The first teaching scene occurs between the young Jonathan Shields and Fred Amiel. They are essentially partners, making pictures for Harry Pebbel. The project in the scene is "Night of the Cat Men," and after they spend an afternoon reviewing cheesy cat-man costumes, Jonathan and Fred become distraught. Speechless, they sit down in the screening room, in luxurious leather theater seats. They agree that men in cat suits are unlikely to achieve what audiences desire from such films—being scared. Jonathan rises into a position where he is excitedly lecturing Fred and asks, "What scares the human race more than any other single thing?" During the pause that follows, Jonathan turns off the overhead light and Fred exclaims, "The dark!" But the scene is not completely dark, because that rarely works in film—this one or the one Jonathan is envisioning. Darkness is suggested by semidarkness; a gooseneck desk lamp remains on in center screen. Jonathan moves his hand beneath it and proclaims a central faith of filmmakers (horror and otherwise): "The dark has a life of its own. In the dark, all sorts of things come alive." The scene reminds us visually as well as verbally that filmmaking is a matter of shadows and darkness working on an audience, a point film theorists have made in numerous ways.[8] Jonathan and Fred agree then that it will be more effec-

tive not to show the cat men, but "What," asks Jonathan, "do we put on
the screen that'll make the back of their necks crawl?" As he says this, he
twists the lamp so that, like a projector, it shines on the screen. The dialogue that follows is lit remarkably: half of the screen is illuminated; in the
illuminated arc stands Jonathan in front of the screen (facing the camera)
with his elongated shadow on the screen to his right; in the foreground
Fred, in silhouette, watches him. They plan the movie in rapid-fire collaboration:

> Fred: Two eyes—shining in the dark!
> Jonathan: A dog—frightened, growling, showing its fangs!
> Fred: A bird—its neck broken, feathers torn from its throat!
> Jonathan: A little girl screaming—claw marks down her
> cheeks!

As Jonathan utters the last line such a scream is heard in audio
overlap and the camera then cuts to a girl practicing the scream on the
set. No other scene in the film so effectively equates the Shields magic
with the magical nature of movies themselves. We see Jonathan and Fred
collaborating, but we also see how Jonathan has the talent to pull the
creative ideas out of his director friend by asking the right questions. The
staging and lighting emphasize how Jonathan projects himself on the
screen through the talents of those who work with him: he is illuminated
and it is his shadow on the screen; Fred sits in the dark.

Georgia Lorrison's narrative also demonstrates the Shields magic.
They meet when Jonathan is already an established producer. He is drawn
to her because he identifies with her: they are both children of men who
had succeeded in Hollywood and then been rejected and outcast before
their deaths. Georgia's father was a great dramatic actor turned alco-
holic, that is, a John Barrymore figure. Georgia grew up to be a hard-
drinking bit player in the movies. One of those bit parts is in a Shields
picture. Georgia has one line, delivered from a book stall in a drugstore:
"Read any good books lately?" she says to the leading man. The film
shows her first take, followed by Jonathan's taking her aside and giving
her advice (which we don't hear), and a second take. The single line is
noticeably improved on the second take, mostly because Jonathan has
her speak the line while looking at her book and then only afterwards
raise her eyes to give the leading man a sidelong glance. This brief scene

shows Jonathan's ability to coach actors, and like the line-reading scene in *What Price Hollywood?* it calls attention to the skill involved in acting as well as directing. Later Georgia calls that moment the only good acting she has ever done. Jonathan has run in a screening room her only leading role, "Jungle Tiger," and found it laughable. Like Thelma Cheri in *Stand-In,* she plays "straight man to a chimpanzee." Jonathan decides to make a star of her.

The first step is the standard screen test. As is so often the case in movies about Hollywood, we see the lengthy preparations (including her agent rehearsing her lines with her in the makeup room) and the response to the test without seeing the filming of the test itself. When the test is screened, the camera locates us in the projection room, where Georgia stands beside the projectionist. Then, as the end of the test nears, we see Georgia in the left foreground with the image of the movie doubly framed through the glass in the background. The shot thus offers us double images of Lana Turner, as Georgia watching her own image on screen. But the movie figure is smaller than the "real" figure, thus inverting the proportions of the screen shadow shot of Jonathan, where the screen magnified his presence. Though movies project an image that is larger than life, this shot shows Georgia Lorrison's performance as smaller than life—and fodder for the vitriolic criticism of the powerful men assembled in the darkness below.

Georgia remains in the projection room and hears their verdict: the director calls her "wooden" and "artificial"; Jonathan's assistant says, "She stinks"; and Harry Pebbel philosophizes, "I know we can get her for nothing. For nothing you get nothing. She's nothing." But Jonathan hires her anyway. In a crucial scene, he explains why he places his judgment over that of director, assistant, and coproducer: "I know I'm right about you. I gave you no help. The test was atrocious. But bad as it was, it proved one thing: when you're on the screen, no matter who you're with, no matter what you're doing, the audience looks at you. That's star quality." We are already familiar with this mystifying definition of star quality and how it makes talent a secondary or nonexistent issue. But more important here is Jonathan's emphasis on his role as star-maker, emphasis on what the producer produces. Later he admits, "I wanted to make a star out of someone this town tossed on the ash heap." The same obsessive and vengeful quality that informs Jonathan's desire to "shove [his] name down their throats" motivates his promotion of Georgia Lorrison. Later, when Harry is pleading Jonathan's case to Georgia, he uses similar terms: "You were a drunk and a tramp playing bit parts around town and he made a star out of you."

Jonathan similarly transforms James Lee Bartlow from a novelist into a screenwriter. When he is trying to woo James Lee into signing a

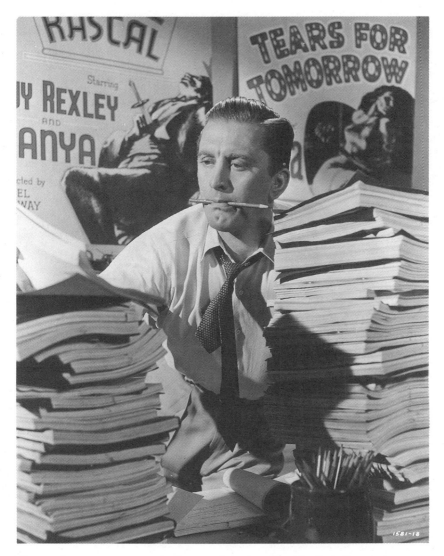

The producer as narrative gatekeeper: Jonathan Shields (Kirk Douglas) reviews scripts to choose what will become a motion picture in *The Bad and the Beautiful*.

contract, he flatters him by telling him his writing is "cinematic." But when James Lee is finally at work on adapting his novel to the screen, Jonathan must tutor him on how to write for a visual medium. Jonathan takes him to a lakeside cabin, where they work together: James Lee writing and Jonathan editing out superfluous material. As we will see in the next chapter, Hollywood faces dramatic limitations when it comes to portraying writing on screen. Contrasting two scenes, as in the Georgia Lorrison line-reading episode, is rarely a workable technique when depicting screenwriting. The scene at Lake Arrowhead in *The Bad and the Beautiful* comes close to showing such a contrast, however. The positioning of the characters is emblematic of the writer's role in film production: James Lee is typing and puffing his pipe in the background of the frame while Jonathan in the foreground strikes through line after line of his material. The producer standing over the writer and revising his best work—this is precisely the picture presented by unhappy Hollywood writers. Again, Raymond Chandler's famous article, "Writers in Hollywood," sums up the feeling most effectively: "In Hollywood the screenplay is written by a salaried writer under the supervision of a producer—that is to say, by an employee without power or decision over the uses of his own craft. . . . This means both personal and artistic subordination [to the producer], and no writer will long accept either without surrendering that which made him a writer of quality" (74).

Yet Jonathan is shown in this scene as wise and benevolent. He explains to James Lee how the emotional climax of the scene he has written (a mother sending her son off to the war) can be rendered by a close-up of her inability to speak instead of a two-page speech. As with Georgia's line reading, we see Jonathan's savvy and his ability to educate in the language of pictures. Further, Jonathan is never shown engaging in the actions most despised by writers: having several writers working independently on a script or farming out different sections for multiple rewrites (recall Atterbury Dodd's complaint in *Stand-In*: "Why does one story have to be written so many times?"). Another dynamic of James Lee and Jonathan's relationship is important here (and unrealistic): James Lee begins by despising Jonathan's egotism and comes to admire and like him (as Georgia Lorrison points out, this pattern is the opposite of the typical response to Jonathan Shields). Producers and writers did not tend to mingle socially or have close working relationships in Hollywood; nevertheless, the relationship between these two men is the closest friendship aside from Jonathan's relationship with Fred, which dissolves.

That Jonathan's closest emotional ties are to men with whom he works is significant in understanding his disastrous relationships with women, a theme relevant to his breaks with Georgia and James Lee. Jonathan's masculine friendships are of the kind Eve Kosofsky-Sedgwick calls "homosocial," meaning powerful male-to-male attachments without apparent or acknowledged eroticism, relationships in which ties to women are seen as an interference or a sign of weakness. Jonathan sees James Lee's wife as his chief distraction and conspires with Gaucho to free him of her interruptions. In his remarkable speech to James Lee some time after her death, Jonathan argues, "I didn't kill Rosemary; she killed herself. Whether you like it or not, you're better off. She was a fool. She interfered with your work. She wasted your time. You're better off without her." This scene concludes James Lee's retrospective narrative. As Jonathan speaks these words, James Lee takes his hat and leaves him forever. The film fades from James Lee exiting to his photograph on the dust jacket of his new novel, *A Woman of Taste*, his Pulitzer Prize–winning defense of Rosemary. Jonathan has converted James Lee into someone who writes to avenge his past.

The fear of women as corrupting poisons the relationship of Jonathan and Georgia. As I have suggested, Jonathan sees in Georgia someone who has been crippled by the same sort of past that empowers him. Her love for her father and bitterness over his decline turn her into a drinker and a failure who keeps a shrine of photos, drawings, and recordings dedicated to her father. Jonathan, on the other hand, has turned his mixed feelings toward his father (he calls him "*the* heel" but resents Hollywood's turning its back on him) into his drive for success. Part of that drive for success manifests itself in making Georgia a star, which means not only teaching her the nuances of acting but also breaking her of her fear of success. The psychological manipulation occurs in two stages: rejecting her advances and accepting them.

After Georgia's drugstore bit, Jonathan shows up at her apartment at four in the morning to offer her a screen test. Georgia naturally assumes this is a casting-couch ploy. She bitterly tells him not to waste his film, but invites him to bed with her anyway (in terms as explicit as the fifties would allow). Of course he rejects her advances: nothing earns the contempt of the tough leading man more than an actual sexual offer. Instead of sleeping with her he lectures her on her morbid obsession with her father. He puts on a recording of her father performing Macbeth's "Tomorrow and tomorrow" speech, as the camera pans her elaborate shrine: "Because he was a drunk, you're a drunk," Jonathan shouts. "Because he loved women, you're a tramp. But you forget one thing—he did it with style." He accuses her of playing the role of "the doomed daughter of the great man," and playing it poorly: "It's the cheap performance of a bit player, not a star. And that's all you'll ever be until you can pull yourself out of this tomb." He draws a moustache on the portrait of her father and smashes the record; she hurls a bottle at him and they wrestle and then violently embrace. Finally he puts her in bed, and she sobs as he leaves. The scene reveals his deliberate manipulations of her psychological state. His contempt for her failure fuels his desire for her, which is desire to aggrandize himself by transforming her into a success. The familiar tropes of desire as control—Svengali, Pygmalion—come to mind.

When Georgia balks out of fear from beginning her starring role, Jonathan romances her to give her the strength to perform. Appropriately (in his mind), he leaves her once the shooting is over, deserting her at the premiere party. When she discovers him with another woman—this time in real casting-couch style (a bit actress who had abandoned Gaucho for Jonathan when she saw Gaucho was not going to advance her career)—Jonathan turns on Georgia with vicious contempt. His remarkable speech reveals the source of his misogyny: "Maybe I like to be cheap once in a while; maybe everyone does. Or don't you remember? Who gave you the right to dig into me and turn me inside out and decide what I'm like? How do you know how I feel about you or how deep it goes? Maybe I don't want anyone to own me—you or anybody. Get lost!" The scene is filmed with noir-style lighting in Jonathan's darkened mansion. Through most of the scene Kirk Douglas is in darkened silhouette or half-light while Lana Turner is fully lit and wrapped in a white fur, lighting that recalls the scene in *Citizen Kane* in which Kane's wife discovers him in Susan Alexander's apartment. As the speech concludes he grabs her and pulls her toward him in a violent parody of an embrace, echoing the earlier scene in her apartment.

From start to finish, Jonathan's "affair" with Georgia—like the affair he furthered between Gaucho and Rosemary Bartlow—is a means toward the end of making a picture. Women represent threats to control, or, as Jonathan phrases it in appropriately economic terms, "ownership." Jonathan's misogyny has economic roots: he is aroused only by the women he can elevate to stardom, only by the women he can transform to fame and profitability with his production magic. In the world of Jonathan Shields, real affection is built in masculine relationships within the industry; women threaten the ultimate goal of getting the Shields name on a great picture. Against this myth of sublimating desire to masculine greatness, we have the comment of Gaucho's girl: "There are no great men, buster, only men."

The strength of *The Bad and the Beautiful* is precisely what makes it seem somewhat dated now: the relatively complex psychological portrait of Jonathan Shields. At its best, the movie shows in considerable detail Shields's producer skills and how they become joined to a tendency to exploit people emotionally as well as creatively. At its worst, the movie presents a schematic "bad and beautiful" hero. The shadow of *Citizen Kane* looms in this portrait of an entrepreneur who pursues public recognition to compensate for lack of love as a child. Producer John Houseman worked with Orson Welles and was present during Herman Mankiewicz's drafting of the screenplay for *Citizen Kane*. Though Welles himself called the "Rosebud" theme of childhood deprivation in *Citizen Kane* "dollar-book Freud," the parallels between Kane, Hearst, and Welles call attention to the hidden theme in *Citizen Kane* of the moviemaker as megalomaniac. Pauline Kael refers to Mankiewicz's "hostile humor" in depicting Kane as "the braggart self-publicist and making Kane so infantile," thus stressing the connection with Welles (55). Welles and Shields are connected by Harry Pebbel's repeated references to Shields as "Genius Boy" (Welles was known as the "boy genius" of Hollywood).

Shields is of course a failure as a director, and he never really spouts Wellesian artistic pretensions; the parallels to a producer like Selznick are closer. The *Citizen Kane* parallels, however, reveal the influence of the stereotype of the emotionally deprived, egomaniacal tycoon motivated by a need for public recognition. The bland but reassuring moral that those you abuse on the way up may scorn you on your way down also lies behind the plot structure of Shields's artistic and financial catastrophe and his appeal to the disaffected trio for help. Thus *The Bad and the Beautiful* presents two related and potentially contradictory aspects of moviemaking: the role of producer as a manager of talent working on the line between art and business and the role of personal desire in shaping production. That is, the movie depersonalizes filmmaking by distancing actors, writers, and directors from the final product and re-personalizes it in terms of the producer as auteur, artistically manipulating "talent." In defense of Shields, Pebbel notes how several of his films always appear on critics' lists of the top ten of all time. He may be a bad man, but he makes good movies.

Such a moral is consistent with the emphasis in Hollywood movies of the fifties on exposing scandal and sordidness. The conduct in *Stand-In* is equally sordid, but it is presented as satire and shares with satire the belief in reform. The good characters (Douglas Quintain, Lester Plum, and—when converted—Atterbury Dodd) rescue the means of production from the corrupt characters (Ivor Nassau, Koslofski, and Thelma Cheri). The resolution of *The Bad and the Beautiful* is much more ambiguous. Fred Amiel, James Lee Bartlow, and Georgia Lorrison have all stood resolutely on their moral principles in refusing to work with the man who betrayed them. Harry Pebbel argues that though they have reason to hate Jonathan they also owe their success and fame to him. This argument suggests that Jonathan represents Hollywood and its compromises. Thus the ambivalence of director, writer, and star reflects the ambivalence of Hollywood insiders who know their criticism of the movie world is ultimately disingenuous. Harry "Money Talks" Pebbel is surely an odd figure to represent the moral center of the highly moralistic universe of *The Bad and the Beautiful,* yet that seems to be his function.

The film appropriately leaves the ending ambiguous. When we see the three principals listening in on Harry's conversation with Jonathan, are we to believe they are ready to relent and help Jonathan? The final shot concludes an unusual sequence of telephone eavesdropping scenes: Georgia listens in when Jonathan renegotiates her starring role; Rosemary listens in when Jonathan makes his initial pitch to her husband. The telephone is a crucial tool in Hollywood deal making, and it becomes more prominent when we move behind the scenes to the world of the producer (it figures very vividly in *The Player*). In each of these scenes, Jonathan is making a pitch (though now from a desperate and powerless position); in each he benefits from the eavesdropper because his remarks persuade the secondary (eavesdropping) audience. His appeal to the eavesdropper suggests the producer's ultimate deferral to the audience, the same deferred justification of Atterbury Dodd's appeal to stockholders. Certainly Jonathan's character is distinguished by his ability to use people to achieve artistic and monetary ends for which they are only vehicles. The telephone scenes also suggest that Jonathan's ultimate power lies in the ability to sell himself, just as Hollywood's power lies to a great extent in how Hollywood pictures, wherever they are set, sell Hollywood. In a strange sense, Jonathan is always talking to a secondary audience, the eavesdropping public whose acclaim motivates all his personal and artistic relationships; similarly, he is always selling Hollywood and himself, his sense of self transferred to the logo that begins his films.

The Bad and the Beautiful shares an essentially negative portrayal of Hollywood with three other films about moviemaking made in the fifties—*The Big Knife* (1955), *The Barefoot Contessa* (1954), and *The Goddess* (1958). Patrick Anderson suggests that the fifties offered "a cycle of anti-Hollywood films which explore the negative side of the industry" (200). But *The Bad and the Beautiful* possesses the same basic contradiction of earlier exposés of Hollywood: successful filmmakers cannot in good conscience attack Hollywood wholesale. As in *What Price Hollywood?* and *A Star Is Born, The Bad and the Beautiful* presents contrasting character trajectories—Jonathan Shields has fallen while the aggrieved trio have all risen. Anderson admits that the characters in *The Bad and the Beautiful* "pay their dues as a means of attaining success rather than as a consequence once they have reached the top" (268-69), the latter being the more common Hollywood formula. And the film shows how Jonathan has suffered from his own ruthlessness as well. Jonathan represents Hollywood as an embodiment of the force that grants success yet takes away happiness, what William James called the wholly American preoccupation, the "bitch goddess success." Thus the richly ambivalent portrait of Jonathan Shields evokes a Hollywood that is criticized for its heartlessness while it is celebrated as the source of glamour, a medium for creativity, and, ultimately, a fount of great movies. *The Bad and the Beautiful* relies on the love of movies, not the imitative adulation of stars, to excuse inhumane manipulation of workers. Justifying destructive business practices in terms of the quality of the final product implies that show business is more like other businesses than it cares to admit.

6 Picturing Writers

Boy Meets Girl (Warner Brothers 1938). Producer: George Abbott. Director: Lloyd Bacon. Screenwriters: Bella Spewack and Sam Spewack.

In a Lonely Place (Columbia 1950). Producer: Robert Lord. Director: Nicholas Ray. Screenwriter: Andrew Solt. Story by Edmund H. North based on the novel by Dorothy B. Hughes.

The story pitch at its most dramatic: J.C. Benson (Pat O'Brien) and Robert Law (James Cagney) enact a story idea to cowboy star Larry Toms (Dick Foran) and producer C. Elliott Friday (Ralph Bellamy) while their inspiration, commissary waitress Susie (Marie Wilson), listens bemusedly in *Boy Meets Girl*.

In *Sunset Boulevard,* Norma Desmond snarls with disdain when she asks Joe Gillis if he is one of those who have "written pictures." Her dismissive formulation highlights the dilemmas of the screenwriter, the writer who has entered a medium in which words are no longer primary. It also invites us to consider how Hollywood has *pictured writers,* how screenwriters are imagined and dramatized in films about Hollywood. "Not often," might be a good first response. In all the movies about Hollywood discussed so far, only *The Bad and the Beautiful* includes a screenwriter (although *Sullivan's Travels,* by writer-director Sturges, perhaps implies that Sullivan will write his next film himself). A director pitches a movie in *The Star,* but the star films are devoid of writers and virtually devoid of scripts (we briefly see Constance Bennett studying her lines, and shots of the script of *A Star Is Born* [1937] frame that movie). *Singin' in the Rain* shows us a songwriter and dialogue coaches but makes no mention of the importation of writers necessitated by the coming of sound. *Stand-In* alludes to using several writers for a script, but, amidst the mass of studio personnel, we never see one. In *In a Lonely Place,* Mildred, the hatcheck girl, tells writer Dix Steele that she used to assume the actors made up their own lines in front of the cameras. Indeed, this assumption is borne out by films about Hollywood, particularly in the films of screen passage. Though the screen persona Tom Baxter in *The Purple Rose of Cairo* considers screenwriters to be gods because they bring him into being, the animation of the screen characters in the disrupted film-within-the-film encourages the illusion that they simply invent their lines, an illusion that is even stronger in *Last Action Hero.*

The invisibility of the writer is a natural consequence of the mimetic illusion, of the invisibility of the Hollywood style. In films about Hollywood, however, the rarity of portrayals of screenwriters stems from three additional sources. First, picturing writers is difficult: that is, showing writers at work lacks the visual and dramatic possibilities of showing actors, technicians, directors, and producers. Producers negotiate deals, directors instruct actors and cameramen, actors declaim lines—writers merely type, or they scribble on legal pads. Second, the lowly status of writers in Hollywood during the studio era militated against their portrayal: producers weren't much interested in stories about writers (particularly if they bit the hand that fed them by casting the studio in a negative light), and writers themselves often viewed their lot so negatively or with such embarrassment that they were unlikely to portray themselves in film scripts.

Third, writers are distinguished from other Hollywood workers by having an outlet other than movies in which to express themselves. Many screenwriters have written about screenwriting, but not in screenplays; they have written about screenwriting in novels and in newspaper and magazine articles. As early as 1930, Stephen Vincent Benet declined to write an article on his experiences as a screenwriter, commenting that he would "rather be the person who went [to Hollywood] and didn't" (Fine 1).

So it is no surprise that one of the first feature films to focus on screenwriters, *Boy Meets Girl,* would be based on a Broadway play lampooning Hollywood (the play was written in 1935 by Bella Spewack and Sam Spewack, who then adapted it for the screen). The movie's theatrical source calls attention to the New York–Hollywood rivalry of which writers were very much a part. The status of the screenwriter, in the thirties and forties at least, was defined by the fact that most screenwriters were first established in another medium (novels, plays, or newspapers) before coming to Hollywood. Thus, they viewed the circumstances of writing in a studio against a norm defined in another medium. As a result, they could not help but be struck by the lowly status of the writer in the making of a movie, as opposed to his or her much greater importance in producing a play, a novel, or a newspaper article. As Richard Fine explains in the definitive study of the relationship of screenwriters to their original media, *Hollywood and the Profession of Authorship, 1928-1940,* "The writers' situation in Hollywood . . . differed radically from that in New York. Writers were completely stripped of . . . their basic right of legal ownership and creative control of their work" (122). They were compensated with higher pay (particularly in the depression years, in which traditional publishing suffered financially), and thus they often felt they were prostituting their talent, working in a medium that was more lucrative but less fulfilling. Consequently, the New York publishing world, and even more so the Broadway theater, felt they were competing with Hollywood for talent—and losing. Writers and critics who never left the East bolstered the myth that Hollywood destroyed writers, in spite of the fact that many important writers were able to sustain work in their original medium through the monies they earned in Hollywood (examples range from William Faulkner to P.G. Wodehouse to Clifford Odets).[1] And for every well-known writer who failed in Hollywood (most famously, F. Scott Fitzgerald) or fled disillusioned (like Theodore Dreiser or John Dos Passos), there were many writers who made successful careers writing for the screen, success they might never have achieved in other genres.[2]

Hostility toward Hollywood was central to the world of screenwriters in a way that it was not with other constituencies of the film world. And that hostility included intellectual condescension. Not only did screen-writers rightfully complain about the inefficiencies and indignities of endless story conferences, team writing, enforced collaboration, numerous rewrites and polish jobs by different writers, and the unfair system of awarding screen credit, they also felt that they were in service to producers who were intellectually inferior to themselves. Screenwriter Ben Hecht put it bluntly: "The pain of having to collaborate with such dullards and to submit myself to their approvals was always acute" (*Child of the Century* 476). Many also felt that the film medium itself was lowbrow (Hecht called it "an eruption of trash that has lamed the American mind and retarded Americans from becoming a cultured people" [*Child of the Century* 468]), and thus they were all the more furious if they did not succeed in it.

Films about screenwriters present a particularly volatile version of the central ambivalence of the Hollywood-on-Hollywood genre. By exposing the absurdities of writing in the studio system and by leveling a cultural critique at the anti-intellectualism of Hollywood, these films undermine their own ambition to be high-quality, successful movies. In the films discussed in this chapter and the next, the screenwriters' distinctive anxiety that working in Hollywood was a squandering of talent looms large. This anxiety manifests itself in the theme of narrative formula in tension with a postulated higher realism. Novelist and screenwriter W.R. Burnett, for example, complained that "in the motion picture business, the plot takes the place of everything else. The plot's all there is, and the characters are names" (qtd. in McGilligan, *Backstory* 58). The films about screenwriters all express this idea that Hollywood genre formulas corrupt artistic integrity. Thus it becomes particularly interesting to see how these films themselves play off of—and submit to—popular narrative formulas.

The films grouped in this chapter present a contrast very similar to that presented in the last chapter: a madcap thirties comedy paired with a dark fifties drama. The contrast here is even more extreme; *Boy Meets Girl* is a wild, antic comedy (the kind of movie in which everyone is speaking loudly and rapidly), and *In a Lonely Place* is a brooding tale of violence and unhappiness. In *Boy Meets Girl*, the protagonists are a pair of highly esteemed writers accustomed to collaborating. Robert Law (James

Cagney) and J.C. Benson (Pat O'Brien) have been extremely successful in adapting the "boy meets girl" formula to various studio projects. They are so confident that they spend most of their time clowning around the studio lots and pretending to work, behavior that has gotten them fired from every other studio in Hollywood. Nevertheless, they are the top writers at Royal Studios (the movie is obviously filmed on the Warner Brothers lot). Cowboy star Larry Toms (Dick Foran) arranges for Law and Benson to script his next picture because he needs a big hit before his contract comes up for renewal. The two writers spin story ideas off the tops of their heads to an increasingly frustrated Larry and producer C. Elliott Friday (Ralph Bellamy), whose nickname is C.F. When a pregnant commissary waitress, Susie (Marie Wilson), faints in the office, Law and Benson hit upon the idea of putting Larry in a picture with an infant: "The Cowboy and the Baby." Against Larry's protestations they develop the idea further by proposing the studio use Susie's baby. They become godparents to—and agents for—her newborn baby, Happy. The movie is a success and Happy an even bigger one. But Larry and his agent conspire to steal away the contractual power Law and Benson have over Happy, and the writers respond with an elaborate plot to regain that power. In their plot, an extra, Rodney Bevan (Bruce Lester), pretends to be Happy's father and creates a scandal at an Errol Flynn premiere. Though not Happy's father, the extra is in love with Susie. The comic machinations result in the firing of Law and Benson, but eventually (thanks to a fake telegram) they are rehired and Susie is united with the British extra who loves her. Since he conveniently possesses a family fortune, baby Happy no longer needs to work for a living.

In a Lonely Place could not be more different. It focuses on Dixon Steele (Humphrey Bogart), a respected screenwriter known for his violent tendencies. Though Dix is a well-established screenwriter, his last effort was a flop and he needs a success. His agent, Mel Lippman (Art Smith), convinces him to consider adapting a popular novel, "Althea Bruce," as his next project. Instead of reading it, Dix invites a hatcheck girl at a Hollywood restaurant, Mildred Atkinson (Martha Stewart), to tell him the story, since she announced that she was a big fan of the novel. Mildred breaks a date with her boyfriend and returns to Dix's apartment and tells him the story, which he finds trite. After leaving Dix's apartment to return home, Mildred is murdered. The police investigation focuses on Dix, in part because of his violent background. But an alluring woman from a neighboring apartment, Laurel Gray (Gloria Grahame), gives Dix an alibi (telling police she saw the victim leave Dix's apartment alone). Their meeting in the police station kindles a romance, which furthers the suspicion of the police. Dix's love for Laurel Gray helps him get back on track with his writing; he becomes astonishingly productive and completes the adaptation of the novel, improving it in the process. But as Laurel encounters displays of Dix's violent temper (he beats up the driver of a car he runs into, for example), she becomes afraid of him and fears he may even have committed the murder of Mildred Atkinson. Dix proposes to Laurel, and she accepts but secretly plans to flee. When Dix discovers her plans he nearly strangles her in his rage. The phone rings as he is strangling her. He releases her and learns from the police that he has been cleared of the murder (Mildred's boyfriend, Henry Kesler, has confessed). But the news comes too late; the love of Laurel and Dix has been destroyed.

It is worth noting at the outset that the depictions of screenwriters in both films are quite unrealistic, or at least exceptional. Both *Sunset Boulevard* and *The Player* provide more typical portraits of screenwriters. The pair in *Boy Meets Girl* have an elaborate office, they cause commotion all over the studio, and they pal around with and tease the head producer. Studio writers tended to have tiny offices and to keep to themselves, both on the lot and off. Screenwriting team Albert Hackett and Frances Goodrich echo a lot of writers when they refer to the "caste system out in Hollywood": "When we got to California, if you were a writer the only people you ever knew were writers. The actors, the big ones, all were friendly with producers. . . . There were layers and other layers . . . and the lowest layer was the writers" (McGilligan, *Backstory* 205). Producers may well have been as obtuse as C.F., but none would have tolerated the treatment Law and Benson gave him. Dixon Steele similarly socializes above his class in the Hollywood hierarchy, and his insistence on working at home is uncharacteristic of writers during the studio era (though not unheard of). Writers were expected to work regular hours; indeed, in some studios, they punched a time clock.[3] Law and Benson seem aware of such studio surveillance, since they equip their office with the recorded sounds of working typewriters. Even given that these are particularly successful writers, their independence and ability to hobnob with studio executives is exaggerated.

The two writers' belief in their intellectual superiority to their bosses is probably typical, however. In *Boy Meets Girl* the theme of intellectual snobbery is presented comically, through the caricatures of Larry and C.F. and through Law and Benson's handling of them. When Larry defends his lack of fan mail by pointing out that most of his fans cannot write, Law dubs him "the idol of illiteracy." More blatantly, the film begins with the two writers making up nonsensical plots to bewilder Larry into believing they have a good story idea for his next film. Similarly, their comic banter in the presence of C.F. is predicated on his stupidity. C.F. views himself as cultured, the only college-educated producer on the lot. He wants Larry's new picture to be "a sort of 'Charge of the Light Brigade,' but as Kipling would have done it," though he comments (to the writers' derision) that he prefers Proust to Kipling. The stage directions of the original play call for a volume of "*Swann's Way* (leaves uncut)" to be visible in his office (Spewack and Spewack 9).

Ralph Bellamy has played his share of genial buffoons, but the point here is the importance of his cultural aspirations. Like many producers and studio moguls, C.F. is insecure about his cultural status and longs to use movie production to enhance that status.[4] Like the producer in *Sullivan's Travels*, C.F. wants to make a picture that will be simultaneously "important" and a box-office smash: "Not just a good story—I want to do something fine, sweet, with scope, stark, gripping—but with plenty of comedy and a little hokum." The intellectual superiority of J.C. Benson and Robert Law is revealed in their lack of cultural pretension. Secure in their own learning, they are free to pursue the "boy meets girl" formula with impunity. But their confidence masks a greater fear that they have squandered their talent. This theme is clearest in the character of Law, who, like so many screenwriters, insists on viewing his sojourn in Hollywood as a temporary hiatus from his real writing. When faced with being fired, Law invokes returning to Vermont and his novel, a novel that he insists will not have a "boy meets girl" plot. "I was a promising young novelist," laments Law. "Almost won the Pulitzer Prize in 1930. Now, in 1938, I'm writing dialogue for a horse." His sentiments epitomize the feelings of a host of Hollywood writers, and they reflect, of course, a certain degree of self-dramatization and self-aggrandizement.

These feelings of intellectual superiority and of squandering one's talent motivate the pair's fondness for gags and practical jokes. That is, practical jokes indicate their refusal to take their trade seriously and their insistence on seeing themselves as above scripting scenarios. Though the Spewacks deny it, it was widely reported that J.C. Benson and Robert Law were based on the screenwriting team of Ben Hecht and Charlie MacArthur. Certainly there are significant similarities. Hecht and MacArthur liked working as a pair, were highly successful in Hollywood and highly paid, and viewed screenwriting as lesser (though not easier) work than literary writing. Hecht famously commented that movie writing was not easier than "good writing": "It's just as hard to make a toilet seat as it is a castle window" (*Charlie* 159). And in the stage version of *Boy Meets Girl,* Robert Law complains, "That's the worst of hack writing. It's hard work" (Spewack and Spewack 50). Hecht and MacArthur were productive and gregarious, and MacArthur in particular was a great storyteller who did earn the admiration of Hollywood executives. The two were also fond of practical jokes. Benson and Law's oddly decorated office suggests an office shared by Hecht and screenwriter Gene Fowler, which they decorated as a red-velvet "brothel parlor." When they were refused a couch because of studio policy, Fowler insisted on hurling all the furniture out the window until his demands were met (Hecht, *Letters* 42-45). The bizarre scene of Benson and Law rallying Indian extras to a revolt in which they hurl a stone into C.F.'s office is in a similar spirit. Screenwriter Niven Bush discusses planning such elaborate practical jokes with collaborator Tom Reed: "In those days you could stop for a week and design a practical joke!" (McGilligan, *Backstory* 95). The most elaborate such joke was surely one concocted by MacArthur and Hecht in which, disillusioned with the workings of MGM, MacArthur arranged for studio chief Bernie Hyman to hire a British gas station attendant by convincing him the man was a highly respected novelist. According to Hecht, the gas station attendant earned a thousand dollars a week for a year (*Charlie* 172-73).

Dixon Steele in *In a Lonely Place* manifests thoroughly contrasting behavior arising from similar motivations. Dix is a brooding loner who insists, "I won't work on something I don't like." When the producer tells him it is just another picture, an enraged Dix accuses him of being "a popcorn salesman." The producer sagely observes, "That's right—so are you. The only difference between us is that I don't fight it." Dix does; his character is defined by that internal fight. "One day I'll surprise you and write something good," he says, expressing his conflicted feelings about the intellectual value of his work. Dix is presented as a character smart enough to know that most of what he creates is not good—and sensitive enough to suffer as a result. His friendship with a downtrodden Shake-spearean actor turned alcoholic represents his alliance with high culture. It is a defensive alliance, and in the first scene of the film we see Dix getting in a fight defending his drunken friend. Dixon Steele epitomizes the alienated intellectual, and the film's emphasis on his essential loneli-ness and his explosive qualities furthers that stereotype. But the film ques-tions that stereotype as well. A friend of Laurel's defends Dix by arguing, "He's a writer—people like him can afford to be temperamental," to which Laurel replies, "I'm afraid he'd be that way no matter what he did." Dix is a macho artist, a writer in the Hemingway tradition of toughness that held such sway in the American forties and fifties. Even his name (which is the first utterance of the film) suggests a metal phallus. The image of the writer as heroic male nonconformist is important to Hollywood screen-writers in general. Hecht's memoirs of his male friendships in *Letters from Bohemia* further this image of tough-guy writers in Hollywood, their toughness often a veneer for their tortured feelings about selling them-selves short.

The opening sequence of *In a Lonely Place* brilliantly depicts Dix's divided nature. I have mentioned the phallic connotations of his name; Dana Polan notes how the name Dix suggests a division, which he char-acterizes as a split between the "man of culture" and the "man of vio-lence" (34). The beginning of the film displays Dix's ambivalence about his own cultural status, which fuels that division. When an actress hails him from a nearby car, he does not remember her. She reminds him that she acted in a picture he wrote, and he responds, "I make it a point never to see pictures I write." When he pulls up to Paul's restaurant, he is ap-proached by kids seeking autographs:

Boy: Can I have your autograph, mister?
Dix: Who am I?
Boy: I don't know.
Girl: Don't bother—he's nobody.
Dix: She's right.

Though Dix confirms that he is nobody, the film shows him signing his autograph in close-up (the first shot of the writer writing). He signs his name with an exclamation point. Opening with his name shouted from a passing car, the film calls attention to Dix's problematic identity in the

Hollywood world: is he just a nobody; does his writing for films really bear his signature? As Polan points out, the question of how good a writer he is remains ambiguous throughout the film (36).

The two films display differing compensatory strategies for coping with the ego-deflating status of screenwriters; in comic and tragic ways, both Dix Steele and the team of Benson and Law are dancing around an essential doubt about the artistic validity of their work. As Ben Hecht reflected about screenwriting: "I've written that it was easy money—and that's a misstatement if you examine the deed. Writing cheaply, writing falsely, writing with 'less' than you have is a painful thing. To betray belief is to feel sinful, guilty—and tastes bad" (*Charlie* 159). Both films show the screenwriter's behavior warped by this internal conflict—though warped in different directions.

So how do these movies picture the act of writing, as opposed to the behavior of writers? In *Boy Meets Girl*, which takes place almost entirely within the studio, as opposed to *In a Lonely Place*, which never enters one, we never see the writers write. The film's avoidance of depicting writing is signaled in the opening scene, in which Larry Toms and his agent discover the recorded typing sounds emanating from the office of Benson and Law. Instead of showing actual writing, *Boy Meets Girl* dramatizes the act of constructing narrative through story pitches. The two writers collaborate on performances in which they develop the narrative together in rapid-fire build-up (similar to the "in the dark" scene in *The Bad and the Beautiful*). These collaborative oral narrative summaries make for some of the liveliest humor in the film. Part of the humor stems from the improvisatory quality of the pitches, and part stems from the way a plot summary emphasizes the clichéd elements of Hollywood formula more than a fully detailed scene would. That is, the story pitches emphasize Burnett's point that Hollywood conceives of writing almost solely in terms of plot.

In a Lonely Place, as the title suggests, is not likely to show collaboration. It does, however, include oral story pitches—first when Mildred summarizes "Althea Bruce" for Dix (which is a parody of the classic Hollywood producers who were too busy to read and relied on oral summaries or "treatments") and later, more provocatively, when Dix uses his narrative talent to imagine how the murder must have been committed. But this movie does show writing: Dix working at his desk writing on a legal pad while Laurel Gray straightens the apartment and turns down his bed. In this movie of gazes through windows, this depiction of Dix writing is oddly presented as a point-of-view shot from the perspective of Dix's agent, Mel Lippman, who is peering through the window. Eventually Laurel and Dix are both at work on the screenplay, with Laurel typing Dix's manuscript drafts in her neighboring apartment. The work scene is thus interwoven with the (somewhat ambiguous) domestic arrangements, which reflect the California garden apartment design so important to the movie. The film emphasizes Dix's renewed appetite for work once Laurel has reinvigorated him. In one of the movie's most tender scenes, Laurel, Mel, and the drunken actor, Charlie, put Dix to bed after he has spent the entire night writing. The film communicates the image of writing as solitary and difficult labor, of writers burning the midnight oil in a lonely occupation. At the same time, it suggests that Laurel serves as a sort of inspiration if not collaborator, a combination secretary and muse who alleviates some of Dix's loneliness and furthers his creative work.

The content of the pitch narratives (spoken and written) creates the most self-referential moments in both films, the places in which the narratives created by the writers parallel the narrative of the framing film. The self-referentiality applies both to the overall scripts written in each film ("The Cowboy and the Baby" and "Althea Bruce") and to the smaller mini-narratives articulated by the writers. Such framed narratives form occasions to satirize Hollywood convention, but in doing so the films must position the framing film as the exemplar of the real world. In another version of the fundamental contradiction of the Hollywood-on-Hollywood genre, the framing narrative of the Hollywood film stands for the extra-Hollywood world. When the framing narrative exhibits the same conventions that are parodied in the framed narratives (as in *Boy Meets Girl*), the contradiction emerges most clearly. When the framing narrative studiously avoids the conventional formulas exhibited in the framed narratives (as in *In a Lonely Place*), the contradiction is hidden but still exists because the framing film remains, ultimately, within the Hollywood system.[5] Much can be learned, with both films, by comparing the examples of screenwriting exhibited in the movie with the overall narrative pattern of the movie itself.

In *Boy Meets Girl*, the story pitches delivered by Benson and Law are the finest comic moments, particularly for James Cagney, who acts out the story he is inventing and pitching. The first pitch is wholly a cover designed to obscure the fact that the writers have done no work on their

assignment. Such a subterfuge is common in Hollywood myth. James
Cain, for example, describes pulling off such a feat during his first assignment at Paramount in 1931, in which, at a story conference, he "knocked
them out of their seats with an account of where we were at on this story,"
and afterward did not have any recollection of what he had told the producer and director. Cain points out, though, that "you can't get away with
that for long" (McGilligan, *Backstory* 116), and Benson and Law eventually pitch a real (though still largely improvised) scenario. Susie's preg-
nancy is the seed of their idea for "The Cowboy and the Baby"; a lamp
with a cupid carving at the base serves as the prop for the baby:

> Law: He finds a baby in the Rockies. . . .
> Benson [inventing a "backstory"]: Girl with a no-good
>   gambler out of Las Vegas has a baby. Gambler is killed.
>   Bang! [he gestures with Larry's six-gun]
> Law [falling]: Ahhh!
> Benson: Girl leaves baby on the ranger's doorstep. Larry is
>   the ranger. He finds the baby. A baby!
> Law [imitating Larry's accent]: My goodness, he says, a
>   baby!
> Benson: A baby! The most precious thing in life. The cutest,
>   goddam little thumbsucker you ever saw. Tugging at
>   every mother's heart. And every potential mother.
> Law: And who isn't?
> Benson: A love story between Larry and the baby . . .
> Law: The two outcasts.

And so on—through Larry's joining the Foreign Legion, illustrated by Law's
marching on top of C.F.'s desk wearing the headpiece of a British guards-
man.

The scene allows for much antic comedy and makes use of Cagney's
considerable and often neglected comic skills. The comedy comes from several sources: the ability to invent the germ of a major motion picture instantly,
the reduction of narrative to plot and cliché ("the virgin of the Foreign Legion
and the West Point man who wanted to forget"), and the use of office props
to suggest the theme and visual effects of the finished movie. Benson and
Law proceed from the idea sparked by the pregnant waitress to a fever-pitch
conclusion in which Larry is united with the mother of the baby:

Law: Boy meets girl!
Benson: Boy loses girl!
Law: Boy gets girl!
C.F.: Boy, I think you've got something. Let's try it on B.K.
   while it's still hot.

This conclusion summarizes the theme signaled by the movie's title: predictable narrative formula sells movie ideas to producers and through
them to audiences.

But *Boy Meets Girl* follows these formulas while in the act of revealing and criticizing them. Susie is not reunited with the father of her child
(a deceased bigamist), though Benson and Law, as we will see, attempt to
stage such a reunion. But she is united with the British extra who has lost
her in the Hollywood shuffle. The plot of *Boy Meets Girl* assures that this
Hollywood satire will include a boy-meets-girl plot that will resolve simultaneously with the restoration of Benson and Law to their jobs in the
studio. Like so many comedies about Hollywood, the film engineers a
climax in which the studio is saved and the appropriate couples are united.
In this case, the film must go to some lengths to make the mother of
Happy the eligible partner in a love match, and it even develops a plotline
about Benson's failing marriage with his (wholly offscreen) spendthrift
wife so that relationship also can be preserved at the film's end. The
central relationship, however, is the bond between the two writers, which
also threatens to break up when they are fired (Law decides to head back
to Vermont, while Benson plans to hang on in Hollywood). As in *The
Bad and the Beautiful,* two men uniting to succeed in the crazy milieu of
Hollywood becomes the primary emotional relationship of the film and
relegates heterosexual pairings to the background. Joining Larry Toms
with Baby Happy—the two outcasts in the wilderness—creates a similar
effect.

On the surface, "The Cowboy and the Baby" appears to be significant only in its utter conventionality, given that it is touted as "combin[ing]
the best features of motherhood and horse operas." But when the writers
crack that "A Star Is Born" would be a good title for the newborn feature
except that "it's been used," we get a glimpse of how the plot parodies
Hollywood in a way similar to that of the framing film, *Boy Meets Girl.*
Benson and Law want to film a newborn through its development (both
for the film and for pre-release publicity), and they insist on using the

"same baby—no switching." In making the baby a star who will outshine Larry Toms, the writers mock Larry's empty celebrity (recall Margaret Elliot's ploy in *The Star* of making a carpenter a star to spite an actor who refused to share billing with her). And as the "star is born" allusion indicates, the marketing of Baby Happy exaggerates the way in which stardom is wholly a studio construct.

In lampooning the invention of stardom and talent's irrelevance to it, *Boy Meets Girl* participates in a Hollywood tradition (in novels, see the elevation of a pig to stardom in Ludwig Bemelmans's *Dirty Eddie*, the story of a studio-publicized search for an Irish peasant girl in Liam O'Flaherty's *Hollywood Cemetery*, or the tale of Juanita del Pablo in Evelyn Waugh's *The Loved One;* film examples include Cagney's previous movie, *Something to Sing About*, as well as *Merton of the Movies* and its many "accidental fame" successors, up to *Won Ton Ton—The Dog Who Saved Hollywood*). That the new star is named Happy because Susie wants "him to be happy—even if he's a girl" suggests the incessant drive for happy endings and optimism in Hollywood films. Putting a newborn child named Happy in the midst of a Western (having the cowboy find "happiness," so to speak) stands for the very formula quality indicated by the title *Boy Meets Girl.*

Happy's stardom is indicated by a montage showing his success through a newspaper article, a fan-magazine spread, and a poster for an upcoming feature in which the baby clearly has top billing over Larry Toms. The montage ends with a full trailer for Happy and Larry's next picture. Shown in a crowded movie theater, it is the only glimpse of Happy (or Larry) on film that we get. And it is the only framed film or film-within-a-film in *Boy Meets Girl*. Lloyd Bacon uses the familiar grammar of shots to show the framed film: framed shot with backs of audience visible, full screen, reaction shot of audience, framed shot, full screen. The preview offers another way of encapsulating the movie-within-the-movie into a brief scene. If the story pitch turns a film into its crudest plot essentials, a preview turns the film into its most basic genre clichés. Happy is billed in big-screen letters as the "CROWN PRINCE OF COMEDY!" and then (shown in tears) the "KING OF TRAGEDY" and finally the "EMPEROR OF EMOTION." The story is described as "THE COLOSSAL EPIC OF A DESERT WAIF WHO MADE A SOFTIE OF A BAD MAN." The credits add: "From the story by William Shakespeare; directed by Serge Borodokov; adapted by J. Carlisle Benson and Robert

Law." The credits allude to the famous credits listing Shakespeare as the author of the 1929 *The Taming of the Shrew* and crediting "additional dialogue by Samuel Taylor."[6] They also include the standard foreign director. The credits and the trailer in general mock Hollywood hyperbole, but the hyperbole of promotion differs little from the hyperbole of the screenwriters selling their story pitches.

Boy Meets Girl depicts a system in which formula plots are repackaged and hyped, from inception through final product. The trailer-within-the-movie emphasizes how the methods of promoting films can come to dictate how films are made. The familiarity both of stars and of entire genres was closely tied to the successful marketing of films. "In economic terms, stars created the market value of motion pictures" (Balio 144).[7] Similarly, Thomas Schatz argues that "box-office returns provided sufficient criteria for continued genre production" (9). Series pictures—such as the series of Happy and the Cowboy movies—provide the most extreme examples of how the feedback system of marketing reinforces conventionality. As *The Player* also suggests, the cartoonish outline of a plot is the basis for highly consequential production and marketing decisions. *Boy Meets Girl*, as we have seen, uses formula to mock formula. In buying a successful Broadway play and pairing the familiar Cagney and O'Brien, Warner Brothers was also following the safe road to film success that the play and film make fun of. And, as we will see later, Cagney's appearance in this film immediately after his legal tangle with Warner Brothers heightens the self-referential irony.

Boy Meets Girl shows us two other important story pitches or mini-narratives. The first is not consequential to the plot, but simply shows again how Benson and Law work. Here they are dreaming up a Happy sequel, this one set (or at least beginning) in a zoo. The inspiration is a tiger-striped throw pillow in C.F.'s office (recall Judy Garland's similar use of props in her living-room performance in *A Star Is Born*). The development of the narrative is similar to that of the original Happy story, but this scene makes more reference to film techniques (fade-ins, pan shots, and so forth) and theatrical business. The scene does contain a subtle interchange between the invented narrative and the primary diegetic narrative. Susie interrupts the writers to ask whether she should marry Larry Toms, who has proposed to her. They tell her no and brush her off, but suddenly they introduce "the fiancé—a pale anemic nitwit" into the narrative they are composing. "The minute the audience sees him," says

Law, "they yell, 'Don't you marry that heel!'" This minor point reminds us to be alert to parallels between framed narratives and the larger framing narrative; and it reminds us that the story critiquing Hollywood plots is itself a Hollywood plot.

More significant is the narrative that Benson and Law actually "direct" as well as script. When Larry's agent gains control of Happy and Larry begins to woo Susie, Benson and Law plan a scene to embarrass Larry and scare him away from Susie. The plan depends on the public and theatrical nature of movie premieres. Knowing that Susie and Larry are attending a premiere, Benson and Law hire an extra (the one who eventually marries Susie) to play Happy's real father and to burst on the scene when Susie and Larry are at the microphone. The brief scene showing Benson and Law scripting the scene unfolds in the same fashion as their other story compositions: they alternate inventing clichéd lines. The befuddled extra is convinced that they are filming a trailer live at the premiere. The strategy allows *Boy Meets Girl* to include a premiere scene, certainly one of the staples of the Hollywood-on-Hollywood genre. This premiere features a young Ronald Reagan as the radio announcer at the Carthay Circle. The requisite limousines, searchlights, flash photographers, and pressing crowds are present. The film alludes to the potential violence of the audience (as does *A Star Is Born* of the preceding year): it shows a fistfight while the radio announcer gleefully explains, "only two injured and they've both refused medical treatment." The treatment of the scene deemphasizes glamour and excitement; instead, it furthers the film's critique of Hollywood promotional hype. In particular, the scene emphasizes the role of radio in film promotion. It also intimates how such live events were scripted to promote stars. When Susie chatters on about her fan mail and Happy's diet (and admits that he can't eat every food he has been advertised with), the radio announcer rolls his eyes. Susie is, in a sense, trailing off the script. Meanwhile Benson is dressed as a parody of a director—in a beret, dark glasses, and a scarf. At the right moment he pushes the extra forward, and the extra successfully executes the embarrassment of Susie and Larry.

This scene has the familiar elements of the comedy about Hollywood. Larry Toms, the not-too-bright but sincere melodrama star, is the villain or at least the character blocking the comic resolution—much like Lina Lamont in *Singin' in the Rain* and Thelma Cheri in *Stand-In*. Though Susie is played as a "dumb blonde" like Lina and Thelma, her position here is more akin to that of Kathy Selden in *Singin' in the Rain* and Lester Plum in *Stand-In*. That is, she is the unaware beneficiary of a supposedly benevolent plot hatched by the men. As in the other two comedies, the plot involves disgracing a celebrity, using gossip to achieve a putatively positive end. As such, the plots are all predicated on the dependence of celebrities on public image, which makes them particularly vulnerable to such ploys. The plots also exploit the fictionality of star personae and the staged quality of public celebrity gatherings such as premieres or stars dining at Hollywood nightspots.[8] If the writers can plot movies, they can also plot publicity (the scene also parallels the elaborate stratagem to return Jean Harlow's character to Hollywood in *Bombshell*). Significantly, Benson and Law are discovered and implicated (and fired) because of their authorship when it turns out that the extra's lines are written on the back of one of their screenplay drafts.

The comic irony of the scene emerges from its results. Benson and Law are trying to save their commission on Happy (and Susie's lucrative earnings from Happy) by breaking up Susie and Larry and keeping Happy in pictures. The stratagem unwittingly unites Susie with the young man she has been seeking, and eventually he marries her and takes Happy out of pictures. In the meantime, Benson and Law are able to restore their jobs by arranging a forged telegram from a London firm purporting to offer five million dollars for the studio (and requiring Happy to be on contract). Benson and Law's schemes cleverly apply fiction writing to Hollywood business dealing. That the screenwriters' skills are used to fake a scandal and forge a telegram represents the extent to which they have prostituted their talents.

Though *Boy Meets Girl* cleverly achieves its comic resolution, it does so only by brushing aside Law's desire to write seriously. Like John Sullivan, Law wants to write something wholly opposed to the comedies he churns out for Hollywood: "I'm going to write life in the raw. I've got the beginning all planned out—two rats in the gutter. No Boy. No Girl." Not only does he want to avoid the Hollywood formula, but he wants to focus on urban poverty. Indeed, the rats in the gutter seem to be shorthand for the realism not allowed in motion pictures: we see similar images in the openings of aborted screenplays by David Kahane, the murdered screenwriter in *The Player*, and by the title character in *Barton Fink*. We are led to suspect that Law is no longer serious about giving up Hollywood work because he has fallen in love with Hollywood high living. He says to Susie:

"I've given up Vermont for a whole year . . . sacrificed a great book—for what? A paltry fifteen hundred dollars a week?" The film acknowledges that its ending reinforces Hollywood formula and resists Law's idealized pseudo-realism. When Susie and the British extra, Rodney, walk out arm in arm, Benson comments to Law: "Well, it checks. Cinderella, Prince Charming. Boy meets girl. Boy loses girl. Boy gets girl. Where's your realism now?" Law shrugs in response; for once, he has no words. Since the alternative to novelistic realism is depicted here as trite formula (rather than as spirit-lifting comedy, as in *Sullivan's Travels*) the unresolved conflict is more troubling. The film's comic ending insures that Robert Law's inner conflict, the fundamental artistic bind of the screenwriter, will remain unresolved.

In a Lonely Place is less obviously a movie about Hollywood. Indeed, part of its resistance to narrative formula stems from its mixing of genres. It appears to be a murder mystery, and yet the solving of the mystery becomes increasingly inconsequential. As James W. Palmer remarks, "Anyone viewing *In a Lonely Place* solely as a murder mystery will surely be disappointed. Dix Steele all but solves the case twice . . . [and] the case is resolved off-handedly and off-screen" (203). Yet, as I will argue, the form of the detective story is important to the film's play with narrative and narrative expectations. Similarly, the film has been connected with female gothics such as *Rebecca* and other films in which the guilt of the central male character is in doubt, such as *Suspicion* (Polan 21; Palmer 200). Polan even notes affinities with the screwball comedy in the way in which the romantic relationship develops (16-18). And though the film never shows the inside of a studio or an event like a premiere, it strikes many critics as essentially a movie about Hollywood. Parish and Pitts call it "one of Hollywood's most intelligent self-analytic efforts" (189). Polan argues, "As much as anything else, *In a Lonely Place* is a Hollywood narrative, joining in a tradition of depictions of that world that range from the fictional (Nathanael West or F. Scott Fitzgerald or Norman Mailer) to the non-fictional (for instance, Hortense Powdermaker's ethnographic *Hollywood, the Dream Factory,* whose cataloguing of hierarchies and conflicts of Hollywood power parallels that of *In a Lonely Place*)" (30). In that spirit, V.F. Perkins compares the cops in the movie to "the film industry establishment" (223), and Palmer parallels the film's concern with betrayal and suspicion to the Hollywood blacklist (203-4). Polan suggests a connection between the ordinary guys Dix Steele gets in fights with and the mass audience catered to by Hollywood (31). I would like to consider the mixing of genres in terms of Steele's position as a screenwriter, his position as an inventor of narratives who strives against the constraints of genre and formula.

The detective story is a fascinating vehicle for the exploration of narrative because detection is ultimately concerned with constructing a narrative. The detective plot works retrospectively to assemble a coherent narrative to explain what has happened in the past (often prior to the beginning of the novel or film). And the successful resolution generally involves the detective's narrating a scenario that explains the clues. *In a Lonely Place* makes this connection explicitly in several scenes. First, when Dix returns from the police interview and is greeted by his anxious agent, he tells him the police let him go because of his superior narrative skills: "I told my story better." Later, dining with friends Brub and Sylvia, Dix offers to solve the crime because "I've had a lot of experience in mat-

Screenwriter Dixon Steele (Humphrey Bogart) uses his scenario skills to imagine a murder in *In a Lonely Place.* As he invents the story, he directs Brub Nicolai (Frank Lovejoy) and Sylvia Nicolai (Jeff Donnell) in enacting the killing.

ters of this kind. I've killed dozens of people—in pictures." The scene, in which Dix narrates and "directs" Sylvia and Brub in a reenactment of the crime as he imagines it occurred, is one of the most gripping in the picture. Dix asserts that the police "don't see enough whodunits—we solve every murder in less than two hours." As he speaks these lines to Brub, the camera oddly focuses on Sylvia, showing her smile fade into a look of concern. Dix's relish for depicting the violent crime—and his confidence in its details—make him appear suspicious or at least morbid and sadistic in the eyes of Sylvia and Brub, the paradigmatic normal couple of the film. Dix directs their movements to show how the killer could strangle Mildred Atkinson while driving. But, as a good screenwriter, he also supplies motive and character: "She's telling you she's done nothing wrong. You pretend to believe her. . . . It's wonderful to feel her throat crush under your arm." As the scene intensifies, director Nicholas Ray adds menacing music and lights Bogart's face with a dramatic stripe across the eyes.

The scene plays on Dix Steele's ambiguous status in the film—villain or victim of false suspicion. But it also exploits his narrative skills and suggests a causal relationship between his writing and his violent tendencies. More importantly, the scene draws a contrast between the typical Hollywood detective narrative and *In a Lonely Place*. The film never shows us the scene Bogart describes, even though Dix's theory is correct. It never shows us the police detective giving such a summary narrative or the real murderer, Kesler, confessing. Instead it shows us the screenwriter imagining how the murder plot should be resolved. Though the framing film does replicate the internal narrative (as it does in *Boy Meets Girl*), this film chooses to de-emphasize the parallel. To put it another way, the scene with Brub and Sylvia mixes two formula elements: the plot in which a suspect's knowledge of how the crime was committed incriminates him exists in tension with the plot in which a crime writer uses his writing skills to solve a case and exculpate himself (as in *The Big Clock*, *The Glass Web*, or the television series *Murder, She Wrote*). As is the case throughout the movie, neither Dix's actual innocence of the crime nor his appeal to artistic temperament succeeds in freeing him from the suspicion of his friends, his colleagues, and the police. In some mysterious sense, Dix is guilty—of not trusting Laurel, of giving way to violent rages, of "killing dozens of people in pictures," and of squandering his talent.

Boy Meets Girl reminds us that most Hollywood narratives are love stories, and *In a Lonely Place* is no exception. Indeed, the chronicle of a romantic relationship is more clearly central to the narrative structure than is the detective plot. The two plots, however, are complexly interwoven: Laurel and Dix's relationship begins in a police station and ends with a call from the police that solves the murder the initial meeting was investigating. Similarly, love and death are interwoven in the internal or framed narratives, the screenwriter stories that get told within the film. Recall that Dix produces romantic jealousy as the motive in his scenario recreating the murder. When Dix imagines the killer's state of mind—"She's telling you she's done nothing wrong. You pretend to believe her"—he foreshadows his own rage toward Laurel in the final scenes of the film.

Similar parallels abound in the romance novel "Althea Bruce," which Dix is charged with adapting for the screen. The story of "Althea Bruce" may seem just a throwaway example of an unappealing screenwriting assignment. But the adapting of the novel structures the entire plot. Dix's assignment is what brings Mildred to his house (and thus, ultimately, to her death); the adaptation of "Althea Bruce" is the project that occupies Dix during his romance with Laurel; the completed screenplay (which Perkins calls "their baby . . . what [Laurel] and Dix have made together" [230]) is approved by the producer on the last night of the drama; and a quotation from Dix's script makes up the final and most memorable words of *In a Lonely Place*. The few weeks that Dix lives while Laurel loves him are the few weeks he spends on the "Althea Bruce" project.

The story of "Althea Bruce" is told by Mildred in a scene that underscores the condescension to her taste by having her mispronounce many words, including the title. The point of the scene seems initially to lie solely in Dix's disdain for Mildred's taste, especially in the context of Mel's reminder, "Remember, she's your audience." The plot itself, as narrated by Mildred, is simple: a rich Long Island widow with many men in her life falls for a handsome lifeguard named Channing; they fall in love and it is revealed he is actually a scientist; after a whirlwind romance begins to fade she tries to make him jealous by seeing a lawyer; when that further alienates him, she swims out to sea while he is lifeguarding and pretends to be drowning; he ignores her cries until it is too late and she drowns, "join[ing] her husband, Lester, in the sea." Dix asks for one clarification during the narrative: did she kill the first husband? "That's not really clear," Mildred explains. Thus the mini-narrative of "Althea Bruce" offers many parallels to *In a Lonely Place*: like Mildred, Althea dies as the result of actions designed to make her lover jealous; like Laurel and Dix, Althea and the scientist-lifeguard enjoy only a few "dreamy weeks" before jealousy and suspicion destroy their love; and, most importantly, like Dix's, Althea's guilt in a previous act of violence is ambiguous. To understand the significance of this inner narrative, though, we must pay attention to how Ray contextualizes it.

First of all, the scene of Mildred narrating the story reverses the intellectual stereotypes: ordinary Mildred is the reader, playing the role of the intellectual story consultant, while intellectual Dix is settling for a synopsis in the mode of semiliterate producers. But Dix's invitation to Mildred has, from the start, deliberate overtones of the casting couch. Dix invites Mildred to his place without explaining that he wants her to tell him the story until after he gets the expected shocked reaction to his proposition. Similarly he shocks her by changing into a robe at his apartment. In both cases, Mildred is mollified when Dix explains he just wants her assistance with his work. She is so thrilled to be helping a real screenwriter adapt the novel she loves that she willingly breaks a date with her boyfriend (an act that costs her her life). Dix mocks her enthusiasm to a waiter at Paul's: "There's no sacrifice too great for a chance at immortality." That line is ironically chilling in retrospect, given Mildred's fate. Though Dix assures Mildred that he has no designs on her, we don't really know that: the scene in his apartment does have a sexual charge. Probably only the appearance of Laurel, who walks between them in the courtyard, and the revelation of Mildred's shallowness deter Dix from making a pass. In his toying with Mildred, Dix demonstrates why his ex-lover, Fran, might say, in the earlier scene, "Do you look down on all women or only the ones you know?"

The brief summary of the plot of "Althea Bruce" is given, then, in a setting charged with sexual threat and intellectual snobbery. Listening to Mildred read, Dix looks out the window to see Laurel Gray looking at him. Ray times Bogart's action to coincide with Mildred's description of Althea looking longingly at the "bronze Apollo" lifeguard. Listening to a woman narrating a scene of a female gaze, Dix discovers another woman gazing at him.[9] When Mildred, dramatizing Althea, screams for help, Dix has to quiet her and remind her of his neighbors. Again, Mildred's eventual fate renders this scene ironic: Dix's neighbor Laurel will provide him with an alibi by telling police she saw Mildred leave his apartment unharmed (her mock screams for help—which could have worked against

Dix—turn out to be a red herring). This early scene mingles the seemingly incompatible aspects of Dix's character: his intellectual nature, his somewhat predatory interest in women, his avoidance of emotional expression.

The parallels with the "Althea Bruce" narrative point up how *In a Lonely Place* struggles with and resists Hollywood formulas. Most obviously, the movie avoids a happy ending. Indeed, it turns a happy ending into a sad one—Dix is cleared of suspicion in the murder of Mildred at the very moment that he is attempting to strangle Laurel. When his script is accepted on the very night he is cleared of the murder and is to be married, we see all the elements of the typical resolution of the film about Hollywood in which the studio and romantic plots resolve simultaneously. But the movie veers deliberately away from such a resolution—as noir films are wont to do. Yet it also avoids the tearjerker ending of "Althea Bruce": neither Laurel nor Dix dies; they merely part having realized the love they had felt could not be sustained. This conclusion represents a radical departure from the Dorothy Hughes novel on which the film is based and in which Dix Steele is a serial killer. More significantly, the filmed ending represents a deliberate alteration from a neater ending that was originally scripted for the film. In Andrew Solt's original ending, Dix strangles Laurel and then writes the final words of his screenplay, which are shown in close-up on the typewriter as the final scene of the movie: "I was born when she kissed me / I died when she left me / I lived a few weeks while she loved me" (Polan 61). As Polan points out, this version brings to simultaneous conclusions the script of "Althea Bruce," the life of Laurel, Dix's love and career, and the framing film, *In a Lonely Place* (59). That is, it makes the parallels between the internal and framing narratives almost exact. Apparently Ray reshot the ending precisely to avoid this neatness, which he found false. "In the original ending we had ribbons so it was all tied up into a very neat package. . . . And I thought . . . I just can't do it" (qtd. in Eisenschitz 144).[10]

Nevertheless, the final version of the film still makes use of the suggestive parallels. These final lines of Steele's screenplay are the only example of Dix's screenwriting that we see or hear, and they clearly apply to Laurel and Dix even more than they apply to Althea and Channing in Dix's screenplay. They are introduced in a context that vividly juxtaposes violence and love. Dix has just handed the wheel over to Laurel after his enraged high-speed drive, which culminated in an accident and his nearly beating the other driver to death. Laurel manages to chide Dix for his extreme reaction. And, somewhat calmer, he speaks these lines and makes Laurel repeat them. She then suggests presciently that they would fit in his script as a "farewell note." Ray's placing these lines in the context of Dix's revealing his violent nature signals the theme of doomed love. As Dix's agent, Mel, realizes, violence "is as much a part of him as the color of his eyes, the shape of his head. . . . if you want him you have to take the bad with the good." Indeed, Mel is the only one in the film who can really love Dix Steele on those terms (and the language of his summary to Laurel reminds one of *The Bad and the Beautiful,* in which the very different figure Jonathan Shields is equally incapable of a lasting heterosexual relationship).

Laurel makes one comment to Dix about his script: "I loved the love scene. It's very good." This comment occurs in the celebrated grapefruit scene, in which Dix prepares breakfast for a sleepy Laurel. The scene brilliantly encapsulates their doomed relationship through Ray's manipulation of point of view.[11] Dix Steele sees this scene as precisely a case where his screenplay parallels his life; but Laurel Gray, awaking from a night of tortured sleep that we have just seen presented in vivid montage, has just concluded that she is truly afraid of Dix and thus she sees the screenplay in contrast to the scene they are currently enacting. Dix makes the parallel explicit in response to her praise of his love scene: "Well, that's because they're not always telling each other how much in love they are. A good love scene should be about something else besides love. For instance, this one: me fixing grapefruit; you sitting over there dopey. Anyone looking at us could tell we were in love." But anyone looking at the scene as Ray has shot it, including Laurel's troubled looks and menacing music, sees something different.

During Dix's speech the camera cuts from a medium shot of him to a full two-shot that emphasizes the space between them and the grapefruit knife that Dix has comically straightened (a prop that suggests how his gesture of love is connected with his phallic threat and his tendency toward violence). Dix plays out his love scene, proposing to Laurel. She tries to say that she will not be rushed, but the coffee boils over at that instant. Dix's love veers toward the violent as his proposal becomes a threat: "The ten seconds are up. . . . A simple yes or no will do very well." She says yes, but means no. Ray has followed Dix's advice by letting the dynamics of the love scene be communicated through actions and implications, not direct statement. But Dix has violated his own advice by in-sisting on being satisfied by Laurel's explicit statement—"yes"—and refus-ing to read the complexities of the scene. The entire scene is predicated on how differently Dix and Laurel view the grapefruit moment, and thus it summarizes their split and also demonstrates how *In a Lonely Place* will resist the romantic formula. As a proposal scene, it is more chilling than "dreamy."

Though *In a Lonely Place* never takes us inside a movie studio or shows us a film-within-a-film, it does give us these glimpses of the script Dix Steele is writing. Each glimpse suggests parallels and contrasts with the framing film and underscores the struggle with Hollywood conven-tion and formula that besets the screenwriter. In films about Hollywood, that struggle typically remains unresolved (it is sometimes fictively re-solved in other media, such as the Hollywood novel written by the novelist cum screenwriter). The film similarly displays a shifting concern with whether or not Dix's screenplay is faithful to the book "Althea Bruce." We learn that it is not faithful but that the producer who insisted on following the book likes it anyway. This issue is all the more intriguing in a film that deviates as radically from its novelistic source as does *In a Lonely Place*.

Boy Meets Girl and *In a Lonely Place* also exhibit the kind of self-referentiality in which the public persona of the lead actor echoes and contrasts with the character he plays in illuminating ways. We have noted such connections before: how Bette Davis's portrayal of an aging actress in *The Star* reflects her own career struggle with Hollywood's appetite for youth; how Judy Garland's playing opposite a self-destructive alco-holic character creates ironic poignancy; and how Arnold Schwarze-negger's screen persona is used as a source of humor throughout *Last Action Hero*. *Boy Meets Girl* and *In a Lonely Place* present some more complexly coded parallels since the actors are portraying writers, not actors, but they are parallels that a savvy audience would have under-stood.

Cagney and Bogart are, of course, actors who are often grouped together: they both came to Hollywood from Broadway, and at about the same time, and they both starred as tough guys in Warner Brothers pic-tures. They also both made a surprising number of Hollywood satires—surprising not only in number but because most of their Hollywood sat-ires cast them against their tough-guy types. Bogart played a producer in *Stand-In*, a screenwriter in *In a Lonely Place*, and a director in *The Bare-*

foot Contessa. Cagney played a gangster-turned-actor in *Ladykiller,* a bandleader turned into a reluctant movie star in *Something to Sing About,* a screenwriter in *Boy Meets Girl,* and Lon Chaney in *The Man of a Thousand Faces.* Both actors rebelled against the way in which they were typecast under the studio system, and both worked independently at some time during their careers in an effort to escape that casting.

Cagney walked out on Warners three times in the thirties. In 1936, he successfully won a court battle that led to the renegotiation of his contract (McGilligan, *Cagney* 52; Balio 159). During this last split from Warners, Cagney made two films for the low-budget Grand National studio—*Great Guy* and *Something to Sing About.* Both films "distinctly mark a denial, a disavowal . . . [of] his Warners image" (McGilligan, *Cagney* 65). The latter was a musical satire on Hollywood, a kind of reverse *A Star Is Born* (which was released in the same year). In *Something to Sing About,* Cagney plays a bandleader who is dragged into the movies by producers intent on making him a star. The movie lampoons makeup artists and diction coaches in much the same way that *A Star Is Born* does. Cagney's character becomes a star, but he ends up fleeing Hollywood when his stardom threatens to break up his marriage. The musical comedy's happy ending is the hero's escape from Hollywood. Sklar calls the film "one of the most cynical and angry films made in that era in the genre of Hollywood movies about Hollywood" (*City Boys* 78). In his book on Cagney, McGilligan notes how the film comments on Cagney's frustration with producers and studios; he also observes that, as part of his contractual control over film content at Grand National, "Cagney sat in on all of the story conferences" (65).

After that experience with story conferences and Hollywood satire, it is especially fitting that Cagney's first film on returning to Warners should be *Boy Meets Girl,* a movie of a satirical play about Hollywood in which he portrays an intellectual screenwriter dishing out pap for a mindless producer. McGilligan comments that after each walkout, Cagney received a role from Warners that deviated from the tough-guy image with which he was so frustrated (*Cagney* 52). *Boy Meets Girl* certainly provides that deviation, and Cagney must have enjoyed the theme of Robert Law's cunning manipulations of his contract with the studio, especially since the real-life Cagney's contractual disputes were so well publicized and so heavily criticized in the trade press and fan magazines. Indeed, *Boy Meets Girl* paid Cagney $150,000, provided for as a special bonus or rider in his renegotiated contract (Sklar, *City Boys* 79). Yet *Boy Meets Girl* is not kind to actors or to their presence in story conferences, so there are limits to the extent to which the Spewacks' satire reflects Cagney's perspective on Hollywood. The premiere scene, however, contains an inside joke relevant to the questions about the status of writers and actors in the studio system. Larry and Susie attend the premiere of " 'The White Rajah,' starring Errol Flynn" (a fact reinforced by Ronald Reagan's incessant repetition of that phrase in the scene). "The White Rajah" was a story that Flynn had sold to Warners but that the studio refused to produce. Within the context of the light comedy of *Boy Meets Girl*, some of the profound criticisms of Hollywood (as voiced by screenwriters and by the outspoken Cagney himself) find cinematic expression.

In a *Lonely Place* has its share of sly self-references. Some, like "The White Rajah," are comic inside jokes, for example, the assigning of the associate producer's name, Henry Kesler, to the murderer. Others are more serious, most notably the parallel between director Nicholas Ray's disintegrating marriage with lead actress Gloria Grahame and the relationship portrayed in the film. Though this film offered Bogart an alternative to playing gangsters and private eyes, he still plays a tough guy of sorts. Indeed, Bogart's reputation for violent outbursts was not wholly unlike Dix Steele's. Polan points out that Bogart was banned from the El Morocco Club for shoving a female model to the floor in an event that preceded the filming of *In a Lonely Place* by only a month (24-25). His occasionally violent marriage to Mayo Methot was as well known to audiences as was his subsequent marriage to Lauren Bacall, a significantly younger actress, as the Laurel Gray character is younger than Dix Steele.

But more intriguing is the general sense in which the film replicates the paranoia and suspicion of Hollywood during the years of investigations into Communism. The film was made at the height of that suspicious climate, just three years after the Hollywood Ten hearings and in the midst of the growing blacklist. That *In a Lonely Place* focuses on a Hollywood screenwriter who is innocent of a murder but suspected by police, studio officials, and friends suggests that it may be deliberately representing the climate of suspicion that poisoned Hollywood (and hit screenwriters particularly hard). Palmer provides the best analysis of the film's relation to blacklist politics: "In holding the mirror up to Hollywood, the film exposes that community's complicity in creating the conditions under which people betrayed their friends" (204).

Indeed, there are a variety of betrayals of Dix in the film: Laurel hides her interview with detective Lochner from him, consults with Sylvia behind his back, and passes the completed script to producer Barnes without Dix's approval; Brub uses his friendship to continue investigating Dix; and even loyal Mel is capable of suspecting him initially in the murder. But Dix, as I have pointed out, is also guilty of other acts of violence: in the past and in the present of the movie against the young actor, the driver, Mel, and Laurel. The film's essential ambiguity—that Dix is both innocent and guilty—also parallels the suspiciousness of the times in which one could be guilty through association or sympathy as well as through active party membership.

More pointedly, the ambiguity suggests Bogart's personally ambiguous stance toward the congressional hearings on Communist influence in Hollywood and the so-called Hollywood Ten. Bogart was an outspoken liberal and the most prominent actor associated with the Committee for the First Amendment, which flew to Washington to protest the hearings as a violation of the subpoenaed persons' civil rights. But Bogart also publicly apologized for his involvement, in part to protect his career but probably also in anger over the strategies taken by the Hollywood Ten and the revelation that some were indeed Communists. Bogart published a defense entitled "I'm No Communist" in the March 1948 *Photoplay*, in which he defended liberalism but suggested that Congress should have used FBI records to identify Communists in Hollywood. Bogart's situation was not unusual. The pressure of the House Un-American Activities Committee's investigation forced people of various political persuasions into uncomfortable compromises; the fervor of anti-Communism poisoned personal loyalties and complicated professional responsibilities. It is this very sense of unease and contamination that *In a Lonely Place* captures.

The self-reference of *In a Lonely Place* and of Hollywood-on-Hollywood films generally is captured in the famous opening shot of that film: Bogart's eyes peering back at the audience from a rearview mirror while a dark road visible through the windshield unrolls before us. The glance in the rearview mirror suggests menace, being followed. But such shots are usually point-of-view shots that show us what the character sees in the mirror. Here we see the character's reflected eyes, a signal that the voyeuristic situation of the movies is two way. As when Dix looks out his window and discovers Laurel looking at him, the audience begins a viewing and discovers the eyes of the star glaring their way. That the eyes appear in one shot over Bogart's starring credit establishes Bogart as both source and object of the gaze. Throughout the movie, when Dixon Steele looks for who is after him, he will see himself. More importantly, he will see himself reflected in the distortions of the movie world, tested and haunted by the demands of the screen. So too is the screenwriter's relationship to the images that ultimately appear on screen one of distorted reflection. Writers became an unusually alienated cohort in the studio system, an alienation more commonly expressed in Hollywood novels and tell-all magazine pieces. In the Hollywood movie about Hollywood, the writer is frequently elided. When present, the writer highlights the tension between the formulaic and the authentic, a tension that works comically in *Boy Meets Girl* but boils over into rage in *In a Lonely Place* and to murder in the films discussed in the final chapter.

7 Offing the Writer

Sunset Boulevard (Paramount 1950). Producer: Charles Brackett. Director: Billy Wilder. Screenwriters: Billy Wilder, Charles Brackett, and D.M. Marshman Jr.

The Player (Fine Line 1992). Producers: David Brown, Michael Tolkin, and Nick Wechsler. Director: Robert Altman. Screenwriter: Michael Tolkin.

Joe Gillis (William Holden) finally gets his swimming pool. Police fish his body out of Norma Desmond's swimming pool in *Sunset Boulevard*.

A dead writer in a swimming pool: that is one way of describing the most famous single image in all the films about Hollywood. It refers, of course, to the shot of Joe Gillis that occurs about two minutes into *Sunset Boulevard*. The image exploits the iconography of Hollywood dreams in which the swimming pool is the ultimate symbol of success, and the corrupted pool—empty, decaying, or tarnished with a corpse—is the ultimate symbol of the failed dream. The private swimming pool glistening blue in the desert landscape signifies luxury, as do chauffeurs, private tennis courts, and home screening rooms (all present in *Sunset Boulevard*). All these indulgences represent luxuries because they are strictly private versions of amenities usually shared publicly—through mass transportation, public parks, movie theaters, and so on. But the swimming pool has special resonance in arid southern California. Where water is in short supply, a private pool is an especially dear luxury. And the private swimming pool (which came to prominence originally in southern California)[1] celebrates the sunny climate and the leisure to enjoy it.

Pools are also visually stunning, a sort of jewelry for houses. Some Hollywood pools have become legendary: Alla Nazimova's pool at the Garden of Allah apartments, shaped like the Black Sea; George Cukor's secluded garden pool in which famous actresses are said to have cavorted naked; the popular party sites at the pools of Joseph Cotten, Tyrone Power, and Errol Flynn; Hearst's famous pools, including an elaborately tiled indoor pool at San Simeon, with a shallow section for nonswimmer Clark Gable, and a Greek-style pool at Marion Davies's Ocean House that offered more than one thousand lockers for guests.[2] Swimming pools possess iconic status in a great deal of Hollywood representation—from glamour shots in fan magazines to Jean Howard's documentary photos of forties and fifties Hollywood to David Hockney's paintings. And swimming pools are standard fare in movies about Hollywood and southern California. They symbolize wealth in *A Star Is Born, Inside Daisy Clover,* and *Barton Fink,* for example. People are thrown into them in *Sullivan's Travels* and *The Bad and the Beautiful*. Robert Altman lingers on their photographic possibilities in *The Long Goodbye* and *Three Women*.[3] The swimming pool is an essential part of how the meaning of Hollywood is constructed.

The elegant swimming pool is an obvious symbol for Hollywood success; but equally important is the empty or decayed swimming pool as a symbol for the corrupted or elusive dream. Raymond Chandler writes in *The Long Goodbye* that "nothing ever looks emptier than an empty swimming pool" (82). The tarnished swimming pool recurs throughout Hollywood fiction: in Pat Hobby's "long lost swimming pool" in Fitzgerald's series of stories about a failed screenwriter (129); in the inflatable dead horse garnishing the pool at the home of the more successful screenwriter Claude Estee in West's *The Day of the Locust* (70-71); in Alison Lurie's *The Nowhere City*, where a mudslide has spoiled a perfect tableau: "Wicker and wire furniture, beach umbrellas, bright cushions, and orange trees in tubs surrounding a swimming-pool. A beautiful girl in a bikini lay on the diving-board. It was like an advertisement for success, or pleasure, or Los Angeles—except that the pool was completely dry" (218). In *Sunset Boulevard*, struggling screenwriter Joe Gillis tells us through ironic and posthumous voice-over that he had "always wanted a pool." But when he first discovers the swimming pool of Norma Desmond it reveals the state of her decay and fall from celebrity grace:

> *Gillis's Voice:* And of course she had a pool. Who didn't
> then? Mabel Normand and John Gilbert must have swum
> in it ten thousand midnights ago, and Vilma Banky and
> Rod La Roque. It was empty now, except for some
> rubbish and something stirring down there. . . .
> *The swimming pool.*
> At the bottom of the basin a great rat is eating a decaying
> orange. From the inlet pipe crawl two other rats, who join
> battle with the first rat over the orange. (Brackett, Wilder,
> and Marshman, *Sunset Boulevard* 109-10)

The decaying orange in the stage directions suggests a symbol for more than the aging star's decline, since the orange was carefully developed into a symbol for California itself.[4] And the literal rat race—competing over scraps of the great tropical harvest promised in California—suggests the lowly status of the writer, at least as screenwriters rendered it into myth. Like Gatsby, Norma Desmond has the pool cleaned and filled for the object of her affections only to have it turn into a grave. As this scene demonstrates, *Sunset Boulevard* is thoroughly immersed in the iconography of the Hollywood Dream and its corruption.

At the end of the movie, the pool is polluted by a dead writer, and his occupation is not incidental. This famous image looms large over the history of films about Hollywood. The oft-echoed and -parodied shot gains further weight by what follows on the soundtrack: voice-over from the dead body. Joe Gillis looms over us visually and verbally. The movie begins with its ending, and the writer who has been silenced by the silent-screen star speaks on preternaturally. With *In a Lonely Place* in mind, we might ask why the connection between screenwriters and violent death? Why in 1950 do two films about screenwriters present them as pursued but morally ambiguous victims? Forty-two years later, *The Player* similarly connects screenwriters and murder, suggesting all the more clearly that Hollywood kills writers. *The Player*, a film rife with allusions, makes the connection with *Sunset Boulevard* explicit when producer Griffin Mill gets a crank call from "Joe Gillis . . . the writer who gets killed by the movie star in *Sunset Boulevard.*" Gillis, the murdered screenwriter, continues to make words, not only in narrating *Sunset Boulevard* after his death, but in making a phone call four decades later in *The Player*. Both films examine the writer's role in Hollywood and use elaborate self-consciousness to identify movies as the site of a struggle between the written word and the moving picture. More than any other films, these movies explore the collision between practitioners of the ancient art of writing and workers in the new technology of filmmaking.

The two films are historically complementary: *Sunset Boulevard* examines the aftermath of the transition to sound, in which the power of the writer (and the spoken word) displaces the acting skills of the silent stars; and *The Player* explores a world in which the visual impact of film threatens to make writers unnecessary. In both films there is a struggle between old and new Hollywoods. The new Hollywood of *Sunset Boulevard* becomes the model for a nostalgically imagined old Hollywood of *The Player*. In *Sunset Boulevard* the writer represents the future of film, the forgotten star the past. In *The Player*, the dashing and aggressive movie executive represents the future, the slain writer the past. Both films "off" the writer—not only by killing him but by moving him off screen. Joe Gillis speaks in voice-over narration from beyond the grave; the unnamed Writer in *The Player* (represented with a capital *W* in the original novel) communicates through written messages in the form of threatening postcards sent to Griffin Mill—only at the very end of the film does he speak, and he does so off screen. The postcard threats, voice-over narration, and mysterious telephone messages all ring changes on how words get into pictures.

The struggle between writer and industry drives the plots of these films. In *Sunset Boulevard,* Joe Gillis (William Holden) is established as a down-on-his-luck writer: "I seemed to have lost my touch; maybe [my scripts] weren't original enough; maybe they were too original." Though a script reader, Betty Schaefer (Nancy Olson), admits she had "always heard [Joe Gillis] had some talent," she pans his latest effort as "from hunger," and the Paramount producer refuses the desperate Joe not only a job, but a loan. Fleeing the men who want to repossess his car, Joe turns into the driveway of an old mansion on Sunset Boulevard. It turns out to be the home of famous silent star Norma Desmond (Gloria Swanson). With the aid of her butler, Max von Mayerling (Erich von Stroheim), Norma persuades Joe to stay and review her script for a return to movies, "Salome." The desperate Joe negotiates a deal to edit the script for her, and Norma insists that he live at the mansion. Gradually her attentions turn amorous, and Joe becomes a kept man, provided with elegant clothes and chauffeured about by Max. Norma gets the script reviewed by her old director, Cecil B. DeMille (playing himself), who tries to find a gentle way to decline it. Meanwhile, Joe longs to return to his familiar world, and he ends up working nights on a new script with Betty, with whom he falls in love. Eventually, in desperation, he confesses his living situation to the horrified Betty, and he walks out on Norma. Crying "No one ever leaves a star—that's what makes one a star," Norma shoots Joe, who falls dead into the swimming pool she had refurbished and filled for him. "This is where you came in," Joe remarks, but the film adds one more scene in which the police (and hordes of journalists) come for Norma. Sunken into dementia, she takes the newsreel cameras for studio cameras and descends the staircase playing Salome.

The writer is no longer the central character in *The Player.* Instead, the film focuses on highly successful producer Griffin Mill (Tim Robbins). Griffin seems to spend his day listening to story pitches from writers, most of which he has to turn down. When he starts receiving threatening postcards, Griffin assumes they must be coming from a vengeful writer he failed "to get back to." He guesses it may be an uncredited writer, David Kahane (Vincent D'Onofrio), and he goes to visit him one night to make peace and beg him to stop the threats. David becomes abusive and mocks him; a shoving match ensues in which Griffin knocks David into a puddle of water, where he drowns. Griffin flees the scene and tries to cover up his involvement, but he soon becomes the subject of a police investigation.

Meanwhile, he is struggling with studio politics in which his position seems endangered by a newly hired producer, Larry Levy (Peter Gallagher). To Griffin's surprise, the postcards keep coming—he has killed the wrong writer. The ruthless Griffin woos David Kahane's girlfriend, June Gudmundsdottir (Greta Scacchi), and drops his own girlfriend, Bonnie Sherow (Cynthia Stevenson), a story editor. Just when everything threatens to collapse on Griffin, he encounters good fortune. The police abandon the investigation after a witness fails to pick Griffin from a lineup; he is promoted over Larry Levy rather than fired to make room for him; and he marries June. The final shots show him approaching his flower-bedecked estate in a Rolls-Royce as he is greeted by his pregnant wife. On his car phone, Griffin listens to a "pitch" from the writer who has been pestering him and knows what he has done. For a million dollars, he secures the happy ending.

Both films satirize their contemporary Hollywoods in some detail. Filmic self-referentiality echoes several of the themes we have examined in earlier chapters. *Sunset Boulevard* examines the plight of the aging star and the transition to sound (as discussed in chapters 1 and 2); *The Player* examines the business end of Hollywood and how that shapes film content (as discussed in chapter 5). Both contrast the present Hollywood unfavorably with a past golden age, and both use star cameos to heighten the insistent self-referentiality. Though I want to focus on the role of the writer in both films, it is worth paying some attention to the other aspects of Hollywood lampooned in these extraordinarily self-reflexive movies.

When Joe Gillis turns into the driveway of Norma Desmond's mansion he explicitly evokes Dickens's Miss Havisham. Indeed, Norma's house, overstuffed with thick draperies and fringed furniture and filmed in noir style with all sunlight excluded, is a space that tries to stop time. Norma Desmond lives surrounded by representations of herself, the production stills and glamour photographs that were such an important adjunct to the moving picture business. Here, Billy Wilder's choice of a real silent-screen star proved useful, for there was no shortage of glamorous photographs of the young Swanson (and some shots were so famous as to be recognizable in the background of scenes). In one sequence the camera follows Joe from Max's organ, which has two framed photos of Swanson/Desmond on it, past a chest with four photographs and a table with eight, to a sofa where Norma lies recumbent surrounded by eleven more photographs. In another scene, the camera moves from Norma autographing publicity photos to track along her framed photographs in close-up while Joe speaks in voice-over, "How could she breathe in that house so crowded with Norma Desmonds, more Norma Desmonds, and still more Norma Desmonds?"

The grotesque number of photographs establishes Norma's mansion as a monument to her ego, but, more specifically, the photographs preserve her youth and fame. Amidst photographs of her younger self, Norma's age stands out to an outside observer like Joe Gillis. "There's nothing tragic about being fifty," Joe comments late in the film, "unless you try to be twenty-five." In contrast to the photographs recalling her celebrity and various cinematic roles, the limitations of the virtually housebound Norma Desmond stand out as well. But to Norma, the photographs keep alive her image, the face that made her career and gave her life meaning, as expressed in the memorable line "We had faces then!" Of course, silent film acting, with its reliance on gestures and close-ups, puts more emphasis on acting with the face than do stage acting or talking motion pictures. *Sunset Boulevard* reminds us frequently that the face of Desmond/Swanson is cinematic property.

If photographs offer a limited immortality, motion pictures with their animation and realism promise a victory over the grave. We have seen that early experimenters and audiences responded to the realism of moving images with just this thought.[5] Norma Desmond's wealth allows her a private screening room; her vanity and craving to halt time's progress ensure that her own silent films will be the entertainment. Private screening rooms frequently exhibit what is forbidden to the general public. They are used to show pornography in *The Day of the Locust*, pre-theatrical releases in *A Star Is Born*, and the new experimental talking pictures in *Singin' in the Rain*; but in *Sunset Boulevard*, Norma Desmond's private theater screens *old* movies, movies no longer seen in the world outside her mansion on Sunset. The situation points up the contradiction of filmic immortality: movies preserve the youthful image while the real self ages, but movies themselves are transitory phenomena, popular for a brief run and then forgotten (especially in the era before television and videotape).

The framed movie within *Sunset Boulevard* emphasizes the tension between the enduring image and the decaying body. Joe speaks in voice-over as he and Norma watch one of her silent films. The screen emerges from behind an oil painting—the moving picture replacing the older means of memorializing the past. Her living room is darkened, illuminated only by the shaft of light from the noisy projector that Max operates. The image of the young Norma Desmond fills the screen, which is itself surrounded by photographs of her. Wilder's use of Swanson's unreleased film directed by von Stroheim *(Queen Kelly)* is one of the most appropriate of the film's insider self-references (because Max will be revealed to have been Norma's director and husband, having fallen to butler—just as von Stroheim fell from respected director to type actor).[6]

The camera tracks in (though never entirely full screen) and shows a close-up of the young Swanson lighting a candle in a church. The candlelit church setting fits nicely with the shrine Norma Desmond has constructed out of the representations of herself that surround the movie screen. Moved by the glory of her work, Norma stands up in the projector light and curses those "idiot producers," swearing that she will "be there again—so help me!" Joe's voice-over gives way to melodramatic background music as Norma turns her head so that her profile is illuminated in the projector beam. The Norma Desmond that is haloed by the projector contrasts with the girlish figure framed on the movie screen. Clearly, the overacting Swanson still has star power, but like Bette Davis of *The Star* and *All about Eve*, her physiognomy seems garish, even (intentionally) grotesque. Swanson's very role (playing an aging and demented screen has-been) highlights Norma's dilemma: aging unfairly and ruthlessly limits her future in a medium that relies on faces (and youthful charm and sex appeal). Mae West and Mary Pickford refused the Norma Desmond role for that very reason, and Swanson admitted that her performance in *Sunset Boulevard* typecast her for the rest of her career. More than any other film, *Sunset Boulevard* demonstrates the cost of motion picture fame, the transformation of the self into ageless but insubstantial images, and the tyranny—especially for women—of a culture of youth and physical beauty. As Lucy Fischer observes in arguing that Norma Desmond's "special status as a maturing woman is central to an understanding of the film," "the figure of the aging actress tends to 'violate' certain cherished cultural myths concerning both Hollywood and woman" (100, 104).[7]

Planning her return to films, Norma begins to work on her face in a sequence that echoes the makeup montages of *A Star Is Born* and *What Price Hollywood?* In less than a minute, Wilder reveals Norma's facial regimen: using a sweatbox, a sander, heat treatments, lotions, massage, rubber masks, and mudpacks, Norma tries to recapture the face of her celluloid image. The sequence ends with a pair of shots that emphasize her face as spectacle, as object of visual inspection. First a shot through a magnifying glass shows Norma's eye, grotesquely enlarged and illuminated by a pen-size flashlight; then we see her from behind in a more conventional shot but looking into a lighted and magnifying makeup mirror that projects her image back to her and to the film audience. Light, mirror, magnifying glass, and giant eye symbolize the remorselessness of the close-up and its demands.[8] Indeed, cowriter Charles Brackett found the whole montage cruel and is said to have exchanged blows with Wilder over his insistence on including the scene (Zolotow 163-64). The scene communicates more than Norma's desperation, however. Like the "star is made" sequences in *A Star Is Born* and *What Price Hollywood?* the makeup montage stresses the celebrity image as a studio construct, but what the studio can do for the young faces of hopeful starlets, it cannot do for Margaret Elliot in *The Star* or Norma Desmond in *Sunset Boulevard.* There appear to be no second acts for the aging star: Norman Maine ends his own life, Norma Desmond becomes a deluded murderer—only Margaret Elliot is offered some happiness in an imagined world off screen and out of Hollywood.

There are no aging stars in the world of *The Player* (though an early story pitch comically suggests an aged "The Graduate—Part Two"). Even the studio bosses are young (and the one who is middle-aged, Joel Levison [Brion James], loses his job). The movie captures the culture of youth that dominates contemporary Hollywood. Post-studio-era Hollywood is also characterized by independent deals, and the "players" are agents and money men. In the tradition of *Stand-In,* but to a much greater extent, *The Player* reveals the business behind show business, and it does so as the executives in the movie deny the importance of the business end: "Movies are art—now more than ever," says Griffin, adapting the studio's slogan to a speech at a museum gala. Though *The Player* takes us deep inside a studio, it never shows scenes being filmed or writers writing. The closest it comes to showing the making of films occurs in two framed scenes—watching dailies and previewing a rough cut. The making of pictures is shown rather through the negotiating of deals and the playing of studio politics. The insider look at Hollywood is not the backstage revelation of special effects or makeup or lighting but a view into the heart of business relations. One of Altman's triumphs in the film is how he makes such studio business so dramatically compelling.

The much-commented-on opening shot (an uninterrupted eight-minute-long take) provides a good example. The camera tracks in and out, up and down, and around the studio, peering voyeuristically into offices from outside, thus suggesting that the film to come will expose the inner sanctum of the movie business. The scene shows us numerous story pitches, which I will discuss later, but it also shows the rhythm and intrigue of office politics. It begins and ends with a ringing phone, which presages how the film will reveal the telephone as the latest talisman of Hollywood power—cell phones, speaker phones, fax lines in cars and offices. An executive assistant chides a new secretary for admitting that head producer Joel Levison is out, saying, "He's either in conference, [or] in a meeting—he's *always* in." Levison's importance is signaled in several ways: the assistant hurriedly dispatches the secretary to make sure the trade papers are on Levison's desk when he comes in, and when Levison arrives the secretary must park his Mercedes. Shots of the parking lot show us the studio traffic in golf carts and bicycles swirling around the potent status symbols parked in the lot. Griffin Mill's Range Rover represents a newer fad than the more familiar Mercedes automobiles driven by Joel Levison and Larry Levy.[9] The opening shot also points out the relationship between the studio and the East—both the East Coast and Japan. A group of Sony executives are getting a tour of the studio (along with an assurance that "we are going to continue using Sony products").[10] Altman also eavesdrops on gossip about eastern banks "putting the screws to us"; as in *Stand-In* a representative from an eastern bank is arriving to check out the studio, and people fear that "heads will roll." The opening shot establishes office politics, status consciousness, and one-upsmanship as central to how movies are made.

Later scenes off the lot demonstrate how jockeying for position dominates Hollywood social life. At lunch with representatives from another studio, Griffin asks, "Can we talk about something other than Hollywood for a change?" Silence and embarrassed laughter follow. Seeing his competitor Larry Levy lunching with movie stars, Griffin opines that Larry is out of his depth and makes a point of greeting both of the stars. But he also knows the proper limits of conducting business at social occasions. At a party that night, Griffin criticizes Bonnie Sherow, "You don't talk about script changes at parties." You do, however, make contacts, and later in the film we learn that Larry Levy attends Alcoholics Anonymous because he fears all the good deals are being made there. *The Player* closely observes how social nuances reveal competitive relations. Altman's comments on the movie also indicate his disgust with the effect of Hollywood business structures on how films are created and marketed: "[In the old days] there was still greed but it worked. The idea was that if you got a guy that was a good actor and the people liked him, and a good writer and a good director, let those people make the movie and then they'd figure out how to sell it. Now they try to figure out how to sell it first and then try to make the picture they've sold. . . . These corporations have nobody running them—that's the change" (Altman, "The Movie" 28-29).

The Player implicitly contrasts the bottom-line orientation of the contemporary studio with the grandeurs of the past, specifically the glories of the studio era. Many of the allusions to a glorified past are visual: the studio is decorated with colorful posters of B movies (on which the camera often lingers ominously), and the movie opens with a shot of a tapestry depicting an old Hollywood scene, Charles Bragg's "The Screen Goddess" (the director in the tapestry looks suspiciously like DeMille). That opening shot juxtaposes old Hollywood and new with a self-referential signature: the movie shows the opening clapboard, labeled "The Player," banging shut in front of the depiction of old Hollywood. The shot tells us not only that we are about to see a movie about movies, but that we are seeing the new Hollywood contrasted with the old. Studio security chief Walter Stuckel (Fred Ward) discusses classic films and their superiority to contemporary, MTV-styled efforts in the opening scene. Walter is second-generation Hollywood, his father having worked as a key grip at the studio, so it is not surprising that he dwells on the glories of the past.

The Player also takes care to include a museum banquet in which the studio is shown donating classic films to be preserved as art: "The art of motion pictures [is] a serious and valuable art form," Griffin asserts in his banquet speech. All of these touches reveal how studios market and mythologize their past to trade on the accumulated glamour of Hollywood. The glimmers of old Hollywood heighten the contrast with the money- and power-driven studios of the present. Even the studio's vacuous slogan—"Movies—now more than ever"—reveals a consciousness of decline that must be gainsaid. In the scene in which the executives discuss eliminating writers from the filmmaking process, no one in the assembled group can recall when he or she last paid to see a movie. The satire in

The Player contrasts Hollywood reality with two related idealizations: what the public imagines Hollywood filmmaking to be, and what the public and contemporary Hollywood players imagine Hollywood was in the height of the studio system. The myths of the studio system form the backbone of the overall Hollywood myth, in part because Hollywood has furthered those myths in films about Hollywood, furthered them even in the process of criticizing or exposing them.

Sunset Boulevard more insistently contrasts old Hollywood with new, though in this paradigm, old Hollywood is the world of silent films, a world of cinematic novelty and tremendous stardom, and new Hollywood is the studio system of talking pictures, a newer novelty. The film also explicitly contrasts age and youth. We see that contrast in the two New Year's Eve parties Joe Gillis attends. At Norma Desmond's party, Joe realizes only well into the evening that Norma has invited no one else. The mise-en-scène reflects the eerie gap between Norma's fantasy and reality. Joe and Norma tango to the music of a hired chamber group on the tile floor where Valentino once danced while Max refills the champagne glasses. High-angle shots isolate the two figures against a ballroom set for dozens: gigantic floral arrangements, garlands wound around the pillars, silver candelabra and champagne buckets on a table with an enormous cake. After Norma and Joe quarrel about her romantic intentions and his indebtedness to her, Joe flees and hitches a ride to a party given by his friend, assistant director Artie Green (Jack Webb): "I had to be with people my own age," he says.

Artie's party is not simply new Hollywood but young Hollywood: "writers without a job, composers without a publisher, actresses so young they still believed the guys in the casting offices." Now Norma Desmond is also a writer without a publisher and an actress without a job, but, in Hollywood terms, she is finished (and determined to delude herself about that), while these young party-goers are hopeful and on the rise. They are perhaps equally deluded about their chances for success, but they are hardly embittered. This party contrasts completely with Norma Desmond's: wall-to-wall people dancing to piano music; a group singing a satirical song about Hollywood; dime-store decorations and cheap punch. Joe Gillis stands out in his evening clothes and camel-hair coat, but he feels at home with the youthful conviviality.

As Joe leaves Norma's mansion to head to Artie's party, his watch chain catches on the door. This little detail foreshadows how he will be drawn back to the home of the woman who bought him the watch and the rest of his outfit. The watch chain also underscores the passing of time, the theme that differentiates the two New Year's parties. New Year's parties look two ways by nature: back over the year just completed (and New Year's parties past) and forward to the birth of the New Year. Norma's plans for the future are distorted by her living in the past. To Joe, the future lies with Artie Green and Artie's fiancée, the story editor Betty Schaefer. But Norma's suicide attempt draws him back to Sunset Boulevard.

The party scenes present old and new Hollywood in two discrete scenes, connected only by the presence of observer-narrator Joe Gillis. Swanson comments that "Billy Wilder and Charles Brackett had cleverly kept [the] ghostly world of oldies separate from the young Hollywood. . . . therefore, I had no scenes with Nancy Olson or Jack Webb. I only saw the rushes, and even that, in this Pirandello framework, was somehow perfectly appropriate" (500). The actual collision of the two worlds is shown more dramatically when Norma Desmond visits DeMille at Paramount studios. She and Joe have finished the script, and she has completed her beauty treatments. Driven by Max, they arrive at the Paramount gates in her Isotta-Fraschini with leopard-skin upholstery. Immediately the contrast between young and old Hollywood is drawn. The security guard at the gate fails to recognize her or her name. An older security guard remembers her and lets her on the lot, explaining that Miss Desmond does not require a pass. Norma asks him to remind his younger colleague that "without me he wouldn't have any job, because without me there wouldn't be any Paramount studio."

They arrive at Stage Eighteen, a real soundstage where DeMille was actually shooting *Samson and Delilah*. Though he found her script awful, DeMille is conscious that "thirty million fans have given her the brush," so he treats Norma with special kindness. He invites her to sit in his director's chair and watch how movies are made today. What follows is a brilliant sequence highlighting the changes in Hollywood. As Norma sits in DeMille's chair, a boom microphone gently brushes the feather on her hat; in disgust with the symbol of sound technology, she pushes it away. Then a light technician recognizes her and turns a spot on her. Illuminated by the spotlight, Norma suddenly becomes the center of attention as technicians, grips, hairdressers, makeup artists, and extras rush over exclaiming, "It's Miss Desmond! It's Norma Desmond!" DeMille returns to this scene and instructs the light technician to "turn that light back where it belongs." The spotlight leaves Norma Desmond for good, and we are reminded of the transforming power of movie technology, its power to turn a person into an icon and, conversely, to extinguish that transfiguring light. The scene shows her star power on the set, but it also reveals that she does not belong in the world of sound motion pictures. To the admiring crowd, she is a wonderful figure from the past, whom they had forgotten (one extra even exclaims, "I thought she was dead!"), but there is no place for her on the soundstage. Ironically, many of the crew, including DeMille himself, are older than she is and still making movies: it is the star, and particularly the female star, who becomes obsolescent. Norma Desmond will act only one more scene in her life, when Max (her one-time director and husband) directs her descent into police custody. Her last words are spoken as she moves her famous face into close range for the camera: "All right, Mr. DeMille, I'm ready for my close-up."

DeMille plays DeMille; one-time Swanson director von Stroheim plays one-time Desmond director von Mayerling. *Sunset Boulevard*'s use of star cameos heightens its self-referentiality. It reminds us that this view of the movie industry is directed and enacted by insiders, and it feeds on our interest in stars as well as characters. The DeMille-Swanson relationship is particularly effective. Swanson became a tremendous star in silent pictures during the period she worked under DeMille's direction (1918-25). She worshipped him, and refers to him in her memoirs as "Almighty God" and as being "on another plane altogether from the rest of Hollywood" (198). Though her worship of him abated during disputes over her second divorce and her joining United Artists, she continued to view DeMille as the most significant influence in her career. DeMille did indeed refer to her as "young fellow," as he does in *Sunset Boulevard*, in tribute, Swanson relates, to her willingness to perform some dangerous stunts in the silent days. In the crucial scene between DeMille and Swanson, Wilder is able to capture the dynamics of their actual relationship, forged in the early days of cinema. More importantly, he is able to capitalize on the associations his audience would bring to the personas of DeMille and Swanson.

Much of that public interest centered on the figure of Gloria Swanson. In the DeMille scene, DeMille is playing himself, and, though he reads scripted dialogue, his public image as a great director fits his part in the movie. The situation with Gloria Swanson is more complex, since she is playing a fictional character and yet bringing her biographical persona to bear on that role. This intentional double focus—that Wilder would use an aging silent star to play Norma Desmond—was obviously important to the film's conception and promotion. As I mentioned, the premise scared away several actresses (as a similar idea frightens and disgusts fictional Margaret Elliot in *The Star*). In radio interviews and promotions for *Sunset Boulevard,* Gloria Swanson was careful, however, to emphasize her differences from Norma Desmond: she did not live in seclusion nor revel in the past, she acted in many talking pictures and hosted a television show, she had many other career interests, including a patent company and a fashion line.[11]

Yet these important distinctions did not obscure the parallels that Wilder exploited and the audience perceived: Swanson was one of the first screen millionaires and lived lavishly and married many times, and her career declined after the coming of sound and never recaptured its earlier glory. Zolotow argues that Wilder's memory of "the aged Swanson vainly trying to recapture her lost youth in *Music in the Air* [a 1934 musical on which Wilder had been a writer] had first planted the seed of *Sunset Boulevard* in his subconscious" (160). Swanson recalls the experience of *Music in the Air* quite differently, as one might expect, and Zolotow's reference to a thirty-five-year-old Swanson as "aged" speaks volumes. But from the start Wilder sought a silent-screen diva for the Desmond role, and he responded enthusiastically to George Cukor's suggestion of Swanson. Indeed, she tested so well that Wilder and Brackett expanded the part of Norma Desmond in the screenplay. The self-referentiality of Swanson's playing the faded silent star grew in importance in the conception of *Sunset Boulevard.* Not only did Wilder borrow Swanson's photographs and oil portrait for the elaborate set, but he also cast other figures from the silent films as her bridge partners, "the waxworks." Anna Q. Nilsson and H.B. Warner, who had starred together in the twenties, were likely to be recognized only by older theatergoers (their names are never spoken, although, like DeMille, they portray themselves), but Buster Keaton's grave face was still widely familiar. Their cameos deepen the film's evocation of old Hollywood, as does Hedda Hopper's brief scene telephoning in the final scandal.

This use of self-referential star cameos to add verisimilitude to the representation of Hollywood is not uncommon in films about movie-making; it is especially prevalent in films from the studio days, where contract players could be trotted out en masse for self-promoting films such as *Hollywood Canteen*. When lesser-known Hollywood figures play themselves in cameos, the result is a sort of in-joke, such as the self-referential humor involved in using von Stroheim's *Queen Kelly* for the home-screening scene in *Sunset Boulevard*. The cameos that occur throughout *The Player* work very much in this way. The extras filling restaurants and parties and walking on the studio lot are easily recognizable actors playing themselves; they function as living set decoration, making the celebrity parties and hangouts look authentically Hollywood. When the actors playing fictional roles (e.g., Tim Robbins, Peter Gallagher, and Cynthia Stevenson) greet the cameo actors, we smoothly forget the star identities of the actors playing roles. Whoopi Goldberg (as police detective Avery) seems convincingly starstruck to be at a studio; Cynthia Stevenson gushes praise to Harry Belafonte; Robbins and Gallagher compete for Anjelica Huston's attention. But the extreme use of such cameo appearances makes the audience complicit in the stargazing. Particularly in the party scene, the audience is invited to locate the celebrity images in the crowd.[12] Altman cleverly involves the audience to exploit imitative desire: while the movie satirizes Hollywood "players," it tantalizes us with images of how appealing being a player might be.

In both films, having recognizable celebrities portray themselves heightens the self-consciousness. In *Sunset Boulevard*, the young and new Hollywood is free of celebrities and the famous faces exclusively represent the glorious but moribund past. In *The Player*, young Hollywood is a sea of hipness and cool in which well-dressed celebrities nod casually to one another while we become excited voyeurs. The celebrity scenes evoke the world of publicity ancillary to Hollywood glamour, from gossip columnist Hedda Hopper in *Sunset Boulevard* to the televised fan magazine *Entertainment Tonight*, which appears in *The Player* as itself reporting on the museum banquet. The inclusion of *Entertainment Tonight* demonstrates how the experience of Hollywood is purveyed by other media. It also reminds us of the fictionality of actors playing themselves, when such things as talk-show appearances and fan-magazine publicity are openly part of the maintenance of a favorable public image. Once again, a fictional construct (the celebrity as real person) functions in the movie as the reality against which other fictions are contrasted. That is, within the fiction of the movie, the appearance of movie stars portraying themselves adds verisimilitude at the very same time that Altman and Wilder are exposing Hollywood phoniness: it makes the fakery more realistic.

Sunset Boulevard and *The Player* include several examples of the paradigmatic Hollywood gatherings, the party and the funeral. We have already contrasted the two parties in *Sunset Boulevard*. In that context, the ghastly funeral for Norma Desmond's pet monkey emphasizes her loneliness and neurotic seclusion. The solemn affair, with Max, Norma, and a pet mortician, echoes Waugh's novel *The Loved One* (as several contemporary reviewers noted), and it contrasts with the stereotype of the grand and garish star funeral. As with Norma's New Year's Eve party, the monkey funeral suggests that there are few to accompany her as she faces death, few to accompany the woman once adored by millions. Altman uses the parties in *The Player* (a gathering of "movie stars and power players" and the museum banquet) to evoke the star-studded milieu and to show the struggle for power and position that shapes leisure as well as work in Hollywood. At both parties, Griffin Mill is slick and comfortable: he pontificates on "movie as art" at the museum while publicly humiliating his lover, Bonnie, by bringing June. Altman wishes to show Griffin as a product of his environment, or, rather, as one who has risen to the top through a ruthlessness appropriate to the company he keeps. Thus the party scenes in *The Player* are as crucial to showing the Hollywood milieu as the party scenes in *Sunset Boulevard* are essential to demonstrating Norma Desmond's distance from it. The funeral of writer David Kahane offers a sobering glimpse of those who are not power players, a group of disaffected writers and their friends. The eulogy celebrates the writer's struggle against the "shitbag producer" and it reads from a pretentious noir script the deceased had just begun. The eulogy ends with the words "fade out." Though Griffin, the player, attends, the funeral underscores the outsider status of writers. And it deliberately echoes *Sunset Boulevard*. Filmed at what is apparently Hollywood Cemetery, in the shadow of the Paramount studios of *Sunset Boulevard* and near the actual grave of Cecil B. DeMille, the scene cuts away to a dead carp floating in a pond, like Joe Gillis in the beginning and end of *Sunset Boulevard*.

The central conflict in both films is the battle between the writer and Hollywood; both films articulate the anxieties of writers about their place in the making of movies. In *Sunset Boulevard* that conflict is oddly staged as a struggle between writer and actor, but, as we will see, Joe's relationship with Norma is a direct consequence of his failure in the stu-

dios. *The Player,* on the other hand, simply updates (and gives fuller treatment to) the classic struggle between writers and producers. When Joe
Gillis fails to secure work in the studios, he flees into Norma Desmond's
Sunset mansion and escapes his poverty by accepting the unusual working relationship she proposes. Mistaken for the pet mortician, Joe identifies himself as a writer and receives Norma's scorn: "Writing words, words,
more words! You've made a rope of words and strangled this business!
But there is a microphone right there to catch the last gurgles, and
Technicolor to photograph the red, swollen tongue!" Norma's vitupera-
tion presents the flip side of the dismissal of silent pictures as "dumb
show" in *Singin' in the Rain.* And it introduces the association between
writing and violence, particularly strangulation, that runs through *In a
Lonely Place* and these two movies.

But Norma needs a writer to edit her screenplay and facilitate her
return to cinema. The mixture of scorn and dependence in her character
is revealing. It illuminates the strange interdependencies of collaborative
art for the masses: actors need writers, directors, cinematographers, technicians, and makeup artists to translate their acting to the screen; screenwriters need the elaborate film industry to survive as writers; and all are
mysteriously dependent on the public, what Norma Desmond calls "those
wonderful people out there in the dark." Casting the relationship between
Norma and Joe as a business arrangement between an older woman
and a gigolo is also suggestive. Certainly the relationship evokes the screen-
writer-as-prostitute conceit that is so familiar in writing about Hollywood.
But in placing Norma and Joe, actor and writer, in a collaborative relationship that turns mutually destructive, *Sunset Boulevard* implies that
the much-vaunted audience is a fickle and pitiless taskmaster. Though
Joe and Norma represent youth and age, new Hollywood and old, they
are drawn together by their mutual failures, their shared inability to sustain their careers.

The relationship between Joe and Norma is what made the film, at
the time of its release, disturbing. And, indeed, the dynamics of power,
age, and money in that relationship continue to be unsettling. The movie
thus threatens to exhibit the very sexism and ageism it critiques: the age
difference between Joe and Norma would seem insignificant if the gender roles were reversed. But, more powerfully, Norma's fate gives the lie
to the paternalistic view of the studio. Perhaps this theme explains why
Louis B. Mayer was so enraged by the movie. And the vision of the stu-

dios as uncaringly exploitative of talent (despite the benevolent DeMille) foreshadows the characterization of the studio and producer in *The Player.* Thus, both Joe Gillis and Norma Desmond are defined by their alienation from the institution that had once employed them.

Their collaborative work on Norma's "Salome" becomes primarily a matter of Norma's forcing Joe to restore scenes of her that he has cut: "Cut away from me!" she roars in disbelief. Since she has been forced to be her own writer, Norma rudely experiences having her work edited: Joe explains sympathetically that his last screen credit, for a script about Okies in the dust bowl, ended up being shot on a torpedo boat. All the artists in the filmmaking process struggle with the final authority of the studio and producer. Thus the character of Griffin Mill in *The Player.* Though Griffin has a reputation as "the writers' producer," the movie presents him as the ultimate arbiter of what sells, of what will please an audience. Griffin is sharp and young; he appears to be a long way from the sort of producer Raymond Chandler characterized as "a low-grade [individual] with the morals of a goat, the artistic integrity of a slot machine, and the manners of a floorwalker with delusions of grandeur" ("Writers" 74). *The Player* develops a slicker caricature, a chic power player whose morals and artistic integrity are ultimately pretty much as Chandler describes.

Griffin's conflicts with writers are established at the very start of the movie, as he hears his first pitch, and those conflicts structure the plot through the harassment of the nameless Writer who threatens Griffin. Griffin tries to explain his image as a factor of sheer numbers: "I can only say yes . . . twelve times a year and [the studio] hears about fifty thousand stories a year." But for the nameless Writer, Griffin Mill epitomizes Hollywood. The Writer's postcards are often Hollywood scenes; one is altered to read, "Your Hollywood is dead!" Another card challenges Griffin's reputation as the "writer's producer" by calling him "the writer's enemy" and threatening, "I'll get back to you!"

Both films explore that crucial narrative question: what kind of stories do people want? Within that broader question, they explore the conflicts between entertainment and politically responsible art (as examined in *Sullivan's Travels*) and between formula pictures and aesthetic integrity (as exemplified in *Boy Meets Girl* and, to some extent, *In a Lonely Place*). Interestingly, both films use a female script reader or story editor to raise the questions of artistic integrity. *Sunset Boulevard* sets up the conflict with a pitch scene in the office of Paramount producer Sheldrake

(Fred Clark). Sheldrake gives Joe Gillis five minutes (just as Griffin Mill will repeatedly warn writers to keep their pitch to "twenty-five words or less"). Joe outlines the story of a star baseball player with a hidden crime in his past, called "Bases Loaded." Sheldrake immediately guesses that the plot will involve the player's being blackmailed to throw the World Series. Joe suggests that the film would be a good vehicle for Alan Ladd; Sheldrake wonders (oddly) if it might be turned into "a Betty Hutton." All these elements will characterize the many story pitches in *The Player*: extreme brevity of synopsis, familiar genre and formula that allow the producer to guess the outcome, and application of the plot outline to casting. Sheldrake calls for a script reader to bring in her report on Joe's outline, and Betty Schaefer cheerfully pans the work to Sheldrake as "just a rehash of something that wasn't very good to begin with." When she deems it "flat and trite," Joe angrily asks her, "Exactly what kind of material do you recommend? James Joyce? Dostoevsky?"

As in *In a Lonely Place* and *Boy Meets Girl*, the screenwriter is depicted as a well-read intellectual who sees screenwriting as intellectual slumming. But Betty criticizes Joe's attempt to write down. "I just think pictures should say a little something," she ventures, echoing Sullivan before his travels. Joe dubs her one of the "message kids." She will continue to play this role throughout the movie, representing youthful idealism and artistic integrity blossoming in the Hollywood desert (she is a second-generation studio worker). Joe is convinced that such attitudes will not earn him a living, so he ends up polishing Norma Desmond's script, which is admittedly poor (he calls it "a silly hodgepodge of melodramatic plots").

But Betty Schaefer reappears in the story, praising an early script of Joe's, "Dark Windows," and offering to collaborate on it with him. She rekindles in him his original enthusiasm for writing, and thus she functions to highlight the compromises he has made. If his relationship with Norma represents the corruption of the writer, Betty represents youthful idealism uncorrupted. Joe is caught between both potential lovers—art and money, or aesthetic integrity and formula plot, if you will—and the tug-of-war proves fatal. But the dichotomy is not so simple. As the romantic scene with Betty acted out on the back lot reveals, her youthful integrity involves considerable self-mythologizing, too. That Joe lives and works with Norma by day and collaborates with Betty by night suggests how he is torn between these two ultimately unsatisfactory approaches to his trade and the industry. He is too cynical to go the way of the message kids and not cynical enough to continue living off Norma Desmond. Striking out for his independence, he is shot dead by Norma. In a business of interrelated dependencies the dream of artistic independence becomes folly; Joe Gillis discovers the only way he can have his artistic integrity and his swimming pool too. *Sunset Boulevard* demonstrates allegorically how Hollywood can kill a writer, and it does so in concert with the more familiar story of the star's destruction at the hands of heartless fame.

The spellbinding opening sequence in *The Player* plunges us into the world of screenwriters in conflict with producers. But while *Sunset Boulevard* shows several scenes of writers writing, *The Player* never does— it only shows us writers groveling before producers with story pitches. The movie contains at least ten such pitches, five in the opening uncut scene. When Adam Simon tries to pitch a story about "a planet with two suns," Bonnie Sherow tells him to write it down, and he responds: "It's not about words—it's about pictures. You've got to visualize it." As he speaks these words a bicycle and a golf cart collide, as if to underscore the collision between writing and film that lies behind the anxieties of the Hollywood writer. Altman uses the story pitches to comment on how the film industry shapes the nature of film narrative. Each pitch is a mini-narrative, a summary of narrative essentials that reveals what aspects of a story are valued in the filmmaking process. The mini-narratives are screenplay abstracts; in narrative terms, they provide what Seymour Chatman calls "content based plot typologizing" (88). Griffin Mill becomes a sort of practical narrative theorist, listening to thousands of pitches, his ear attuned to the right combination of elements that will make for a successful film.

The pitches function comically by showing hyperbolically how Hollywood retells the same handful of stories—thus many of the pitches conclude with references to other films. "So it's a sort of *Gods Must Be Crazy* with a woman instead of a Coke bottle," Griffin summarizes. The pitching writers agree, "Right! *Out of Africa* meets *Pretty Woman*." "*Ghost* meets *Manchurian Candidate*," concludes another pitch. The pitches provide a bare plot outline, but they pay more attention to identifying milieu and genre: "So it's a psychic political thriller comedy with heart," summarizes Griffin, sounding a bit like Polonius. Finally, as in Joe Gillis's baseball story pitch, the brief narratives characterize the movie by identifying likely stars (the running joke in *The Player* is that everyone phrases their pitches in terms of Julia Roberts and Bruce Willis, the hottest stars of the moment). Identifying narratives as star vehicles is a holdover from the days of studio contracts, but it illustrates how the Hollywood process works backwards from audience to star and genre to script. The star system and the reliance on genre formulas are essentially marketing tools designed to insure commercial viability by combining familiar and tested elements. How a film will be marketed thus shapes how it will be written, as Altman complains. The one thing wholly absent from an oral pitch is writing—actual dialogue, stage directions, and so forth.

In a crucial scene late in the film, Griffin tries to explain his function as narrative gatekeeper. Most pitches will not make good films, he explains, because they "lack certain elements we need to market a film successfully. . . . Suspense, laughter, violence, hope, heart, nudity, sex, happy endings—mainly happy endings." "What about reality?" queries Griffin's companion, echoing Betty Schaefer in *Sunset Boulevard* and the early Sullivan in *Sullivan's Travels* and foreshadowing Bonnie's response to this movie's film-within-a-film, "Habeas Corpus." These characters voice one side of Hollywood's continuing dialogue with itself about art and entertainment, realism and escapism. Though Griffin's list enumerates familiar Hollywood qualities, it hardly explains why virtually all pitches are rejected, since most would include such points formulaically. Griffin Mill's definition of the Hollywood style is not as fully articulated as the definitions put forth by film theorists, but, like those analyses, it emphasizes the importance of familiarity, optimism, and narrative pattern in producing mass entertainment. Similarly, the question about reality, while not theoretically sophisticated, neatly summarizes the recurrent disaffection many feel with Hollywood narrative formulas.

The pitches demonstrate how movies are assembled out of the parts of earlier movies. Even scenarios derived from the news are patched together by identifying the news stories with earlier Hollywood films. When Larry Levy suggests dispensing with writers, he tries to illustrate how one can generate movie plots from the daily paper. An accountant reads the headline "Immigrants Protest Budget Cuts in Literacy Program"; Larry improvises: "Human spirit overcoming economic adversity. Sounds like Horatio Alger in the barrio. Put Jimmy Smits in it; you've got a sexy *Stand and Deliver.*" Another person reads: "Mudslide Kills Sixty in Slums of Chile"; Larry responds: "That's good. Triumph over tragedy. Sounds like a John Boorman picture. You slap a happy ending on it, the script will write itself." Altman suggests here the two-way process whereby current events stimulate film content while events themselves (and how they are reported) are shaped into filmlike narratives.[13] Larry's pithy illustrations lay bare the formula for filmmaking: genre plus star plus happy ending (and then the writing ceases to be important, since "the script will write itself").

Larry Levy's illustration occurs in the context of his argument that the studio overprizes writers and could perhaps get along without them. His central example is the actual movie *Fatal Attraction*, in which "[the audience] wrote the new ending." He is referring to preview screenings where the original ending (in which the obsessed woman commits suicide) tested poorly and was rewritten until an ending that tested well was achieved.[14] This example clarifies the complex reciprocity between industry and audience that is ultimately at issue in debates about the content of movies. Griffin realizes that he derives his gatekeeper power by virtue of being in touch with the mass audience. A particularly vitriolic passage of his interior monologue from the novel *The Player*, by Michael Tolkin, defends producers in just these terms:

> [Those critical of film] didn't love the movies the way he did. They asked, "Why does Hollywood make such awful movies, why must it pander to the lowest common denominator, why does it persist in making movies that demean us all?" They liked movies from Europe. They couldn't enjoy an American action movie, but let the Japanese copy a Western and they tripped over themselves adoring it. Creeps. Film buffs. Pear-shaped morons with their shirts buttoned to the collar, whining about the *cinema*. Their fucking *cinema* was subsidized by government television stations; it was all a European scam to pretend to America that someone else had real culture. And their precious little negative stories failed over here the way they failed over there. Griffin saw it all as a giant circle jerk, phonies with prissy taste, with their Saabs, and here he realized that David Kahane was as much a loser as the Writer, their precious European taste and their precious taste for old movies, against the big virile American public, those millions who create the movie

stars, who demand polish, who demand emotional roller
coasters, big laughs, big explosions, big tears. . . . Now he
hated the Writer. What are you doing in this business? he
wanted to ask him. You don't understand why the audience
loves a good silly movie. You think we make them because
we're stupid, but you're the one with contempt. What kind
of stories did the Writer like? The Writer probably loved
film noir. He probably loved shadows and moral ambiguity.
He probably hated slapstick, or movies where the audience
cries because a wonderful person dies of a disease. . . . If
[the Writer] thought himself better than the movies, better
than Hollywood, then Griffin wanted the last words the
Writer would ever hear to be the player's credo: "I love the
audience, I am the audience." (91-92)

The final peroration is worthy of Norma Desmond in the way it
moves from claims about talent to an ecstatic, ego-inflating identification
with the audience. Nevertheless, Griffin's formulation bespeaks a certain
truth: Hollywood has succeeded in capturing the national imagination to
a degree that other narrative media, such as the novel, have not in this
century. Yet, at the root, Griffin's angry defense of Hollywood as self-
justifying reveals an egotistic naïveté. The relationship between audience
and product is considerably more mediated (and even whimsical or un-
predictable) than Griffin's literal identification allows. The fiction of a
cohesive mass audience remains a powerful one—to Norma Desmond as
well as to Griffin Mill or Larry Levy. And the passage reveals different
ways of insulting that audience—by writing down, as Joe Gillis tries in
"Bases Loaded," or by ignoring the audience and writing from artistic
pretension, as Griffin believes David Kahane does.

The reciprocal relationship between film and audience—the way the
audience figuratively becomes the writer, as Larry Levy insists is the case
with *Fatal Attraction*—is demonstrated in the movie-within-the-movie in
The Player, "Habeas Corpus," a courtroom drama. In this movie of pitches,
we hear "Habeas Corpus" pitched three times. Each time writer Tom
Oakley (Richard E. Grant) and agent Andy Civella (Dean Stockwell) stress
that the film will aspire to a higher artistic realism: it will end unhappily
with the execution of an innocent woman ("She's dead because that's the
reality—innocent people die"); and it will feature no box-office stars ("No

stars—because this story is too damned important to be overwhelmed by personalities. . . . No stars, no pat happy endings, no Schwarzeneggers, no hostages"). In short, the pitch violates Griffin's central principles (though it does have violence, suspense, and, as Sturges would put it, "a little sex"). Griffin tricks Larry Levy into taking on the film, hoping to set him up for failure. But when Griffin gets promoted over Larry, he rescues the film by translating it back into his formula. Altman shows us the end of "Habeas Corpus" in a screening-room scene: in front of a star-studded crowd, Bruce Willis smashes the glass of the gas chamber just in time to save Julia Roberts from being wrongly executed. Bonnie Sherow, in a clear echo of Betty Schaefer, asks, "What about truth, what about reality?" The once idealistic Tom Oakley, now flushed with intimations of fame and fortune, invokes the audience in response, "What about the way the old ending tested in Canoga Park? Everyone hated it. We reshot it and now everyone loves it. That's reality." Tom's citation of reality echoes the book's Griffin asserting, "I am the audience": the audience shapes films to their desires, and thus they get what they deserve. Bonnie gets fired for her honesty.

The framed film, "Habeas Corpus," comments on the framing film, *The Player,* in a complex way. Altman commented in an interview that *The Player* exhibits all the qualities in Mill's list of "certain elements we need to market a film successfully." The most troubling is, of course, the happy ending. The final pitch of the movie is made by the threatening writer who pitches the movie we have just seen: "It's a Hollywood story, Griff. A real thriller. It's about a shitbag producer, studio exec, who murders a writer he thinks is harassing him. The problem is he kills the wrong writer. Now he's got to deal with blackmail as well as the cops. But here's the switch: the son of a bitch, he gets away with it." Pitching the movie we have just seen is the ultimate gesture of self-referentiality, a conclusion that says this movie is about itself. Altman notes how he attempted such a self-referential signature at the end of *M*A*S*H* by having that movie announced over the public address system on the Korean base. Similar gestures are made in several of the films about Hollywood we have discussed: *Singin' in the Rain* ends with an advertisement for "Singin' in the Rain," and *A Star Is Born* (1937) ends with the concluding page of its own screenplay. Breaking the illusion at the end of the film anticipates the break that comes with the lights coming up, and it may underscore a film's claim to be entertainment and nothing more. But as *The Player* exemplifies, the self-referential ending—it is only a movie—implies the importance of movies as *content* by having them replace reality as the subject matter of the film.

The villainous writer-blackmailer dubs Griffin Mill's getting away with murder as a happy ending. Surely this definition offers an ironic yet appropriate conclusion to the film's satire of Hollywood convention: the bad are rewarded and the good (particularly Bonnie Sherow and murder victim David Kahane) are punished. This conclusion reverses the original conclusion of "Habeas Corpus": there an innocent woman goes to the gas chamber; here a guilty man prospers. The *revised* "Habeas Corpus" and *The Player* share the swelling, feel-good ethos of what the Writer appropriately calls a "Hollywood ending." Indeed, Altman underscores the connection by having the framing film end with the same line as the revised framed film: "Traffic was a bitch."

Altman knows that while the film ostensibly urges us to despise and condemn Griffin Mill, it covertly invites us to envy and admire him, particularly through its vivid iconography of success. Altman clothes Mill in the trappings of wealth and power that make the romance of Hollywood so potent. Altman, as William Luhr suggests, has it both ways, deriding Hollywood and improving his bankability. Frank Pilipp argues that "the film cannot transcend the boundaries of the system it disputes" (83). Michael Wood, writing before *The Player*, discusses in similar terms the irresistible power of the success myth: "If winning is made so marvelously appealing, it doesn't matter whether the hero wins or loses, and it doesn't matter how many subtle and decent sermons against winning you sneak into the movie. For all the film's real energies come to it from the myth it sets out to criticize, and it ends up not as a correction of the myth but as another fine instance of it" (95). As I suggest in the introduction, this contradiction defines the genre of films about Hollywood. Altman's particularly self-conscious use of the unjust happy ending ultimately implicates the audience by offering the successful resolution of the American Dream at any cost, much as the revised ending of *Fatal Attraction* does. If the audience of that film can be said to have drowned and shot the seductive woman who threatened the family, so too have we provided Griffin Mill with his Rolls, his flower-bedecked estate, his lovely ice queen, and his clear conscience. The writer is out of the picture.

Griffin Mill must "off" two writers. The one he actually kills is neither the author of the threatening postcards nor the blackmailer. The one he pays off remains off screen. Both are effectively silenced. One of the postcards (an accordion album of Hollywood attractions) threatened, "In the name of all writers, I'm going to kill you." But the plot of the movie suggests that Griffin kills the writer in the name of all producers who refuse to have their success undermined by ungrateful pseudo-intellectuals. *The Player* makes it clear that the murder of the writer is a silencing that symbolizes Hollywood's corruption of the written word.

We see this symbolic connotation through the filming and placement of the actual murder scene. Richard P. Sugg notes how the "killing of Kahane is best understood as the middle scene of a triptych which begins with Griffin's visit to *The Bicycle Thief* and concludes with Larry Levy's executive meeting to discuss eliminating writers from the movie production process" (13). The final sequence of the actual movie *The Bicycle Thief* is shown as a framed film, and like "Habeas Corpus," it comments on the framing film, *The Player*. Sugg notes that it is "the antithesis of . . . the Hollywood system Griffin represents" (13). David Kahane makes that clear, sneering that Griffin's studio would "probably give it a happy ending." When Griffin mentions at the executive meeting that he attended the film, Larry Levy says, "It's an art movie—it doesn't count." The passage from the novel *The Player* also clarifies Griffin's scorn for foreign films and ambiguous endings. Thus it is typical of Griffin that he would attend such a film for ulterior purposes (looking for Kahane) and then lie about it.

Though David Kahane turns out not to be the postcard writer, he shares that writer's scorn for Griffin. He distrusts Griffin's peacemaking offers and treats him rudely. This symbolic dialogue between representatives of writing and film takes place in a karaoke bar, and the background of singers reading lyrics off of videotaped song accompaniments provides a fascinating intersection of audience, written word, and film. Griffin is cool to David's hostility until David starts taunting him about Larry Levy's ascendancy and making fun of Griffin for "making promises to writers in parking lots." This taunt moves Griffin to silence the writer, and he does so by screaming "Keep it to yourself!" repetitively, while smashing David's face against the concrete ditch and leaving him gurgling in a puddle of water. Altman bathes the scene in red and overlaps the dialogue from the next day's meeting where Larry proposes eliminating the writer. *The Player* gives us two producers and two writers; both producers find ways to silence the writers, to kill them, bribe them, push them off screen, or fundamentally change their work. In an interview in *Cineaste*, Altman put it tersely, "Hollywood is about greed . . . and trying to get rid of all the artists" (Altman, "The Player" 61).

Griffin's tirade about intellectual film buffs notes that film noir licenses unhappy endings and ambiguity. Certainly the conclusion of *Sunset Boulevard* provides one of the few unequivocally unhappy endings in the films studied here (*The Purple Rose of Cairo* and *In a Lonely Place* conclude with sad separations, but at least no one is headed to the morgue or prison). *Sunset Boulevard* ends (and begins) with the murder of the writer, the event that is located in the middle of *The Player*. The murder is the conclusion of Norma Desmond's desperate search for the Hollywood ending that eludes her. The possibility of that happy ending motivates her delusions: her belief that fans still write her in great numbers, that "Salome" is a brilliant script for her return to film, that DeMille loves the script, that Joe Gillis loves her. Contained in her delusions is a Hollywood story of the great star returning in glory to the "millions of people who have never forgiven me for deserting the screen."

Producer Griffin Mill (Tim Robbins) arrives at a studio conference after murdering a writer in *The Player*. At the conference, Larry Levy (Peter Gallagher) will suggest doing away with writers altogether.

Again, the writer represents the unwelcome incursion of a harsh reality. The crisis occurs after Betty Schaefer's visit to the Sunset mansion. Joe cruelly reveals his living situation to her and confesses that he cannot live in poverty with her. In his final confrontation with Norma, Joe reveals that Max writes the fan letters; that the studio was only interested in her car, not her script; and that he loves Betty, not her. She turns to Max for consolation, and he appeals to the myth of stardom, the myth that dominates the final moments of the picture: "Madame is the greatest star of them all." Norma speaks to herself two fundamentals of the mythology: "No one ever leaves a star—that's what makes one a star" and "Stars are ageless—aren't they?" Norma Desmond murders Joe Gillis in a desperate attempt to force those beliefs to be true, to insure the happy ending.

Joe Gillis is fished out of the pool the next morning and carted away to the morgue. But the film does not end strictly full circle ("where you came in"). Instead, Wilder violates voice-over narrative convention and allows Joe to narrate the final scene, a scene in which he is not present. In a study of voice-over narration in film, Sarah Kozloff notes that "the presentation of scenes in which the I-character is absent" does not generally "violate our contract with the voice (the narrating-I)" (48). But *Sunset Boulevard* is unusually strict in limiting the entire film—except the last scene—to locations in which Joe Gillis is present. On the other hand, the film's basic premise of retrospective narration by a corpse violates convention and verisimilitude, though the form called "narration from beyond the grave" is not without precedent (Fleishman 92).[15]

The writer will not be silenced; he is given voice by writer-director Wilder to point out the folly and contradictions of the movie unfolding before us. The odd juxtaposition of Joe's voice with the scene from which he is absent is ironically appropriate, because the scene Norma is playing is the happy ending to her imagined movie. Norma Desmond in her delusion is not Salome but rather the great Norma Desmond acting Salome and making her fabulous return to grateful fans. As usual, Joe's voice provides a world-weary commentary on the illusions of the other characters, but here it functions more like an omniscient narrator by telling us that "the dream she had clung to so desperately had enfolded her." Avrom Fleishman connects this scene to "those modern novels—of which Conrad's *Heart of Darkness* is paradigmatic—that begin as an ordinary man's personal reminiscences yet give way to a second and more awesome figure, who arrests our final attention" (96).

In this context, Norma Desmond's final scene comments powerfully on moviemaking and on movies about movies. As the press gathers,
Hedda Hopper dictates her column, and the homicide detectives fire off
unanswered questions, Norma sits staring into her lighted makeup mirror. The scene is composed with six large policemen standing, looming
over the seated Norma Desmond. An overhead lamp illuminates her face,
which we see in profile, and we also see the front of her face reflected in
the makeup mirror. She is appropriately silent, fixed as an image, a face.
Her eyes literally light up when she hears that the (newsreel) cameras
have arrived—a hand mirror flashes a strip of reflected light across her
face. Max asks her to play her scene; standing at the base of the spiral
staircase, he acts the director as he did in the past. But Norma believes
she is acting Salome for DeMille. She descends the staircase before running cameras and accents her face with elaborate hand gestures. At the
base of the staircase she breaks from her part into another—and thanks
everyone for making her return to movies possible. "You see," she concludes, "this is my life. It always will be. There's nothing else—just us and
the cameras and those wonderful people out there in the dark." But what
is the referent for her "this"? Most simply, movie acting, the movie acting
she believes she is engaged in in her great return to the screen. But the
assumption that the screen provides the only source for reality or satisfaction is at the root of Norma's despair and sense of uselessness at fifty.
And to the audience of *Sunset Boulevard* the "this" that is her life is not
stardom and glamour, but delusion.

Sunset Boulevard and The Player provide two different commen-
taries on the Hollywood happy ending, both of which imply its falsity.
The Player provides a happy ending but rewards the wrongdoers in achieving it. *Sunset Boulevard* provides a happy ending only in the mind of its
star—"So they were turning after all, those cameras. Life, which can be
strangely merciful, had taken pity on Norma Desmond." The movie frames
the Hollywood ending within the mind of the Hollywood star and allows
the writer to comment on its falsity. But the writer is dead. Perhaps *The
Player* shows a truer fate when the writer is banished off screen. While
Joe Gillis's fate is hardly a happy ending, the power of his voice and his
ability to tell the story—"the whole truth," as he promises, "before you
hear it all distorted and grown out of proportion [by] those Hollywood
columnists"—offers a Hollywood fantasy of sorts.

I think it is important to avoid any glib assumption that unhappy endings (as rare as they are in film) are intrinsically more authentic than comic resolutions. Almost all of the films we have considered draw attention to the convention of the happy ending and its tendency to skew the narrative as a whole. We have seen strained or cumbersome resolutions in which the happy ending does not entirely fit the plot (*The Star, Stand-In, Boy Meets Girl*, and *What Price Hollywood?*), excessively neat happy endings that self-consciously endorse comedy (*Singin' in the Rain* and *Sullivan's Travels*), parodies of happy endings (*Pennies from Heaven* and *The Player*), bittersweet resolutions in which the power of movies is affirmed against personal sadness (both versions of *A Star Is Born, The Purple Rose of Cairo, Last Action Hero*, and *The Bad and the Beautiful*), and movies in which the power of movies culminates in violence (*In a Lonely Place* and *Sunset Boulevard*). In all these films, the Hollywood ending presents a problem because of its predictability, its tyranny, and its human appeal.

Most of the films (I think *In a Lonely Place* may be the sole exception) try to have it both ways, exposing the bitter truth about Hollywood and celebrating the power of the movies. *Pennies from Heaven* most blatantly juxtaposes tragic and comic endings, in almost nonsensical fashion. And these two bitter satires of Hollywood—*Sunset Boulevard* and *The Player*—ironically became tremendous critical successes for their directors and stars. Altman's film was so true to contemporary Hollywood that Hollywood players endorsed it, as if to say, I can laugh at the others who are like this because I am not. *Sunset Boulevard* did manage to inspire Louis B. Mayer's rage. Mayer is said to have yelled to Wilder at the premiere: "You bastard! You have disgraced the industry that made and fed you. You should be tarred and feathered and run out of Hollywood" (Zolotow 168). Wilder and Swanson (and Holden for that matter) became the toast of the town instead. As cynical as the Desmond-Gillis relationship is, the film still communicates that love of filmmaking and of Hollywood that successful filmmakers so often exude. Mayer was right to detect a biting of the hand that feeds, and it is there in Altman's film as well. That old cliché for disloyalty captures the recurrent contradiction of the movies about movies, that mixture of love and hate for the mythological beast that remains our master—Hollywood.

Epilogue:
California Dreams

We began by considering the multiple associations of "Hollywood" as signifier and asking how movies about Hollywood might explicate some of those cultural meanings. It is worth considering the "sign" of Hollywood as well. For the most famous symbol of Hollywood is the literal Hollywood sign, perched on the Hollywood hills. Its history—from advertisement for the subdivision Hollywoodland to icon for the movie industry, from optimistic newness to disrepair to renewal at the hands of the Chamber of Commerce—seems especially appropriate to Hollywood's self-construction. Like the movies themselves, the Hollywood sign represents a human invention transforming a natural landscape for profit; it grew out of one of the many westward booms from which Los Angeles and California were created. Like the movies themselves, the Hollywood sign is essentially an advertisement for itself, and that it has become the movie capital's best-known symbol confirms Richard Schickel's observation that the idea of Hollywood is Hollywood's most original and powerful creation.

Recall Grandmother Lettie from the original *A Star Is Born*, telling her starry-eyed granddaughter of her trip across the wilderness in a prairie schooner and asserting that Hollywood could be the promised land for Esther's generation. The scene connects the growth of Hollywood with that series of California booms—gold rush, oil rush, land speculation. It connects the hopeful's journey to Hollywood with a history of European westward expansion and conquest. The Hollywood dream articulates a twentieth-century version of eighteenth- and nineteenth-century American expansionism, but in the twentieth century and under the influence of cinematic storytelling, that tale is burlesqued, exaggerated, stylized. Exaggeration and stereotyping are the stuff of Hollywood; its mirror is an unusually distorting one. Recognizing Hollywood's exaggeration of American themes, many of the writers who came west to make Hollywood fortunes went on to depict California precisely as America writ large. Hollywood novels—often written by writers who prospered little in Hollywood or only depended on movie income for a while—tell a less flattering story than movies about Hollywood. Those stories will add to and complicate our understanding of the cultural meanings of Hollywood. But just as history is typically written by the victors, so is the story of Hollywood largely told by the movies and the publications that promote them.

If movies are the dominant narrative form of the twentieth century—if they are, as Gore Vidal asserts, the lingua franca of our age—then how Hollywood represents itself can reveal a vocabulary of American self-representation. Both the insider stories of Hollywood-on-Hollywood films and the outsider genre of the Hollywood novel seem to agree that Hollywood stories are somehow prototypically American stories. And though the movies about Hollywood tend to whitewash the very concerns they raise, they still reveal the collision between culture and democracy so definitive of American self-image. What began as crude entertainment for the masses became a medium of extended narrative and artistry that appealed to a distinctly middlebrow vision of the mass audience. Today, adult movie attendance increases with level of education, while movies are still attacked, as they have been throughout their short history, for pandering to the low and vulgar. Defending themselves—in movies about Hollywood and in the promotional press—moviemakers have argued, contradictorily, that movies are "just entertainment" and that they educate and enlighten. Sullivan's conflict in *Sullivan's Travels* epitomizes the divided nature of filmmaking and film-viewing.

The same conflict emerges when the business side of Hollywood is exposed—from Walter Pebbel's formula ("Give me pictures that end with a kiss and black ink on the books") to Griffin Mill's. "Movies are art—now more than ever," exclaims Mill, and the artful movie *The Player* proves him both wrong and right. Indeed, the aesthetic of movies is an especially compelling, democratic, middlebrow mix of entertainment and art, delighting and instructing in proportions measured to please and generate profit. For all that we might—and do—criticize the business of Hollywood culture, the movies continue to give considerable pleasure to those of us who read and write about them. An adversarial stand vis-à-vis popular culture grows less and less tenable, as the contradictory dynamics of the movies we have discussed reveal. My frequent recourse to terms such as "contradiction," "tension," "paradox," and "ambivalence" attempts to express the cultural uneasiness that surrounds the art and industry of motion pictures, an uneasiness that has its roots in American self-definition. The combination of critique and celebration in the genre of movies about Hollywood captures that central ambivalence that viewers and critics express toward their culture, a resistance to manipulation and a reveling in it.

At the conclusion of a book on Hollywood movies, it is worth recalling the fate of writers in the films about Hollywood. The nimble Cagney of the writing team Benson and Law offers some hope, if one views cynically writing formula scripts for fifteen hundred dollars a week as success. Otherwise the images are of silencing: Dixon Steele crushing Laurel Gray's neck in apoplectic rage, Joe Gillis floating dead in the pool he had always wanted, David Kahane gurgling unto death in a reddened puddle. These perhaps are the casualties of the success of mass culture, casualties that audiences are complicit in bringing about. And the very concept of "popular culture" calls to mind the images of audiences that run through these films: Cecilia choking back tears as Fred and Ginger dance across the screen, Arthur and Eileen dancing before similar screen images miming their movements in a Hopperesque theater, prisoners in chains laughing at a cartoon screened in a church. From all of these Hollywood stories, it seems Sturges's image best captures the mixed fate of the moviegoer. The church may have ceded its role to art, as the modernists envisioned, but the new church is the movie theater, where we are moved to laughter in our chains.

Appendix: Film and Videotape Availability

Most of the films discussed in this book are available in 16mm from film distributors. All are available on videotape, and most are also available on laserdisc. The information below may be helpful for ordering videotapes and laserdiscs.

The Bad and the Beautiful. MGM/UA Home Video M300959.

Boy Meets Girl. MGM/UA Home Video M202944.

In a Lonely Place. RCA/Columbia Pictures Home Video 60940.

Last Action Hero. Columbia/Tri-Star Home Video 27933. Columbia/Tri-Star Laserdisc 19669, 27936, LD19669.

Pennies from Heaven. MGM/UA Home Video M800147. MGM Home Video Laserdisc ML 100147.

The Player. Columbia/Tri-Star. New Line Home Video 75833. Image Laserdisc 2290LI; Criterion Laserdisc 1318L; Pioneer Laserdisc 31251.

The Purple Rose of Cairo. Vestron Video 5068. Image Laserdisc IDVL 5068.

Singin' in the Rain. MGM/UA Home Video M202539.

Stand-In. Monterey Home Video 133-287.

The Star. Warner Home Video 12489.

A Star Is Born (1937). Barr Video HM0026.Image Entertainment Laserdisc 130.

A Star Is Born (1954). Restored Version. Warner Home Video 11335A/B; Warner Home Video Laserdisc 1020, 11335LV.

Sullivan's Travels. MCA Home Video 80551. Pioneer Artists Laserdisc 120.

Sunset Boulevard. Paramount Home Video 4927. Paramount Laserdisc 130.

What Price Hollywood? Turner Entertainment Video 6197. Image Laserdisc ID 7079 TU.

Notes

Introduction: Hollywood Stories

1. Like many famous truisms, this sentiment has been attributed far and wide and was, no doubt, uttered independently by many. Carey McWilliams attributes it to both Rachel Field and Katherine Fullerton, crediting the latter with the specific assertion that Hollywood is "a state of mind" (330).

2. The place of early Hollywood in the history and mythology of southern California is handled better by California historians than by film historians, with the exception of Lary May. See Carey McWilliams, *Southern California: An Island on the Land,* and Kevin Starr, *Material Dreams: Southern California through the 1920s* and *Inventing the Dream: California through the Progressive Era.*

3. Postmodernist literature offers a few exceptions, that is, novels acutely conscious of the publishing industry. The rejection letters from editors that precede Gilbert Sorrentino's *Mulligan's Stew* or the comic treatment of publishing in Martin Amis's *The Information* are interesting exceptions to the general rule that literary self-reference does not call attention to the material circumstances of book publishing.

4. The ideal theoretical position Metz is describing is far more distanced, analytical, and critical than are films about Hollywood. But the language he uses in examining this problem of the placement of the critic vis-à-vis the cinematic institution is so suggestive for the paradoxes of Hollywood-on-Hollywood film that I hope I may be forgiven for applying it well outside its intended range.

5. Behlmer and Thomas note that the genre of films about Hollywood includes "many . . . short subjects. A flood of them were made by Mack Sennett alone" (2). Parish and Pitts provide a brief but detailed discussion of short films about Hollywood (and early television treatments) (306-13).

6. Soroka provides the best survey of early critical attention to films about Hollywood as a genre (12-38).

7. Behlmer and Thomas and also Barris refer to the recent films about Hollywood and those in production at the time their books were written. Soroka provides a list of self-referential Hollywood films of the seventies (21, 40 n).

8. The belief that films about Hollywood are rarely successful has a variety of sources. Selznick had to sell the idea of *What Price Hollywood?* to a

New York office that believed that "Hollywood stories did unfavorable business" (Behlmer 45). Similarly, Selznick saw the making of *A Star Is Born* as an attempt "to disprove what I had long believed had been a tradition until this time, that pictures about Hollywood could not succeed" (Behlmer 96). The same belief was raised as an objection to and was very much in evidence during studio discussions of producing a sequel to the original *A Star Is Born*.

1. Cautionary Tales

1. From a memo from David O. Selznick to Russell Birdwell on how to approach Will Hays, dated 5 April 1937, in the Selznick Archives, Harry Ransom Humanities Research Center, University of Texas at Austin.

2. See the chapter "Mertons and Marys of the Movies" in Behlmer and Thomas (103-24) and the full discussion of "the Merton myth" in Anderson (74-176).

3. Richard Dyer discusses this theme as represented in fan magazines (50).

4. Studlar's detailed article theorizes a complex effect of fan magazines on female readers and moviegoers. What she describes as an "'I-know-but-nevertheless' balancing of knowledge and belief" (10) is quite similar to my conception of how films about Hollywood work. Like Hollywood-on-Hollywood films, fan magazines present views of Hollywood created by those with an interest in furthering the Hollywood mystique while they criticize it.

5. For a thorough account of this oft-told story, see Alexander Walker. For a summary and somewhat revisionist account, see Richard deCordova.

6. Anderson develops a historical theory in which the fifties mark a turn to more negative portrayals of Hollywood. As I indicate elsewhere, I think the ambiguities of such films as *A Star Is Born* (made in the thirties and again in the fifties) complicate such an analysis. On the zeitgeist of the fifties, see Gordon Gow, *Hollywood in the Fifties*. New York: A.S. Barnes, 1971, and Dana Polan, *Power and Paranoia: History, Narrative, and the American Cinema*. New York: Columbia Univ. Press, 1986.

7. Maltby and Craven term this phenomenon the plot of the "reluctant hero," in which the "character . . . eventually displays the skills the audience already knows the performer possesses" (254).

8. After the premiere of *A Star Is Born*, David O. Selznick received a letter from John Gilbert's widow, Virginia, in which she admits that the film made her feel "pretty low" but asserts that it is "the *most* beautiful picture" and thanks Selznick for making it. The letter makes it clear that she thought the film a fitting tribute to John Gilbert. (No date [Selznick Archives], but Selznick's reply is dated 3 May 1937.)

9. Selznick objected to this particular promotion, suggesting that it was unfair to raise the hopes of the winners of the contest and worrying about just what the studio would do with them when they arrived. But it was just a few years later that Selznick would engineer the greatest screen-test hoax in the business:

the publicity-motivated search for an actress to portray Scarlett in *Gone with the Wind*. Selznick also suggested creating a role in *A Star Is Born* for a "dumb girl" and running an ad in the trades "asking for the dumbest girl in Hollywood to report to Wellman's office" (20 October 1936 [Selznick Archives]). Thankfully, this promotion was not pursued.

10. Information in a press release on the back of a production still photo in the Selznick Archives.

11. The film *Stage Door* (1937) is interesting in this regard, though it concerns Broadway actresses. In it we see the supportive boarding house of would-be stars, which continues to be a staple in Hollywood pictures. In Katharine Hepburn's struggles with the famous line "The calla lilies are in bloom," we also see the difficulty of acting.

12. Dyer charts critical disagreement about the importance of talent and concludes that skill in acting is not a relevant criterion for stardom because "not all highly talented performers become [stars], nor are all stars highly talented" (18). I find Dyer's all-or-nothing logic here a bit unconvincing: skill in acting is clearly something performers work to acquire, and though there is surely no precise correlation between talent and fame, it does not follow that the two are unrelated.

13. Before Rita Hayworth, the boldest example of the fabrication of a star persona out of whole cloth was the marketing of Theda Bara as a supernatural Arab foundling. Episodes like these are parodied in Hollywood novels such as Evelyn Waugh's *The Loved One* (in the story of Juanita del Pablo) and Liam O'Flaherty's *Hollywood Cemetery*.

14. A French journalist writing in 1895 about an early demonstration of moving pictures commented: "Everybody will be able to photograph those who are dear to them, no longer as static forms but with their movements, their actions, their familiar gestures. . . . Then, death will no longer be absolute" (Cook 13). Geoffrey O'Brien notes that such commentators envisioned "that people would want to contemplate the simulacra of their relatives and loved ones. [They] could hardly have foreseen that [people] would choose instead to resurrect Maria Montez or Elvis Presley" (63).

15. René Girard discusses the mimetic nature of desire in several of his works. He argues that "rivalry does not arise because of the fortuitous convergence of two desires on a single object; rather, *the subject desires the object because the rival desires it*. . . . The rival then serves as a model for the subject. . . . The subject thus looks to that other person to inform him of what he should desire in order to acquire that being" (145-46). This description of imitative desire applies most directly to fans and to hopeful starlets like Mary Evans who desire the dress and style of stars to become more like them. In the case of the mature screen star, like Margaret Elliot, the aspiration has turned into the desire to be desired: desire me.

16. Letter to David O. Selznick, 3 March 1937 (Selznick Archive).

2. Singin' on the Screen

1. Rick Altman uses the term "show musical" to include traditional "backstage musicals" as well as musicals that "construct their plot around the creation of a show (Broadway play, fashion magazine, high school revue, Hollywood film), with the making of a romantic couple both symbolically and causally related to the success of the show" (200). Altman argues persuasively for the usefulness of this broader definition of "show."

2. "Realism" is a term that is problematic but unavoidable. I think it is most helpful—in discussions of film and literature—to consider realism as a convention, but as a convention that is particularly powerful in creating illusions of lived experience. Ian Watt's discussion of "formal realism" (32) as a convention of the novel genre remains one of the best descriptive applications of the term. His delineation of the conventions by which the novel presents something appearing to be "a full and authentic report of human experience" has clear parallels with classical cinematic realism, except that the present tense of film replaces the "report" quality of the novel with visual analogues.

3. Feuer discusses the prevalence of this theme in musicals (49-65). See also Rick Altman's treatment of the folk musical as subgenre (272-327).

4. Walker discusses the myth of Gilbert's voice by analyzing critical and popular reception of several Gilbert talkies in addition to the notorious "I love you" film, *His Glorious Night* (1929), which was actually his *second* talking picture. Walker concludes that Gilbert's fall from popularity—and the laughter provoked by the "I love you" scene—"[have] nothing to do with the quality of his voice" (183). Walker's analysis is convincing: "What really broke Gilbert's romantic spell was the nature of the sound cinema itself. Speech made some of the most potent archetypes of the silent movies into obsolete caricatures overnight" (183). It is interesting that *Singin' in the Rain* gives the failed "I love you" scene to Don Lockwood (and treats the reasons for the failure realistically) while it transfers wholesale the myth of the comical voice to Lina Lamont.

5. Laura Mulvey discusses the uniting of audience and character gaze during showgirl performances: "A woman performs within the narrative, the gaze of the spectator and that of the male characters in the film are neatly combined without breaking narrative verisimilitude" (809). Mulvey cites Lauren Bacall's songs in *To Have and Have Not* as an example.

6. Mast discusses this scene in detail in *Can't Help Singin'* and comments on the use of the television screen in the Academy Awards ceremony as well (278-79). Anderson discusses "anti-TV" movies of the fifties (196-97).

7. Cukor's biographer, Emanuel Levy, relates a story about Cukor "foolishly explaining" the motivation of scenes such as this one to Garland, who replied to one such explanation, "Who will ever know better than I the tortures of melancholia?" (225).

3. Let a Smile Be Your Umbrella

1. There is some ambiguity about whose film is being screened. Though the scene may suggest the film is Sullivan's, the plot makes it clear that he is contemplating his first serious film. Thus, this excerpted film must be a work by someone else, which Sullivan admires (see Henderson 520).

2. Diane Jacobs discusses the charges raised against *If I Were King* and cites an article in *Redbook* as well as Paramount's defense that the film was "devised solely for entertainment purposes" (183).

3. See Richard Maltby, "The Production Code and the Hays Office."

4. Sturges has been accused of displaying contempt for his audience, and the sole political passage Jacobs cites from his letters shows an elitist disregard for the masses (183-84). *Sullivan's Travels* complicates this attitude significantly, as Jacobs acknowledges and Wineapple discusses.

5. Most critics see *Sullivan's Travels* as Sturges's most personally revealing film; Houston remarks that it is the one film in which Sturges "very nearly came out into the open" (133). Such an appraisal, however, need not lead us to identify Sullivan with Sturges unproblematically.

6. Sturges does use montage for comic effect later in the film, when he shows Sullivan's colleagues reacting to his picture in the newspaper and the news that he is alive.

7. In a discussion of the role of the audience in *Sullivan's Travels*, Wineapple makes a related point: "Sullivan must recognize himself not only as audience but must recognize the audience as prisoners, as it were, of the media 'text'" (155).

8. The NAACP wrote to Sturges lauding his treatment of black people in this scene and distinguishing it from Hollywood's tendency to limit black characters to "menial or comic roles" (quoted in Jacobs 262).

9. My discussion of this unproduced and unpublished screenplay is indebted to Jacobs and Henderson.

10. Jacobs also cites a letter from Crowther to Sturges that elaborates on his objections to the ending of *Sullivan's Travels* (260). For Bazin's discussion of the film, see Andre Bazin, *The Cinema of Cruelty: From Bunuel to Hitchcock* (New York: Seaver Books, 1982), 37.

11. Rick Altman provides the fullest discussion of how musicals contrast the real and the ideal, often in terms of a contrast between extramusical narrative and song (60-65, 185). He applies the distinction revealingly to self-referential musicals: "Stage and backstage space thus serve as a reversible intermediary between two real worlds, that of the audience and that of the actors" (208).

12. Feuer sees this scene as thoroughly ironic, an example of "quotation [with] a critical function" and of the film's "deconstruction" of the folk musical (128-29). I think the scene is multivalent: though the screen illusion is broken it is also celebrated, as is the whole concept of audience projection.

4. Screen Passages

1. The negative response to genre mixing in *Last Action Hero* is apparent in reviews: David Ansen in *Newsweek* complained, "If the film makers don't believe in what they're making, how can we?" (64). He adds that the movie "aims for so many different constituencies . . . that it will likely satisfy none of them" (65). Even one of the rare positive reviews, by Anthony Lane in the *New Yorker*, admits that the film is unlikely to please "all those Danny Madigans out there in the audience" (97).

2. See Robin Wood, *Hollywood from Vietnam to Reagan*, and Michael Rogin, *"Ronald Reagan," the Movie, and Other Episodes in Political Demonology*.

3. Allen is one of the few contemporary directors who has, in his words, "fought for the privilege to tell stories with black and white photography" ("True Colors" 38).

4. See Wernblad (109-10) and Rosen, however, for discussions of the problems Allen had with residents during the location shooting of *Purple Rose*.

5. Polhemus discusses how comic novels take the place of religious faith in nineteenth- and twentieth-century British fiction. His discussion forms an important background to my discussion of faith and comic resolution here and elsewhere in this study (see the discussion of *Sullivan's Travels* in chapter 3).

6. See "A Gimmick Deflated," *Time*, 15 March 1993.

5. No Business Like

1. This argument about the historical progression of films about Hollywood is developed by Anderson. As I suggest in discussing *The Bad and the Beautiful*, however, a celebratory element persists even in stories that picture Hollywood as a corrupt destroyer. Similarly, early Hollywood films (such as the original *A Star Is Born*) are often darker than Anderson's generalizations allow.

2. Fox's version of the story is related in *Upton Sinclair Presents William Fox*, published in 1933.

3. Anderson discusses parties in movies about Hollywood (47-49). I discuss parties in modern literature in an earlier work, *The Life of the Party: Festive Vision in Modern Fiction*. When parties are overtaken by work concerns, the festive spirit of play becomes corrupted and the participants are frequently dissatisfied.

4. Molly Haskell discusses this imbalance and notes: "Directing—giving orders, mastering not only people but machinery—is a typically masculine, even militaristic, activity" (33). The same point might be made of producers as well. Certainly, in fact, those are the positions in the film world that have been most consistently dominated by men.

5. One could argue that marriage comedy in general supports the status quo in its happy resolutions, frequently at the cost of female friendships or careers—from Shakespeare's comedies (see Montrose) to the screwball comedies discussed by Stanley Cavell in *Pursuits of Happiness*. See also Shumway's revision of Cavell.

6. The *New York Times* referred to Los Angeles as "the self-styled open shop capital of America" and as "a militant non-union city" as late as 1937 (9 May 1937).

7. The comments of the Screen Actors Guild apply even more dramatically to studio responses to labor actions attempted by the craft unions. Union-breaking techniques would become more vicious in the forties, when charges of Communism were used to undermine union solidarity (Sklar, *Movie-Made* 258).

8. There are many examples. Laura Mulvey, for one, argues that "the extreme contrast between the darkness in the auditorium . . . and the brilliance of the shifting patterns of light and shade on the screen helps to promote the illusion of voyeuristic separation" (806). Gerald Mast discusses the phenomenon of film projection, the significance of the fact that "the 'material' of projected images is the immaterial operation of light itself" ("Projection" 268). Similar concerns inform Christian Metz's discussion of the "imaginary" and Rudolf Arnheim's analysis of the visual experience of watching films. Geoffrey O'Brien discusses the "watchers in the dark" in the explicit context of horror films (175). The scene in *The Bad and the Beautiful* draws on the work of horror film director Val Lewton.

6. Picturing Writers

1. The contrast between the myth of Hollywood as destroyer of talent and the reality that many writers used Hollywood employment successfully to support their writing is discussed in many sources, including Fine. See also Tom Dardis's study of Fitzgerald, Faulkner, West, Huxley, and Agee in *Some Time in the Sun* and more specifically his article "The Myth That Won't Go Away: Selling Out in Hollywood."

2. Several Hollywood writers make this point—that the complaints about the restrictiveness of writing for the movies do not mean that most Hollywood writers are great artists. Ben Hecht comments: "Before it might seem that I am writing about a tribe of Shelleys in chains, I should make it clear that the movie writers 'ruined' by the movies are for the most part a run of greedy hacks and incompetent thickheads. Out of the thousand writers huffing and puffing through movieland there are scarcely fifty men or women of wit or talent" (*Child of the Century* 474). Raymond Chandler comments similarly in "Writers in Hollywood": "There are writers in Hollywood making two thousand a week who never had an idea in their lives, who have never written a photographable scene, who could not make two cents a word in the pulp market if their lives depended on it. Hollywood is full of such writers, although there are few at such high salaries" (72).

3. W.R. Burnett gives a helpful outline of conditions for writers at different studios: "I don't think any of the studios valued writers very much. If the writer could fit in the Warners system, it was far and away the best place to be. And I wrote everyplace. Metro—you might as well be out in the middle of the desert. Nobody even knew you were there. You could sit there for four weeks and draw your pay and not say anything and you never heard from anybody. Paramount was always hit-or-miss—they had people coming in and out. It wasn't a well-run place, ever. Columbia was a tight ship. Harry Cohn was tough, real tough. Republic was a joke. And Fox, I would say, was very well run under Zanuck" (McGilligan, *Backstory* 75).

4. The best analysis of how movies became a means of attaining cultural respectability is Neal Gabler, who discusses the theme throughout *An Empire of Their Own*: "Making movies was a metaphor for one's entire life—for the imaginative transformation to which those lives would be subjected. . . . [The moguls'] wealth was another way of acting out the genteel" (240). Theatrical producer George Abbott praises *Boy Meets Girl* for its presentation of this quality (in his foreword to the Spewack play): "Most of the writings about the great film colony have overlooked an important expression of the Hollywood consciousness. That is the eagerness for culture" (4).

5. I do not mean to overemphasize the extent to which film content is determined by the system of production—a great deal of variation (ideologically and otherwise) is obviously possible. But if a film remains a marketable commodity in the classical Hollywood period, it is likely to exhibit certain narrative and thematic conventions.

6. The debate over whether this famous credit actually exists (and, if so, on which prints of the film) recently surfaced in the "Forum" section of the *PMLA* (108, no. 1, January 1993, 151-53).

7. Balio provides an excellent overview of studio promotion techniques and their relation to the star system (168-75).

8. For discussion and examples of how Hollywood nightspots were used for photo opportunities and publicity, see Heimann.

9. Polan provides an excellent discussion of "the woman's look" in *In a Lonely Place* and argues that "the film sets up women as figures who look at and thereby interrogate Dix" (41; see 40-44).

10. For a detailed discussion of the earlier ending scripted by Solt, and Ray's reaction to it, see Polan (58-61). Ray's reasons for changing the neatness of Solt's original ending are given in the 1974 documentary *I'm a Stranger Here Myself*, quoted in Eisenschitz (144).

11. Many commentators note that Ray does not follow the Hughes source in restricting or even emphasizing Dix Steele's point of view. He offers many scenes to which Dix is not privy. The fullest discussion of point of view in film noir, Telotte's *Voices in the Dark*, offers an interesting argument about *In a Lonely Place*. Telotte considers the film a "classic third-person approach" (and thus not typical of noir),

but he argues that "the film still manages the sort of discursive focus we have noted in other *noirs* by shifting the effects of the novel's interior voice to the film's new reflexive dimension, its concern with the movie industry. In effect, the adaptation [of Hughes's novel] turns style into subject" (190; see 190-94).

7. Offing the Writer

1. When *Sunset Boulevard* was released in 1950 there were only about 10,000 swimming pools in the United States. By the end of the 1950s there were more than 250,000 swimming pools, more than a third of which were located in southern California. So reports Lefevre (9), who also notes that Los Angeles led the country in swimming pool installation in the twenties and thirties, during which "most of the private pools were built for those in the movie industry" (13).

2. See "Hollywood-at-Home," a special issue of *Architectural Digest* 51, no. 4 (April 1994), and Knight, *The Hollywood Style.*

3. Anderson discusses swimming pools as recurrent symbols in films about Hollywood (16-17) and notes how the state of Norma Desmond's pool parallels the relationship between Norma and Joe. Anderson argues that people are never shown swimming in films about Hollywood, although we do see Joe swimming in *Sunset Boulevard.*

4. A variety of works discuss the development of marketing collectives of orange growers and how the promotion of the orange was closely related to the promotion of California. Particularly interesting are the studies of themes in orange crate art in McClelland and Last and in Salkin and Gordon.

5. See O'Brien (63) and Cook (13).

6. Swanson discusses the debacle of the original making of *Queen Kelly,* a film that went outrageously over budget thanks to von Stroheim and took so long to make that talking pictures had replaced silents before it was finished (382-416). At the time of *Sunset Boulevard,* no print of *Queen Kelly* had actually been released. Swanson also discusses Wilder's screening of the film for von Stroheim and Swanson during the making of *Sunset Boulevard* (499).

7. Fischer's essay argues that Norma Desmond "represents the typical woman in our culture—woman, as it were, writ large" (106). An interesting section of the essay discusses Norma Desmond as vampire, trapped in an existence as one of the post-cinematic "undead."

8. See Wood: "Why are there so many mirrors in movies, for example? Why do we often see a character's face in a looking glass, or reflected in a window or other suitable surface, simultaneously with the back of the same character's head? Why is it that the first appearance of major characters in so many movies is a reflected appearance, rather than a direct confrontation with the camera?" (117). Wood provides two answers: the influence of German expressionism and the tendency of directors to emphasize lighting and composition over character and narrative. His discussion (117-21) provides a variety of examples and also

notes that mirror shots "remind us of what we normally forget in the cinema, unless we are looking for it: the location of the camera" (120).

9. In an interview, Altman used luxury cars to epitomize the character of contemporary Hollywood: "It's a cutthroat atmosphere. These people are all after their own. It used to be every car in the parking lot at ICM had to be either a black BMW or a black Mercedes. Somebody bought a Lexus and they're all Lexuses. They wear these things like you wear a necktie" ("The movie you saw" 28).

10. Sony's takeover of Columbia is one of a variety of instances in contemporary Hollywood of movie studios' being acquired by large firms involved in various entertainment-related ventures. See the discussion in chapter 4 of Sony product placement in *Last Action Hero*.

11. Swanson's insistence on drawing these distinctions is shown not only in her autobiography but also in scripts for radio promotion interviews connected with *Sunset Boulevard* and in her collection of materials at the Harry Ransom Humanities Research Center at the University of Texas at Austin.

12. Various editions of the movie on videotape and laserdisc further exploit fan interest in celebrities by including outtakes of celebrity cameos and stills that help the viewer locate and identify the various players.

13. The symbiosis between movies and news reporting has received considerable attention with regard to recent events—particularly the coverage of the Vietnam War, the Reagan presidency, and the television coverage of the war in the Persian Gulf. See Rogin, *"Ronald Reagan," the Movie*.

14. In a videotaped interview, director Adrian Lyne discussed the importance of a happy ending in terms of audience identification: "If you spend two hours getting an audience to sympathize [with] and enjoy a family, become identified with this family, to then abandon that family at the end of the movie . . . it just doesn't work" ("Director's Cut" videotape of *Fatal Attraction*). Here he is referring to the originally scripted ending of *Fatal Attraction* (never filmed) in which the husband is jailed for the murder of the woman who has committed suicide.

15. Fischer argues that the posthumous narration serves only "to insure that the text is mediated by a man. The narrative voice is entirely denied to Norma Desmond, who remains (in a typically feminine posture) a 'silent' movie star" (101). Yet Joe Gillis also is an outsider character denied a voice in the Hollywood in which he tries to earn a living as a writer. The various codes of Hollywood that would label both Norma and Joe as washed up also conspire to put them at odds with one another.

Bibliography

Studies of Movies about the Movies

Anderson, Patrick Donald. *In Its Own Image: The Cinematic Vision of Hollywood.* New York: Arno Press, 1978. A reprinted dissertation from the University of Michigan (1976), Anderson's study is the best combination of historical perspective and wide-ranging discussion of the genre. Referring to more than one hundred films, Anderson surveys recurrent conventions of the genre and then focuses on how these films reflect American ambivalence about material success. He sees a celebration of rags-to-riches stories dominating films about Hollywood before the 1950s, while films from the fifties and following present "the dark side of the dream." Good bibliography and filmography.

Barris, Alex. *Hollywood according to Hollywood.* New York: A.S. Barnes, 1978. Heavily illustrated, Barris's study presents a popular survey of the genre, emphasizing star performances and box-office results. The chapters divide the genre into categories such as "Hollywood Kids Hollywood" and "Hollywood Salutes the Boys." The book covers many films, most in one or two paragraphs; occasionally a discussion approaches one page. Indexed.

Behlmer, Rudy, and Tony Thomas. *Hollywood's Hollywood.* Secaucus, N.J.: Citadel Press, 1975. This volume surveys more than two hundred films about Hollywood and is copiously illustrated. Behlmer and Thomas divide the films into thematic categories and pay a good deal of attention to the level of accuracy in the depictions of Hollywood and filmmaking. Though the format suggests a coffee-table book, the research is thorough and the discussion of films consistently intelligent--by far the most useful of the surveys of the genre. Discussions of individual films range from a few sentences to three or four pages. Indexed.

Maltby, Richard, and Ian Craven. *Hollywood Cinema: An Introduction.* Cambridge: Blackwell, 1995. This is actually a textbook for an introductory film class, but it is significant for this study in that the authors often use films about Hollywood for illustrative purposes (e.g., *A Star is Born* and *Singin' in the Rain*) in the context of what they call an analysis of the commercial aesthetic. The work positions itself in the tradition of Bordwell, Staiger, and Thompson's *Classical Hollywood Cinema* but with greater attention to the means of production and reception.

238

Parish, James Robert, and Michael R. Pitts, with Gregory W. Mank. *Hollywood on Hollywood.* Metuchen, N.J.: Scarecrow Press, 1978. An alphabetical reference work on the genre, this volume presents entries on virtually all the films about Hollywood prior to its publication. Entries run about a page and include film credits and cast lists, plot summaries, intelligent evaluations, and, often, quotations from contemporary reviews. Contains a fascinating and well-researched essay on movie shorts about Hollywood. This is a very useful work that would benefit from updating and republication. Illustrated.

Stam, Robert. *Reflexivity in Film and Literature: From Don Quixote to Jean-Luc Godard.* New York: Columbia Univ. Press, 1992. A useful reprint of a 1985 study, this critical analysis focuses on the anti-illusionist effects of reflexivity. Though a good portion of the book examines reflexive film, only a small part of that deals with Hollywood film (Godard is treated at the greatest length). A brief section on reflexivity in the Hollywood sound film examines *Sullivan's Travels, Singin' in the Rain,* and *Sunset Boulevard.* A later section discusses the critical reaction to Woody Allen's *Stardust Memories* in ways that anticipate my treatment of the critical failure of *Last Action Hero* and *Pennies from Heaven.* The book does an excellent job of connecting diverse works in an illuminating way. Clearly written throughout, with a good bibliography.

Works Cited

Abbott, George. Foreword to *Boy Meets Girl: A Play in Three Acts,* by Bella Spewack and Samuel Spewack. London: English Theatre Guild, 1947.

Agee, James. "Sunset Boulevard." *Agee on Film.* New York: McDowell, Obolensky, 1958. 411-415.

Allen, Woody. *Three Films of Woody Allen.* New York: Vintage, 1987.

———. "True Colors." *New York Review of Books* 34:38 (13 August 1987).

Altman, Rick. *The American Film Musical.* Bloomington: Indiana Univ. Press, 1987.

Altman, Robert. "The Player." Interview by Janice Richolson. *Cineaste* 19 (1992): 61.

———. "The movie you saw is the movie we're going to make." Interview by Gavin Smith and Richard T. Jameson. *Film Comment* 28.3 (1992): 20-30.

Anderson, Patrick Donald. *In Its Own Image: The Cinematic Vision of Hollywood.* New York: Arno Press, 1978.

Ansen, David. "Bang, Bang, Kiss, Kiss." Review of *Last Action Hero. Newsweek,* 28 June 1993, 64-65.

Arnheim, Rudolf. *Film as Art.* Berkeley: Univ. of California Press, 1957.

Balio, Tino. *Grand Design: Hollywood as a Modern Business Enterprise, 1930-1939.* New York: Scribner's, 1993.

Barris, Alex. *Hollywood According to Hollywood,* New York: A.S. Barnes, 1978.

Basinger, Jeanine. *American Cinema: One Hundred Years of Filmmaking.* New York: Rizzoli International Publications, 1994.

Behlmer, Rudy, ed. *Memo From David O. Selznick.* New York: Viking Press, 1972.

Behlmer, Rudy, and Tony Thomas. *Hollywood's Hollywood.* Secaucus, N.J.: Citadel Press, 1975.

Bemelmans, Ludwig. *Dirty Eddie.* New York: Viking Press, 1947.

Bogart, Humphrey. "I'm No Communist." In *Photoplay Treasury,* ed. Barbara Gelman, 356-58. New York: Crown, 1972.

Bordwell, David, Janet Staiger, and Kristin Thompson. *The Classical Hollywood Cinema: Film Style and Mode of Production to 1960.* New York: Columbia Univ. Press, 1985.

Brackett, Charles, Billy Wilder, and D.M. Marshman Jr. *Sunset Boulevard.* In *Los Angeles Stories: Great Writers on the City,* ed. John Miller, 80-110. San Francisco: Chronicle Books, 1991.

_____*Sunset Boulevard.* In *Best American Screenplays 3,* ed. Sam Thomas, 117-62. New York: Crown, 1995.

Braudy, Leo. *The World in a Frame: What We See in Films.* Garden City, N.Y.: Anchor, 1977.

Busby, Marquis. "The Price They Pay for Fame." In *Hollywood and the Great Fan Magazines,* ed. Martin Levin, 94-96. New York: Arbor House, 1970.

Cameron, Ian, ed. *The Book of Film Noir.* New York: Continuum, 1993.

Card, James. "'More than Meets the Eye' in *Singin' in the Rain* and *Day for Night.*" *Literature-Film Quarterly* 12 (1984): 87-95.

Cavell, Stanley. *Pursuits of Happiness: The Hollywood Comedy of Remarriage.* Cambridge: Harvard Univ. Press, 1981.

Chandler, Raymond. *The Long Goodbye.* Boston: Houghton Mifflin, 1953.

_____"Writers in Hollywood." In *Los Angeles Stories: Great Writers on the City,* ed. John Miller, 71-79. San Francisco: Chronicle Books, 1991.

Chatman, Seymour. *Story and Discourse: Narrative Structure in Fiction and Film.* Ithaca: Cornell Univ. Press, 1980.

Cook, David A. *A History of Narrative Film.* 2d ed. New York: Norton, 1990.

Corliss, Richard. "The Dinosaur and the Dog." *Time,* 21 June 1993, 67.

Cywinski, Ray. *Preston Sturges: A Guide to References and Resources.* Boston: G.K. Hall, 1984.

Dardis, Tom. "The Myth That Won't Go Away: Selling Out in Hollywood." *Journal of Popular Film and Television* 11 (1984): 167-71.

_____*Some Time in the Sun: The Hollywood Years of Fitzgerald, Faulkner, Nathanael West, Aldous Huxley, and James Agee.* New York: Scribner's, 1976.

deCordova, Richard. *Picture Personalities: The Emergence of the Star System in America.* Urbana: Univ. of Illinois Press, 1990.

Doane, Mary Ann. *The Desire to Desire: The Woman's Film of the 1940s.* Bloomington: Indiana Univ. Press, 1987.

Dyer, Richard. *Stars.* London: British Film Institute, 1979.

Eberwein, Robert. "Comedy and the Film within a Film." *Wide Angle* 3 (1979): 12-17.

Eisenschitz, Bernard. *Nicholas Ray: An American Journey.* Trans. Tom Milne. London: Faber, 1993.

Feuer, Jane. *The Hollywood Musical.* 2d ed. London: Macmillan, 1993.

Fine, Richard. *Hollywood and the Profession of Authorship, 1928-1940.* Ann Arbor: UMI Research Press, 1985.

Fischer, Lucy. "*Sunset Boulevard:* Fading Stars." In *Women and Film,* ed. Janet Todd, 97-113. New York: Holmes and Meier, 1988.

Fitzgerald, F. Scott. *The Last Tycoon.* New York: Scribner's, 1941.

———*The Pat Hobby Stories.* New York: Penguin, 1983.

Fleishman, Avrom. *Narrated Films: Storytelling Situations in Cinema History.* Baltimore: Johns Hopkins Univ. Press, 1992.

Friedberg, Anne. *Window Shopping: Cinema and the Postmodern.* Berkeley: Univ. of California Press, 1993.

Frye, Northrop. *Anatomy of Criticism: Four Essays.* New York: Atheneum, 1969.

Gabler, Neal. *An Empire of Their Own: How the Jews Invented Hollywood.* New York: Doubleday, 1988.

Girard, René. *Violence and the Sacred.* Trans. Patrick Gregory. Baltimore: Johns Hopkins Univ. Press, 1977.

Girgus, Sam. *The Films of Woody Allen.* Cambridge: Cambridge Univ. Press, 1993.

Grant, Barry Keith, ed. *Film Genre Reader II.* Austin: Univ. of Texas Press, 1995.

Grover, Ronald. "*Last Action Hero*–or First $60 Million Commercial?" *Business Week,* 12 April 1993, 56-57.

Haskell, Molly. *From Reverence to Rape: The Treatment of Women in the Movies.* New York: Holt, Rinehart and Winston, 1974.

Haver, Ronald. *"A Star Is Born": The Making of the 1954 Movie and Its 1983 Restoration.* New York: Knopf, 1988.

Hecht, Ben. *Charlie: The Improbable Life and Times of Charles MacArthur.* New York: Harper, 1957.

———*A Child of the Century.* New York: Simon and Schuster, 1954.

———*Letters from Bohemia.* Garden City: Doubleday, 1964.

Heimann, Jim. *Out with the Stars: Hollywood Nightlife in the Golden Era.* New York: Abbeville, 1985.

Henderson, Brian, ed. *Five Screenplays by Preston Sturges.* Berkeley: Univ. of California Press, 1986.

Higham, Charles, and Joel Greenberg. *Hollywood in the Forties.* New York: A.S. Barnes, 1968.

Hirschhorn, Clive. *The Hollywood Musical.* New York: Crown, 1981.

"Hollywood-at-Home." *Architectural Digest* 51, no. 4 (April 1994).

Houston, Penelope. "Preston Sturges." *Sight and Sound* 34 (1965): 130-34.

Howard, Jean, and James Watters. *Hollywood: A Photo Memoir.* New York: Abrams, 1989.

Jacobs, Diane. *Christmas in July: The Life and Art of Preston Sturges.* Berkeley: Univ. of California Press, 1992.

Kael, Pauline. "Raising Kane." *The Citizen Kane Book.* Rpt. 1984. New York: Bantam, 1971.

Klawans, Stuart. "Films." *Nation,* 19 July 1993, 115-16.

Knight, Arthur. *The Hollywood Style.* London: Macmillan, 1969.

Kozloff, Sarah. *Invisible Storytellers: Voiceover Narration in American Fiction Film.* Berkeley: Univ. of California Press, 1988.

Lane, Anthony. "Reality Check." Review of *Last Action Hero*. *New Yorker*, 5 July 1993, 94-97.

Lax, Eric. *Woody Allen: A Biography*. New York: Knopf, 1991.

Lefevre, Dorothy Janet. "Geographic Aspects of the Private Swimming Pool Industry in Los Angeles." Ph.D. diss., University of California at Los Angeles, 1961.

Levin, Martin, ed. *Hollywood and the Great Fan Magazines*. New York: Arbor House, 1970.

Levy, Emanuel. *George Cukor, Master of Elegance: Hollywood's Legendary Director and His Stars*. New York: Morrow, 1994.

Luhr, William. "Robert Altman's *The Player* and Masculine Excess." Paper presented at the Florida State University Conference on Film and Literature, Tallahassee, 2 May 1994.

Lurie, Alison. *The Nowhere City*. London: Heinemann, 1986.

Maltby, Richard. "The Production Code and the Hays Office." In *Grand Design: Hollywood as a Modern Business Enterprise, 1930-1939*, ed. Tino Balio, 37-72. New York: Scribner's, 1993.

Maltby, Richard, and Ian Craven. *Hollywood Cinema: An Introduction*. Cambridge, Mass.: Blackwell, 1995.

Mast, Gerald. *Can't Help Singin': The American Musical on Stage and Screen*. Woodstock, N.Y.: Overlook Press, 1987.

————. "Projection." In *Film Theory and Criticism: Introductory Readings*, 3d ed., ed. Gerald Mast and Marshall Cohen, 265-70. New York: Oxford Univ. Press, 1985.

Mast, Gerald, and Marshall Cohen, eds. *Film Theory and Criticism: Introductory Readings*, 3d ed. New York: Oxford Univ. Press, 1985.

May, Lary. *Screening Out the Past: The Birth of Mass Culture and the Motion Picture Industry*. New York: Oxford Univ. Press, 1980.

McClelland, Gordon T., and Jay T. Last. *California Orange Box Labels: An Illustrated History*. Beverly Hills: Hillcrest Press, 1985.

McGilligan, Pat. *Backstory: Interviews with Screenwriters of Hollywood's Golden Age*. Berkeley: Univ. of California Press, 1986.

————. *Cagney: The Actor as Auteur*. New York: DaCapo, 1979.

McWilliams, Carey. *Southern California Country: An Island on the Land*. New York: Duell, Sloan and Pearce, 1946.

Medved, Michael. *Hollywood vs. America: Popular Culture and the War on Traditional Values*. New York: HarperCollins, 1992.

Metz, Christian. *The Imaginary Signifier: Psychoanalysis and the Cinema*. Trans. Celia Britton, Annwyl Williams, Ben Brewster, and Alfred Guzzetti. Bloomington: Indiana Univ. Press, 1982.

Montrose, Louis Adrian. "*A Midsummer Night's Dream* and the Shaping Fantasies of Elizabethan Culture: Gender, Power, Form." In *Rewriting the Renaissance: The Discourses of Sexuality in Early Modern Europe*, ed. Margaret W. Ferguson, Maureen Quilligan, and Nancy J. Vickers, 65-87. Chicago: Univ. of Chicago Press, 1986.

"Movie Men Split by Strike." *New York Times* 9 May 1937. Rpt. in *The New*

York Times Encyclopedia of Film, vol. 3 (1937-1940). Gene Brown, ed. New York: Times Books, 1984.

Mulvey, Laura. "Visual Pleasure and Narrative Cinema." In *Film Theory and Criticism: Introductory Readings*, 3d ed., ed. Gerald Mast and Marshall Cohen, 803-16. New York: Oxford Univ. Press, 1985.

Nugent, Frank R. "Another Dance of the Seven Veils." *New York Times* 3 October 1937. Rpt. in *The New York Times Encyclopedia of Film*, vol. 3 (1937-1940). Gene Brown, ed. New York: Times Books, 1984.

O'Brien, Geoffrey. *The Phantom Empire*. New York: Norton, 1993.

Palmer, James W. "*In a Lonely Place:* Paranoia in the Dream Factory." *Literature/Film Quarterly* 13 (1985): 200-207.

Parish, James Robert, and Michael R. Pitts, with Gregory W. Mank. *Hollywood on Hollywood*. Metuchen, N.J.: Scarecrow. 1978.

Perkins, V.F. "In a Lonely Place." In *The Book of Film Noir*, ed. Ian Cameron. New York: Continuum, 1993.

Pilipp, Frank. "Satirizing Hollywood: The Self-Referentiality of Robert Altman's *The Player*." In *Proceedings of the Conference on Film and American Culture*, 80-84. Williamsburg, Va.: Roy R. Charles Center, College of William and Mary, 1993.

Polan, Dana B. *In a Lonely Place*. London: British Film Institute Publishing, 1993.

Polhemus, Robert M. *Comic Faith: The Great Tradition from Austen to Joyce*. Chicago: Univ. of Chicago Press, 1980.

Potter, Dennis. "Pennies from Heaven." Final Draft. 27 June 1980.

Priestley, J.B. *Albert Goes Through*. London: W. Heinemann, 1933.

Quirk, Lawrence J. *Fasten Your Seat Belts: The Passionate Life of Bette Davis*. New York: Morrow, 1990.

Rice, Elmer. *A Voyage to Purilia*. New York: Cosmopolitan, 1930.

Rogin, Michael. *"Ronald Reagan," the Movie, and Other Episodes in Political Demonology*. Berkeley: Univ. of California Press, 1987.

Rosen, Nick. "Hurricane Woody Hits Town." *London Sunday Times*, 6 May 1984.

Rosten, Leo Calvin. *Hollywood: The Movie Colony, The Movie Makers*. New York: Harcourt Brace, 1941.

Salkin, John, and Laurie Gordon. *Orange Crate Art*. New York: Warner Books, 1976.

Schatz, Thomas. *Hollywood Genres: Formulas, Filmmaking, and the Studio System*. Philadelphia: Temple Univ. Press, 1981.

Schulberg, Budd. *What Makes Sammy Run?* New York: Random House, 1941.

Sedgwick, Eve Kosofsky. *Between Men: English Literature and Homosocial Desire*. New York: Columbia Univ. Press, 1985.

Shumway, David R. "Screwball Comedies: Constructing Romance, Mystifying Marriage." In *Film Genre Reader II*, ed. Barry Keith Grant, 381-401. Austin: Univ. of Texas Press, 1995.

Sklar, Robert. *City Boys: Cagney, Bogart, Garfield*. Princeton: Princeton Univ. Press, 1992.

_____ *Movie-Made America: A Cultural History of American Movies*. New York: Vintage, 1976.

Soroka, Laurence. "Hollywood Modernism: Self-Consciousness and the Holly-wood-on-Hollywood Film Genre." Ph.D. diss., Emory University, 1983.

Spewack, Bella, and Samuel Spewack. *Boy Meets Girl: A Play in Three Acts.* London: English Theatre Guild, 1947.

Stam, Robert. *Reflexivity in Film and Literature: From Don Quixote to Jean-Luc Godard.* New York: Columbia Univ. Press, 1992.

Starr, Kevin. *Americans and the California Dream: 1850-1915.* New York: Oxford Univ. Press, 1973.

_____*Material Dreams: Southern California Through the 1920's.* New York: Oxford Univ. Press, 1990.

Studlar, Gaylyn. "The Perils of Pleasure? Fan Magazine Discourse as Women's Commodified Culture in the 1920s." *Wide Angle* 13 (1991): 6-33.

Sturges, Preston. *Five Screenplays by Preston Sturges.* Ed. Brian Henderson. Berkeley: Univ. of California Press, 1986.

Sugg, Richard P. "The Role of the Writer in *The Player:* Novel and Film." *Literature/Film Quarterly* 22 (1994): 11-15.

Swanson, Gloria. *Swanson on Swanson.* New York: Pocket, 1980.

Telotte, J.P. *Voices in the Dark: The Narrative Patterns of Film Noir.* Illinois Univ. Press, 1989.

Todorov, Tzvetan. *The Poetics of Prose.* Trans. Richard Howard. Ithaca: Cornell Univ. Press, 1977.

Tolkin, Michael. *The Player.* New York: Vintage, 1992.

Vidal, Gore. *Screening History.* Cambridge: Harvard Univ. Press, 1992.

Walker, Alexander. *Stardom: The Hollywood Phenomenon.* New York: Stein and Day, 1970.

Watt, Ian. *The Rise of the Novel: Studies in Defoe, Richardson, and Fielding.* Berkeley: Univ. of California Press, 1957.

Webb, Michael, ed. *Hollywood: Legend and Reality.* Boston: Little, Brown, 1986.

Wernblad, Annette. *Brooklyn Is not Expanding.* Rutherford, N.J.: Farleigh Dickinson Univ. Press, 1992.

West, Nathanael. *Miss Lonelyhearts* and *The Day of the Locust.* New York: New Directions, 1962.

Wineapple, Brenda. "Finding an Audience: *Sullivan's Travels.*" *Journal of Popular Film and Television* 11 (1984): 152-57.

Wollen, Peter. *Singin' in the Rain.* London: British Film Institute, 1992.

Wood, Michael. *America in the Movies or "Santa Maria, It Had Slipped My Mind."* New York: Columbia Univ. Press, 1975.

Wood, Robin. *Hollywood from Vietnam to Reagan.* New York: Columbia Univ. Press, 1986.

Wright, Judith Hess. "Genre Films and the Status Quo." In *Film Genre Reader II,* ed. Barry Keith Grant, 41-49. Austin: Univ. of Texas Press, 1995.

Yacowar, Maurice. *Loser Take All: The Comic Art of Woody Allen.* New York: Continuum, 1991.

Zolotow, Maurice. *Billy Wilder in Hollywood.* New York: Putnam, 1977.

Index